Removed from
library collection
3 3067 00409 9232

CUTTING-EDGE STRATEGIES
to EVOLVE
YOUR VIDEO BUSINESS

RON and TASRA DAWSON

384.558
D
7/10
TS

ReFocus: Cutting-Edge Strategies to Evolve Your Video Business
Ron and Tasra Dawson

Peachpit Press
1249 Eighth Street
Berkeley, CA 94710
510/524-2178
Fax: 510/524-2221

Find us on the Web at www.peachpit.com
To report errors, please send a note to errata@peachpit.com
Peachpit Press is a division of Pearson Education
Copyright © 2010 by Ron Dawson and Tasra Dawson

Senior Editor: Karyn Johnson
Development Editor: Stephen Nathans-Kelley
Production Editor: Becky Winter
Copy Editor: Liz Avery Merfeld
Compositor: Danielle Foster
Proofreader: Kelly Kordes Anton
Indexer: Jack Lewis
Interior and Cover Design: Mimi Heft
Cover Production: Michael Tanamachi, Shelftown

Notice of Rights
All rights reserved. No part of this book may be reproduced or transmitted in any form by any means, electronic, mechanical, photocopying, recording, or otherwise, without the prior written permission of the publisher. For information on getting permission for reprints and excerpts, contact permissions@peachpit.com.

Notice of Liability
The information in this book is distributed on an "As Is" basis without warranty. While every precaution has been taken in the preparation of the book, neither the authors nor Peachpit shall have any liability to any person or entity with respect to any loss or damage caused or alleged to be caused directly or indirectly by the instructions contained in this book or by the computer software and hardware products described in it.

Trademarks
Many of the designations used by manufacturers and sellers to distinguish their products are claimed as trademarks. Where those designations appear in this book, and Peachpit was aware of a trademark claim, the designations appear as requested by the owner of the trademark. All other product names and services identified throughout this book are used in editorial fashion only and for the benefit of such companies with no intention of infringement of the trademark. No such use, or the use of any trade name, is intended to convey endorsement or other affiliation with this book.

ISBN-13: 978-0-321-63530-3
ISBN-10: 0-321-63530-2

9 8 7 6 5 4 3 2 1

Printed and bound in the United States of America

ENDORSEMENTS FOR *REFOCUS: CUTTING-EDGE STRATEGIES TO EVOLVE YOUR VIDEO BUSINESS*

"Video producers, photographers—*any* creatives starting or rebooting a business—*pay attention* to Ron and Tasra Dawson's brilliant new book. Rarely do I come across anything remotely useful in writing about how to solve the business side of a creative life. This book made me sit up and reread each section, paragraph, sentence. Because *ReFocus* combines basic common sense with insightful advice, I learned new things, remembered valuable ideas that I'd forgotten, and was inspired. And they manage this without guilt or attitude, like an intervention with a teenager, so that their words really get through the crazy creative brain. Your life and your business *will* change after you absorb this wise, practical, invaluable guide—the new bible for creative businesses!"

—Doug Menuez, Director/Commercial and Editorial Photographer

"If you want to be a visual artist *and* you want to make a living doing it, there's one cold hard fact you should know right now: You have to concentrate on the business side first. The art comes later. As someone with three decades worth of media experience, I've been looking for people like Ron and Tasra to help spread the word: *Creatives need business skills*. Don't go out and buy a new camera. Buy this book. Learn to build your business. Let your clients buy your gear for you later. Ron & Tasra's passion for life and the video business shine through this book. If you read it, you'll catch the same fire that helped make them successful."

—Scott Bourne, President, Bourne Media Group

"We can often get so lost in the art of what we do that we forget or undervalue what keeps everything running—and that is the business side. Ron and Tasra Dawson have been educating for years on the importance of this side. They are authorities in our industry for everything business, and they always say what needs to be said. As our industry evolves at a record pace, there could not be a better time for these words to be said."

—Patrick Moreau, StillMotion

"There has been a cataclysmic, confusing change in the way successful entrepreneurs market themselves. The old methods are no longer effective, and the new strategies that you desperately need are in this comprehensive, step-by-step guide. Get this book and then you'll get it."

—John Goolsby, author,
The Business of Wedding & Special Event Videography

"*ReFocus* is an incredible resource for all video professionals. If you're just starting out or in the process of making over your business, this book addresses all the major areas to help ensure your career success."

—Tim Sudall, Video One Productions

"Ron and Tasra will help you to move mountains in your business. Who better to guide you on a tour of successful business principles for your video/photo business than a crew that doesn't just talk the talk, but truly walks the walk? It's hard not to imagine success for those who apply what they'll learn in this book!"

—Lance Gray, CEO, PixelPops

"Our experience shows that one thing desperately lacking among small-business video producers is a clear and cohesive understanding of their brand and how to differentiate themselves from others in their industry. That's all about to change."

—Craig Johnson, Brand Strategist, Matchstic

"*ReFocus* is a much-needed, incredibly informative and valuable book, written by a much-needed, incredibly informative and valuable couple named Ron and Tasra Dawson. If you read this book through, and apply the information, it should turn your world around. Please enjoy this very special inspirational and practical guide to event film-making business."

—David Robin, david robin | films

"Ron and Tasra Dawson have demystified what it takes to succeed in the event video industry. With this book, a beginning producer can expect to avoid three years' worth of trial and error while charting a steady path to the top of his or her market."

—Chris P. Jones, Co-Founder In[Focus], Mason Jar Films

"*ReFocus* is a geyser of information about our rapidly changing industry."

—Chase Jarvis, Director/Commercial Photographer

"From big-picture strategy to ground floor tactics, Ron and Tasra Dawson have unlocked it all by offering you turnkey access to the kingdom of commercial creative storytelling. Don't miss this gift. ReFocus *now*. Your future may depend on it."

—Dane Sanders, Author, Fast Track Photographer

"*ReFocus* will inspire you with clear guidelines, precise steps, and solid research to grow your video business. Stand out from the crowd, online and off, with your feet firmly on the ground. Focus and flourish—this book gives it to you straight."

—Victoria Vestal and Brad Kupper, Barndoor Studios, Photo and Video

"Purple Cow? Blogosphere? If you have to ask what these things are—or if you're not sure—you're at a huge disadvantage in today's business world. *ReFocus* is *the* business guide for today's videographer."

—Julian St Pierre, Co-Founder, IN[FOCUS] and Studio Vieux Carre

ACKNOWLEDGMENTS

In the spirit of social media and the changing technological landscape, we give you our list of Twitter-compliant acknowledgments. (Real Twitter handles are listed with the @ symbol.)

@karyn Unwavering editor, patient leader, inspiring cheerleader, let's do it again. :-)

@stevenathans Mastermind and schedule keeper, thx 4 your confidence in us over the years.

@peachpit Mimi, creative designer; Becky and Danielle, amazing interior layout; @DHampson, @Laura7, & @sarajanetodd, marketing gurus.

#eventvideoindustry Thx 2 colleagues & friends in industry who inspired & pushed us to be better & strive higher.

@zacuto Steve Weiss, thx 4 taking time out of your jet-setting 2 write the foreword, luv your tell-it-like-it-is approach.

#davidhebel We are humbled and blown away by your amazing words of encouragement. Keep rockin' the industry w/ Digital Juice.

#johngoolsby Godfather of event video, author of original how-to, thx 4 personal encouragement and mentorship.

#timsudall U went to bat 4 us with top dogs and told Ron his 1st biz card sucked (er, needed work)...many thanks.

#reviewers Thx 4 endorsement...Chase, Chris, Craig, Dane, David, Doug, John, Julian, Lance, Patrick, Scott, Tim, Victoria-Brad.

#twitter & **#facebook** Friends and fans who answered questions, submitted photos, and encouraged progress...u rock.

#photographyindustry You've supported our work & embraced us as one of your own...we're honored.

#wppi & **#skipcohen** Thx 4 opening our eyes to photography industry & being our guinea pigs 4 crazy video ideas.

#jdcochran Thanks for asking the fateful question "What do you want 2 do with your life?"

#harry&yuka 4 being our very first paying clients. Your confidence & belief in us (despite no samples) started it all.

#mentors RoJean DeChantal, Marv Morris, Mr. Crook, Chris Spencer... wouldn't be where we are today without you.

#quickenteam Thx for all the knowledge I (Ron) gained there and 4 encouraging me to pursue what I truly loved.

#imahni Darling daughter, tireless babysitter, patient transcriber, brilliant short order lunch cook...we luv u.

#bubbie We luv u 4 always providing entertainment & joy & getting us 2 stop work by asking, "Who wants to play with me?"

@rondawson Always knew we were polar opposites...writing this confirmed it...luv u because of & despite our differences.

@tasradawson I don't think we're polar opposites sw'art. :) Thx for being an amazing wife, mother, & best friend.

#God All things are possible with you.

FOREWORD

A very wise man once said, "The only constant is change." This bit of practical wisdom is more relevant today than ever before. It's especially applicable to the competitive video business, where technology and equipment need constant update and clients demand the latest creative style or look. But in the race to keep up with rapidly changing technology and ever-evolving styles, we often forget about the changes needed in other areas of the business that are just as important and in many cases more vital to growth and success.

What I love about Ron and Tasra's book is their emphasis on the need to change, really, to evolve the whole of your video business. There are times and situations in business that demand radical change in a very short period of time. In fact, incorporating the concept of continual, methodical, evolutionary change every single day is the only way I've found in the 17 years of running my company, Digital Juice, to keep the business relevant to the needs of my customers and thus successful.

Almost every area of my company is different today than it was just 10 years ago. The products, marketing, Web site, packaging, business model, pricing, and even the way customers buy are all different today than they were then. About the only thing that hasn't changed is the name of the company and our basic mission.

For example, in the early years Digital Juice was known primarily by our marketing efforts through direct mail, advertising in video trade magazines, and going to various industry-related trade shows. As much as 25 percent of our entire budget was allocated to these three areas. Today, we don't spend a dime using these methods. Instead, we focus on reaching customers via the Internet. Why? Because of change. Today, most of our customers get their information, learn about new products, and make buying decisions almost exclusively through the Internet. As a result, we had to evolve.

I'm expecting that things will be even more different tomorrow than they are today, and you should too. Change is inevitable, evolving a necessity. If you want to be in business 10 years from now, you must develop a mindset today that allows for change tomorrow.

Ron and Tasra have written a book that will help you do just that. They will get you thinking creatively and strategizing effectively on how best to grow and evolve your business in new and exciting directions that will keep you ahead of the competition and relevant to your customers, thus allowing you to enjoy the many rewards that come from owning your own business.

David Hebel
Founder & CEO, Digital Juice, Inc.

This book by Ron and Tasra Dawson is about all things I love: marketing, marketing, and marketing.

As far as I'm concerned, the book of marketing has now been rewritten, and Ron and Tasra give you a great insight into what marketing means *now*!

And how is that done in 2009? Create content, build communities, and distribute your news to your communities via videos, photos, and press.

At Zacuto, we call them *gathering spaces*, places like the neighborhood mall, the Diamond District in New York, or gathering spaces on the Internet like Vimeo, YouTube, Blip.tv, Exposure, Facebook, MySpace, Flickr, Zenfolio, Twitter, iTunes, Plaxo, LinkedIn, blogs, forums, and more. If you want to create a community and keep in touch with community members on a daily basis, you need to master these gathering places, and learn how to use their various features to your benefit. This book will show you how.

Things like commercials are really the past. Creating your own content—especially Webisodic audio, video, or photo content—and getting people coming back to your gathering spaces on a regular basis is key. You are now creating a discussion with your community and customers and we love that.

Great book, Ron and Tasra; I couldn't agree more with what you are saying.

Steve Weiss
Partner, Zacuto

INTRODUCTION

NOTHING PERSONAL, IT'S BUSINESS

STOP! DON'T READ ANOTHER WORD of this book...unless you agree to do what we suggest.

You can start by answering one question: Why?

Why in the world have you decided to engage in one of the most difficult industries to succeed in? Why have you decided to enter a business that requires both a significant amount of artistic talent, and perhaps an even greater amount of business skill?

Is it because you love making movies and someone somewhere once told you, "Hey, you should do this for a living"?

Is it because you hope to one day be the next Spielberg, Tarantino, Soderbergh, or [insert name of your favorite filmmaker here], and you figured that launching a videography business would be a good way to get started?

Or, perhaps, you just got tired of shooting all your friends' weddings for free and figured it's about time you made some money at this.

Whatever your specific reason, we're willing to wager that what's really driving your decision is a passion and love for the craft. In other words, money was not the motivating factor that prompted you.

Given that, we have good news and bad news.

The bad news is that unless you're ready to take seriously the reality that what you embarked upon is not a money-making hobby, but a veritable business, you shouldn't even bother hanging out the shingle.

The good news is that this industry can be both artistically fulfilling as well as financially rewarding.

But, are you ready to get uncomfortable and perhaps evolve in order to make that success a reality? Are you willing to step out and venture into uncharted territory, to try something new and daring?

PURSUING YOUR PASSION

Before I met Tasra, I became friends with JD, an independent filmmaker, writer, and graduate of University of Southern California's acclaimed film school. We met at Screenplay Systems, a small software developer of film and television production software located in Burbank, California. During my second year at Screenplay, shortly after JD arrived on the scene, I enlisted his help in the production of a short film I had written. During that production we became great friends (he later was a groomsman in our wedding). I later left the company as VP of Operations to return to Silicon Valley and work as a Business Marketing manager in the Quicken division of Intuit.

It wasn't until January 2002, when I was back in Southern California visiting family and friends during the holiday break, that JD challenged me. He and I were relaxing in his living room, having a philosophical discussion/debate/argument that was going nowhere (as usual). Then he posed a question to me that changed the direction of my life.

"So, Ron, what do you want to do with your life?" (I bet you didn't see that coming.)

I replied, "Well, ideally, I'd love to be able to write and direct my own movie one day."

"Cool. Cool. I hear ya. So, tell me, how are you going to do that at Intuit?"

His question stopped me cold. It was simple, and yet so poignant. How *was* I going to do that at Intuit?

My plan, of course, was to continue earning my comfortable six-figure salary, write and shoot short films on the side, get discovered after entering one of said films in a film festival, then quit my high-paying Silicon Valley marketing gig the day after I signed my million-dollar film deal with Warner Bros., Miramax, or any other major studio wise enough to see the talent burgeoning inside me.

CUT TO: REALITY.

The truth is, most great artists who make it in "the Biz" didn't do so from behind the desk of some "safe" 9-5. They gathered up the courage, or were already imbued with the necessary chutzpah, to jump into the business and go for broke. They realized that they had to put everything they had into it if they were ever to make it big. Playing it safe was not the way to become the next big auteur, turning studio heads and making the cover of *Daily Variety*.

Within a few weeks of that conversation, I marched into my boss' office and told him I wanted to quit. Luckily, he took it extremely well, primarily because he knew my passion for filmmaking. I had made a few short, fun videos for my department, and for colleagues' birthday parties, and I had shared my older projects with my work mates. Everyone always commented that I was wasting my talent at a desk job and that I should pursue filmmaking.

The timing could not have been better. Intuit had undergone some major restructuring and layoffs were in the works for a number of individuals. Instead of "quitting," I held out a few months and accepted a layoff package. By April 2002, I left the company, and a month later I was pursuing my dreams and following my passion.

Three months later I married Tasra, and from that point on, we were business partners as well as life partners.

REFINING THE EVOLUTIONARY PROCESS

When we first started the company, I named it Don Ron Entertainment, based on a nickname I once had. My intention back then was to start off in the wedding videography business to pay the bills until I had the opportunity to make "real" videos (read: music videos). I wasn't particularly excited about starting in weddings, but I knew I had to start somewhere, and that seemed like the easiest thing to do.

After shooting my first wedding in fall 2002, we invited our clients to our home to watch the seven-minute highlights clip I created. Within those seven minutes, they laughed and they cried. A powerful sense of purpose came over me that day. I felt like I found what I was made to do: To use my talents as a filmmaker to help preserve memories and strengthen marriages was a purpose that resonated deeply with both of us. Perhaps one day I'd go off and be the next Spike Lee, but for now, Ron Dawson, wedding videographer was just fine.

Over the next seven years, our company evolved. The name changed from Don Ron Entertainment, to Cinematic Video Productions, to Cinematic Studios, and most recently, to Dare Dreamer Media. Although we still produce wedding movies via a separate division (or as an "off-menu" item if a client wants to hire me personally), our primary focus is now commercial video production with an emphasis in new media marketing.

One thing we've learned in business is that a key ingredient for success is the ability to adapt to change. In an industry as technology-focused as video, that's one aspect of our business we all must absolutely embrace.

Every change we've made to our business over the years was done to propel us forward, to set our company in a position where it could best survive in a competitive industry. We changed our company name to position our brand in such a way that would give us flexibility in the services we offered (we didn't want to be pigeonholed into providing only video services). We changed our focus from weddings to commercial so that we could go after larger corporate gigs. And our latest evolution from a production company to a new media marketing agency is designed to draw focus and attention to our core strength as an idea company.

If nothing else, we hope you'll take away from this book the importance to change and adapt with the times.

EMBRACING YOUR STORY

So, what is your story? Whatever it is, however you got to the point you're at now, in this Introduction we want to set a foundation. We want to get you going in the right direction to sustain a long and rewarding career in this industry.

CHOOSE YOUR PATH

A dear friend of ours is an editorial music photographer named Zack Arias. Zack is a treasure chest of valuable information on lighting, equipment selection, composition, and being a true artist. His blog (www.zarias.com) has a large following, and in early 2009 he was invited by technology and Photoshop guru Scott Kelby to be a guest blogger. The resulting video he made for the site garnered more than 100,000 views and is still going strong.

Zack conducts photo critiques, which he records and adds to his blog. Oftentimes, he'll come across a Web site that has a child portrait gallery, a landscape gallery, a wedding gallery, a family portrait gallery, and a fashion gallery. When that happens, he always says the same thing: "I don't know who you are. Who are you? What kind of photographer are you trying to be? Pick one, and go with that."

Another friend and wildly successful photographer is Kevin Swan. After 15 years as a creative director in an ad agency, Kevin has become adept at the art of marketing. Kevin talks about the importance of picking a "hill" to claim. That is, find out your business specialty, then stick to it. Own it. Be the best at it. If it's weddings, do just weddings. If it's portraits, do just portraits. And if you do decide to expand, then market those services under different Web sites and brands.

Successful business consultant and bestselling author Michael Port writes in his book *Book Yourself Solid* about the important of zeroing in on your specific target market. If you find that it feels like pulling teeth to get clients to book you, it could be because you're getting your message in front of the wrong client.

We could go on and on about successful businesses and authors who extol the importance of picking that hill. So, as you venture forth into the world of video production as a service-based business, ask yourself the same question Zack would ask you: Who are you?

What kind of videos do you want to produce?

Weddings? If so, are you going for a high-end client or the budget bride?

Commercial? If so, what's your focus?

Media duplication? Corporate events? Stage events? Sports events? Corporate training videos? Promotional videos?

You will find that if you focus, your marketing efforts will not only be relatively easier, but more effective.

DIFFERENTIATION DONE RIGHT

We're not saying that you should not differentiate your offerings. In fact, especially if you're relatively new, it may be necessary to differentiate your service offerings. The important thing is how you present those services. A prospective commercial client looking for a company to produce its next promotional video, will most likely be turned off if they come to a site filled with pastels, smiling brides, and blossoming bouquets. Likewise, most brides who are used to visiting feminine bridal sites as they do their wedding planning online will be less than intrigued by your video services if you have a pictures of tall corporate buildings, DVD duplicators, or hulking video cameras.

So, how does one go about offering varying services from the same company? We'll cover some of these concepts later in the book, but the primary method is to use different Web sites for the core business services you plan to offer. For about three years we used Cinematic Video for our corporate work and Cinematic Studios for our wedding work. When we changed our focus to corporate work, Cinematic Studios design became more corporate in feel, and then we used www.WeddingFlix.com as the primary Web site for our wedding work. It does create extra work maintaining multiple sites, but in the long run, it's worth it.

CHARTING THE COURSE AHEAD

In the world of event video production, there are a number of avenues you could travel. You could be a freelance shooter or editor, a "mom and pop," an "auteur" taking on the most exclusive of jobs, or a full-blown studio with lots of projects and a team of shooters and editors at your disposal. Whichever path you take, the concepts described in this book will help you along your journey. Some of the concepts may be better suited towards one path versus another, but by the end, our hope is you'll be further along towards success (however you define it) than if you didn't read this book.

The one rule we have as a central premise, however, is this: you are more than just a "videographer." That term is too limiting. You have to view yourself as a "visual media producer." It may be video today, but could be something new tomorrow. This book will show you how to embrace your creativity and it will empower you to view yourself and your business in a new light. The first section of the book will walk you through how to embrace this new type of thinking.

Once you've got that down, we'll move on to sales and marketing in the second section. It's here that you'll find inspirational and practical ideas and strategies for marketing your business and extending your brand beyond your local market to the world. "Be interesting or be invisible," says Andy Sernovitz from *Word of Mouth Marketing*.

Innovative marketing can pull you out of the proverbial ditch, while poor marketing can leave you there indefinitely. We'll show you how to do the former. Decipher Web 2.0 and the social networking tools worthy of your time and attention. Don't use your creativity just in video production, put it to good use in your marketing communication, materials, and message.

From there, we'll wrap it all up by guiding you to put systems into place that will help you avoid becoming overwhelmed and keep it all in check. Find out and make the changes needed to make sure you're in the driver's seat. Regain your life, and your love for the craft.

This book is a call to action. A raising of the bar. We want to set a new standard in the video production world. Delivering late projects or laughing about a mountainous backlog should no longer be our standard.

In writing this book, we're not saying we're experts. In fact, as we neared the completion, we realized just how much of what we're teaching we need to start doing more of ourselves, or continue to practice. So, we are right there with you. Working harder—correction, working smarter—to meet the new standard.

Let's take this journey...together.

TABLE OF CONTENTS

I
TAKE A STAND

CHOOSE YOUR PATH

PAUL ARDEN, ONE OF THE GREATEST ADVERTISERS IN HISTORY, is quoted as saying, "Your vision of where or who you want to be is the greatest asset you have." In other words, it's not necessarily how good you *are* at something that determines whether you achieve success, but how good *you want to be.*

This chapter opens by exploring some of the strides that have been made in visual arts and showcases a few creative individuals. Then, we'll give you some direction on how to choose your path and what to consider when establishing your business.

IT'S THE TALENT, NOT THE TOOLS

In the fall of 2008, high-profile editorial photographer Vincent Laforet made a short film with a not-yet-released digital SLR still camera, Canon's EOS 5D Mark II. It was the video shoot "heard 'round the world." The high-definition video quality of the camera, combined with the amazing depth-of-field imagery enabled by the Canon lenses, made his short film *Reverie* an instant hit among still photographers and video producers alike (**FIGURE 1.1**). In fact, Internet traffic to his blog to view the video was so great, Canon had to take the video down (it was hosted on their servers) and it was moved to a new server that could handle the bandwidth.

When the camera officially went on the market a few months later, photography and video forums were abuzz in anticipation of how this latest technological achievement was going to change the industry. Many people were scared about what this change meant for their business. Others took advantage of the hype and started offering training

FIGURE 1.1 Vincent Laforet's short film *Reverie* (shot on a digital SLR) sent chills down the spines of videographers and photographers alike. The game has now changed.

DVDs on how to effectively use the camera in video production (these were the proverbial "shovel suppliers" who took advantage of the hype during the great gold rush). There was so much focus on what this tool was going to do for those who were able to get one of these cameras.

The overhyping of a new technology is nothing new to this business. Every few years there seems to be some major advancement that is going to forever change the industry. People start freaking out. Some act as if the sky is falling. It happened when the industry went from Betacam to VHS, from VHS to digital, from digital to HD digital, and so on. There's always some new technology that will be available. Alas, most people focus on the wrong thing. People seem to forget that it's the talent, *not* the tools, that will make you a successful video producer.

We don't mean to downplay the importance of these advancements or the exciting opportunities they offer. But those opportunities are only as good as the talent of the person who wields that technology. Just because you have the best, most expensive equipment does not mean you'll make great art. But it's not all about skill and artistry either. Even if you *do* have the artistic talents necessary, if you lack the business talent (or the wherewithal to find a savvy business partner), your chances of success are even less.

We think this simple statement, "It's the talent, not the tools," is a mantra you need to believe and embrace. Before we venture any further into this journey together, we need to know that you recognize and appreciate your talent and are capable of applying it to your business, no matter what the technology.

Let's look at a few examples of visual artists who prove that regardless of the tool used, great art can be made.

CHASE JARVIS' IPHONE PHOTOS

Chase Jarvis is the youngest photographer to be dubbed both a Nikon and Hasselblad master. He's shot commercial jobs for some of the biggest brands in the world (Nike and McDonald's, to name a couple). His blog is heavily followed and he's one of the hottest commercial photographers on the scene today. He knows his way around a camera. His talent is such that even photos he's shot on an iPhone look great. Every week he posts to his Facebook page or his blog a photo taken with his iPhone. With a few $3 iPhone apps, a steady hand, and a good eye, the results he achieves are amazing (**FIGURE 1.2**).

ZACK ARIAS' TRANSFORM VIDEO

In the Introduction, we mentioned editorial music photographer Zack Arias' invitation to be the guest blogger for www.ScottKelby.com, and noted that a video he produced for the guest blog post has received more than 100,000 views. What we haven't mentioned yet is that Zack shot that video on a Flip Mino HD consumer camcorder—the world's smallest consumer HD camcorder with a 1.5 mm fixed focal length, terrible low-light capability, and for all intents and purposes, no depth of field.

However, the story he told was poignant, moving, and engaging. So much so, that almost two months after posting the video, Zack's video (**FIGURE 1.3**) was still the most popular post on www.ScottKelby.com, based

FIGURE 1.2 An image taken by Chase Jarvis with his iPhone.

FIGURE 1.3 A screen shot from photographer Zack Arias' popular Flip camera–shot video on www.ScottKelby.com.

on the number of comments, which stands at more than 500 as of this writing. If you haven't already seen it, you can watch the video here: www.zarias.com/?p=284.

JASON MAGBANUA'S CELL PHONE VIDEO

For whatever reason, some of the most artistically accomplished event video work in the world is coming from the Philippine Islands. One of the most talented out of the bunch is a wedding cinematographer by the name of Jason Magbanua (FIGURE 1.4). His craft is empirically brilliant. His command of HD cameras, 35 mm adapters, and nonlinear editing software is masterful. But one of the reasons he's a leader in the industry is because he's always pushing the envelope and trying new things.

FIGURE 1.4 Wedding cinematography master Jason Magbanua of the Philippines. Photo by Dino Lara, mangoRED.

If you think Zack Arias shooting a video on a Flip Mino HD is something, try this on for size: in 2008, Jason (or "J-Mag," as he's affectionately known in the industry) won a silver award (second place) in the Wedding and Event Videographer Association (WEVA) Creative Excellence Awards' Love Story category with a video he shot entirely on a Nokia N93 mobile phone. I (Ron) was the judge for another national video contest in which this video was entered, and it was brilliant. Someone who can take second place in an international competition with a video shot on a cell phone will have the talent to succeed in this business regardless of the latest and greatest new gadget.

REBELS WITHOUT A CREW

Indie filmmakers, without the big budgets or big cameras, take whatever they can get their hands on to make their artistic vision a reality. Names like Ed Burns, Robert Rodriquez, Steven Soderbergh, and Spike Lee are all famous for having freshman feature film efforts shot with inexpensive equipment and little to no budgets. And let's not forget Daniel Myrick and Eduardo Sánchez.

Unless you're a very savvy film buff, you may not recognize the last two names. But, we have no doubt you'd recognize the film that put them on the map. *The Blair Witch Project* (celebrating its tenth anniversary this year) was a marketing marvel. Shot entirely with cheap consumer camcorders, this horror/mystery thriller was all the rage the year it opened. Copycat thrillers quickly followed, but nothing quite captured the essence of the first, not even its big-budget sequel.

Don't get us wrong. We're not saying that you shouldn't care about new technology. We get just as excited about the possibilities that open up with new cameras. The danger is that when you put such a high importance on acquiring that technology, you lose sight of what will really bring you success. Just because you shoot a video with a RED One camera (www.red.com) doesn't mean clients are going to hire you and pay you top dollar. Nor does it mean you'll make anything that's worth watching.

From an artistic standpoint, there's so much more than the equipment that goes into a well-produced video or film. And from a business standpoint, you need even more talent if you want to keep from becoming a statistic.

So, as you venture forth in this book, and in your business, keep in mind that the most important factor to your success is not your camera. It's not your computer or NLE system. It's not the filters or plug-ins. Not the camera stabilization device. Not the lens adapters. Nor the format on which you shoot. For better or worse, the most determining factor of your success is...you.

PICK THE RIGHT FORM OF BUSINESS

Earlier, I (Ron) mentioned that I was hit with reality in regard to the prospect of becoming a successful filmmaker. My reality check helped me make a decision that allowed me to pursue my passion and still make a living. If you've entered this business for the reason we stated in the book's introduction, at some point you're going to have your own reality check.

As a business owner, you will be faced with the challenge of making decisions that won't necessarily jive with your artistic passion. As a business owner, there will be times you may have to wear hats you don't want to wear (you may have to be a bookkeeper, salesperson, project manager, and so on).

Truth is, you are a *business* owner. You won't be able to always make the kind of videos you're passionate about. Sometimes you're going to take jobs that you have to take because they'll put food on the table. You don't always have the luxury of making art for the sake of art.

In the confines of these pages, we'll provide a plan for you to effectively manage the business side in such a way that you'll have more freedom to pursue those aspects of your business that excite you. Whether it's putting systems in place to help you delegate the roles you don't want or improving your sales and marketing so that you can afford to do just the kind of work you want (by charging more), our hope is that you'll

(1) act on the information, and (2) you'll find it effective at transforming your business, and by way of that, your life.

So you've got the gear, the computer, and the coolest nonlinear editing applications. Your business license is framed and proudly mounted over your desk. Your URL is secured and you're ready to start hitting the pavement. Now, all you need to do is figure out what path you'll take. In this chapter, we'll give you some direction. We'll briefly touch on business forms, then cover various setups you'll need to consider when establishing your business.

This is not intended to be an in-depth look at the basics of starting a business. There are plenty of other resources where you can get that information. But it seems appropriate to touch on the types of businesses you can form as they relate to the video business.

CONSULT A TAX ACCOUNTANT

We'll address working with CPAs in Chapter 11, but it's worth introducing the topic now. We highly suggest hiring a competent tax accountant, ideally someone familiar with the video business (get a referral from a colleague). If possible, see if you can find an *enrolled agent* (EA). These are professional CPAs regulated by the government who have passed a special examination to be registered. It's a difficult status to attain and includes a background check by the government. EAs have a keen understanding of IRS tax code. Naturally, they may be more expensive, but the money they save you in taxes from what you don't know could pay for their fees.

For instance, when we first formed our corporation, one thing we learned from our EA was that any equipment or furnishings brought into the business could be written off at their fair market value, as if you purchased them. That means, if you found a desk on the side of the road, and officially brought it into your business, you could write it off as a purchase. The year we incorporated, we expensed a few thousand dollars worth of equipment and furniture from this one tip alone. We would not have known that without the assistance of our tax accountant.

As you'll also learn in Chapter 11, the money and time you'll save from hiring the right professionals and outsourcing work will be well worth your investment.

SOLE PROPRIETORSHIP

Sole proprietorship is by far the easiest business form to create. Basically, what you need to do is get your required local, city, and county licenses and permits and you're good to go. Naturally, you'll need to set up a bank account for your business that is separate from your personal account. As a sole proprietor, you'll have to pay self-employment taxes, and some expenses (such as health insurance) may not be completely tax-deductible. Also, as a sole proprietor, you are personally responsible for any debts, lawsuits, and other potential liabilities. That can be a scary thought, for example, if one of your lights on a shoot falls over and injures a guest.

If you do go the sole proprietor route, make sure to get a DBA ("doing business as") fictitious business name. Whenever you do business under a name other than your own, this is necessary. Often this name has to be filed at the county level; this is not the case in all locations and you should check with your local city or county office.

As a sole proprietor, an additional tax form is required to report your business income, but you will be taxed at your personal rate and the business itself won't pay any taxes.

PARTNERSHIP

If you're going into business with a second party (aside from a spouse), and you're not incorporating or forming an LLC, you'll have to set up a partnership. There are many other sources available for learning the specifics of creating a partnership, but the basics are: You'll need to create some form of partnership agreement that lays out details such as how the business will be run, how much of the business each partner owns, and what happens if a partner wants to leave. Also, the tax forms required for a partnership are different from those you'll need to file if you're in business by yourself.

If you enter into a partnership with someone, keep in mind that it's a bit like getting married, and it comes with much of what that implies. There will be great moments of "love and affection" between you and your partner(s). And you can rest assured that there will also be some knockdown, drag-out disagreements and fights. Make sure you partner with someone who can accept the challenges of going into business together and be willing to go the long haul. Your partner(s) should bring to the business talents that complement your skill set. If you're great at artistry, but lousy at business, find a savvy marketing partner. And it goes without saying, partner with people you can trust.

Like a sole proprietorship, the partnership itself does not pay income tax; each partner pays income tax on his or her pro rata share of the business income.

CORPORATION VS. LLC

Two other forms are corporations (**FIGURE 1.5**) and limited liability companies (LLCs). Each provides a layer of legal protection greater than that of a sole proprietorship or partnership. Depending on how much revenue you generate, there may also be some additional tax benefits for forming a corporation or LLC. For instance, FICA taxes that you pay on your employee wages are assessed in lieu of the self-employment tax you pay as a sole proprietor. FICA is only 7.65 percent versus the 15.3 percent self-employment tax. As a corporation, you also have the option to write off your health insurance expenses. (Consult your tax accountant for the best advice for your specific financial situation.)

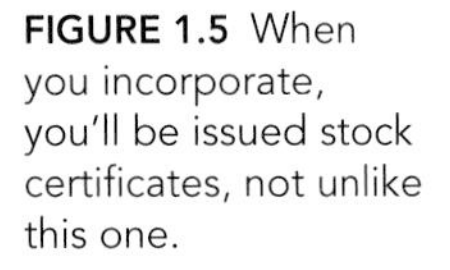

FIGURE 1.5 When you incorporate, you'll be issued stock certificates, not unlike this one.

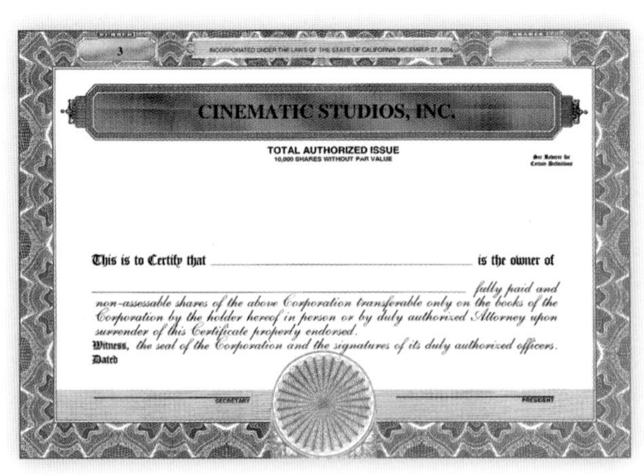

3

INCORPORATED UNDER THE LAWS OF THE STATE OF CALIFORNIA DECEMBER 27, 2004

CINEMATIC STUDIOS, INC.

TOTAL AUTHORIZED ISSUE
10,000 SHARES WITHOUT PAR VALUE

This is to Certify that ______ is the owner of

______ fully paid and non-assessable shares of the above Corporation transferable only on the books of the Corporation by the holder hereof in person or by duly authorized Attorney upon surrender of this Certificate properly endorsed.

Witness, the seal of the Corporation and the signatures of its duly authorized officers.

Dated

SECRETARY

PRESIDENT

When deciding whether to incorporate, you also need to consider what type of corporation to create: a C-Corp or S-Corp. We won't go into all the details of the differences. The most significant difference is that C-Corps pay income tax at the corporate tax rate, then any money taken out of the business also gets taxed at the personal tax rate. With an S-Corp, the corporation pays no income tax. The income (or loss) flows right through to you.

An LLC has very similar tax benefits to an S-Corp, and both offer the same level of legal shielding. Depending on your state, one may be more beneficial than the other. And since there is a minimum tax that corporations and LLCs have to pay regardless of the company's income, depending on your financial status, it may be better to wait. Be sure to consult your tax accountant if you choose this route.

We ran our business as a sole proprietorship for 2 years before incorporating as an S-Corp in 2004. We recommend that as soon as it makes sense for you to do so, either incorporate your business (as an S-Corp) or form an LLC. There will be more responsibilities required (such as keeping annual minutes), but the amount of extra administrative work is worth it.

PICK THE RIGHT SIZE

Part of choosing the right path is determining how you want to grow your business. Some business owners are interested only in having a small, single-person operation that allows them to get paid to do what they love. Others may want a deluxe studio with state-of-the-art editing suites, an amphitheater-style viewing room, and a stylish waiting area with a friendly receptionist. So let's look at the pros and cons of the various company sizes.

FREELANCER

The simplest of the pro video business paths you could choose is that of freelance shooter. There's nothing that says you have to create a formal company and build a big business. In fact, if you got into this line of work because of your love for the craft, and have little or no interest in dealing with the business side of it, we submit that becoming a freelancer is a direction you should seriously consider (**FIGURE 1.6**).

Let's say you love shooting—getting out there with your camera in hand, playing DP (director of photography) or auteur visual artist. You could make a fine living doing just that. Leave the hard-core sales and marketing, human resource management, administration, and other facets of running a company to the more entrepreneurial types. Your love for the art won't be weakened by all the other duties and hats you'd have to wear. You'll just go out, shoot for other studios, collect your paycheck, and call it a day. No customer service. No bridezillas. No "when will my video be ready?" inquiries from impatient clients whose wedding you just shot 2 weeks ago but they forgot or neglected to read the part of the contract that promises a 4-month turnaround on every project. As a freelance wedding videographer, you just go out, get some great shots, have some good food, and vicariously enjoy the celebration. Then you come home, absolved of any further responsibilities.

Maybe shooting corporate gigs is your passion. If you do them as a freelancer, you'll likely have less stress, a planned shot list, more control over the environment, and perhaps a bigger paycheck. The other benefit of corporate work is that most of it will likely take place during the week, leaving weekends free to spend relaxing with your family, reading a good book, or getting more great shooting ideas by going to see a movie.

FIGURE 1.6
Freelancers typically have their own video and audio gear to use on a shoot, although in some cases a larger studio may provide the equipment.

FIND YOUR FOCUS

Naturally, there's no reason you can't do all kinds of video work: corporate, weddings, stage events, and more. But you may find you'll get more work (and higher pay) if you specialize. The discipline and talent needed to shoot a wedding is very different from that needed to shoot a scripted corporate production. A wedding studio looking to hire you as a freelancer will want to have confidence in your ability to think fast on your feet, adapt to changing schedules, and anticipate the shot. Likewise, if a studio needs a freelance shooter for a corporate job, they will want to be confident in your ability to execute flawlessly, perhaps light a shot, bring your own pro gear, and represent yourself professionally. When you focus on a specific aspect of video production, and become known as an expert in that area, you'll be in greater demand.

FINDING WORK

Another huge benefit for the freelance videographer is that you can get a lot of work from fewer sources. Whereas the studio/production company has to advertise, network, and market, freelancers can focus their job search in a few places. You could hook up with just two or three studios that give you most, if not all, of your work. You could find those studios at a local Professional Videographers Association (PVA) meeting. Get up, announce yourself to the group, tell them you're available for freelance projects, and hand out a demo DVD reel of your shooting work. If you're good, studios will want to hire you.

You can also find a lot of consistent work from large video production agencies that have global filmmaker networks. Companies like TurnHere (www.turnhere.com), Sagas (www.sagas.com), and LicenseStream Production (www.imagespan.com/lsproduction) offer thousands of videographers from all around the world consistent commercial work for local small businesses looking for solid shooting and editing. Depending on your level of experience, the pay from companies like these may be lower than what you'd get from a more traditional studio in your area. However, the potential volume of work and the lower complexity level of the shoots may make up for it.

WHOLESALE VS. RETAIL

Many videographers who do freelance work for other studios may also have their own studio/production company. That's fine. In fact, it's good to offer your services to fellow video producers in your area. When you need help, they'll be there for you. One thing to keep in mind, though, is that the rate you'll be paid as a freelancer will most likely be less than the rate you'll receive when a consumer or corporate client pays you directly. This is as it should be.

As a production company serving a client, there are a host of expenses that go into serving that client that need to be covered by your rates, including sales and marketing, customer service, and project management. The rate you charge needs to cover all of these plus overhead and profit. As a freelancer, there may be some similar expenses you'll have, but not nearly the same level of costs invested in that shoot as the studio in charge.

This topic caused a bit of a controversy on my (Ron's) blog last year after posting an article about it. There were those who felt that if they get paid a certain rate to do a job when a client hires them, they should get paid the same rate if a studio hires them. The problem is that if that same rate is similar to or even more than what a hiring studio charges a client, the studio loses money if they hire a freelancer at the same rate. It's a fundamental aspect of any business that you need to charge more than the costs you invest in a job so that you can make a profit. The best analogy is found in the retail business. The freelancer's contribution to a project is the "wholesale" rate, whereas the studio's rate to the client is retail.

INTEGRITY AND HONESTY

Lastly, as a freelancer, you must have a high degree of integrity and honesty. A hiring studio is entrusting you with their client. You are representing that studio, not your own business. Passing out your business cards while on the job for another studio is a good way to get blacklisted. We also believe it's professionally unethical, like soliciting business from the clients of the studios who hire you. In cases like this, the golden rule is good to keep in mind: How would you feel if a freelance contractor you hired started going after *your* clients?

THE MOM AND POP SHOP

The next level up from freelancer is the small studio, typically comprised of one to three primary employees or partners. Many of these are "mom and pop" shops, usually small companies owned by husband and wife teams (**FIGURE 1.7**). The mom and pop business is in many ways the backbone of American business. A majority of small businesses in the United States fall in this category. If your business fits this description, there are a lot of advantages. You get to work alongside your spouse, using each other's respective talents to complement one another. One of you may be the organizer while the other is the artist. You can also save on contractor fees because your spouse can be your second cameraperson.

For the first two years of our business, Tasra was the company's second shooter for all wedding gigs. And having her there was great for other reasons besides not having to pay a second shooter. Her instincts as a woman and her attention to detail caught things I missed. She was also great at providing input during the editing process when selecting shots from a wedding shoot. She'd say things like, "Oh no, you can't use that shot of her. That's unflattering." Or she'd let me know if a particular edit gave her chills or not. The female input was very valuable.

FIGURE 1.7 Husband and wife team Mark and Trisha Von Lanken run Von Wedding Films, one of the most successful event video outfits in the country.

Being a mom-and-pop size business can add a level of intimacy to your relationships with your clients that many people appreciate. Particularly in the personal event video world, clients like to have a strong connection with their visual media producer. If you're going to have someone filming you on the most important day of your life, chances are you'll want someone you're comfortable around—maybe even someone who becomes a friend.

THE LARGE STUDIO

The final common incarnation of your business is that of a large studio. Studios produce an impressive number of jobs in a year (perhaps 100 or more). They may be working out of an actual studio location (as opposed to the living room or basement). There may be a few edit suites where employees come in to work.

As a large studio, your overhead will be significantly higher than if you're a freelancer or mom-and-pop studio. In order to maintain a production studio (**FIGURE 1.8**), the number of jobs you do and the rates you charge need to be pretty significant. Most of the country's largest production studios take on only commercial projects where the fees per job can get into the mid to high five-figure, and even six-figure fee range. Those large studios that primarily do wedding work are doing hundreds (and in some cases thousands) of weddings each year.

If you're hoping to grow your business into a large studio, you need to be ready for all the additional roles that will be necessary. In addition to your key production personnel, you'll most likely also need a full-time studio manager who will typically handle everything from client reception to bookkeeping to human resources to customer service.

FIGURE 1.8 Large studios have significantly more overhead costs than the freelancer or the mom-and-pop studio.

With on-site employees, you'll need to be a good leader and manager and there'll be employee laws and regulations from both the federal and state government with which you'll have to comply.

MAKE A PLAN

Chances are, most of you reading this will be building businesses that fit in the mom-and-pop or large studio categories (or somewhere in between). Whichever path you choose, we encourage you to create a business plan. Actually put down on "paper" what you want to achieve in your business, both personally and professionally. Start by answering the following questions:

- What kind of lifestyle do you want to have for yourself?
- How many hours per week would you like to work?
- Do you want to take vacations?

- How much money does your business need to generate to give you that lifestyle?
- Where will you find most of your business?

The process of writing a formal business plan is beyond the scope of this book, but if possible, we suggest you do just that. Find a good business-plan-writing program (check out Business Plan Pro at www.paloalto.com) if you're not sure how to write one. Find a business school student to write one for you. Once you have it, update it periodically, perhaps every 3 to 6 months. As Paul Arden says, "Without having a goal, it's difficult to score." Nowhere is this truer than in the business of videography.

WAY OUT WEDDINGS

WHAT COMES TO MIND WHEN you hear the term "wedding video"? If you're like most people, you probably get visions of a long, boring, cheesy documentary that only a mother of the bride could love. Corny animations of ringing church bells and bubbling champagne flutes superimposed over a shot of the wedding invitation probably come to mind as well.

If that's what you think contemporary wedding videos look like, it's time to throw those stereotypes away. Sure, there are still a few tucked-away corners of the world where wedding videos are still made like that, but today's wedding video is a whole new animal. (Note that if you're one of the holdouts we just mentioned, we hope this chapter will help you turn over a new leaf.)

The wedding video industry has come a long way. In the early years, weddings were shot with large cameras and lights that involved heavy battery packs, and videos were edited on tape-to-tape editors. The early Video Toaster systems created those aforementioned cheesy effects.

The advent of nonlinear editing, the accessibility of powerful editing tools, and the increased sophistication of today's brides have given rise to the "new and improved" wedding video. The best and most artfully crafted wedding videos today are nothing short of mini-movies. In fact, from here on out, that's how we'll refer to them—as movies. They have dramatic scores, breathtaking cinematography, cutting-edge and clever editing, and they tell stories.

Even though, in truth, every wedding movie is a documentary, the best-edited ones feel like scripted narratives. Instead of 90 minutes or two hours of sheer boredom, today's artistic wedding movies are often 30 minutes or less of tightly edited entertainment. At a recent wedding filmmaking workshop called Re:Frame 09, world-renowned filmmaker Jason Magbanua (remember the guy we talked about in Chapter 1 who made an award-winning video with a cell phone?) went so far as to argue that, with the right shots and effective sequencing, you can deliver more visual impact, emotional depth, and effective storytelling in a three-minute wedding film than in longer efforts, and proceeded to show a series of clips that proved his point. These aren't your mother's old wedding movies.

THE NEW WEDDING CINEMATOGRAPHER

The players in the game today have changed a lot as well. It used to be that most pros in the industry were older men with years of local television experience, or hobbyists with the disposable income necessary to buy the equipment. Expensive and complicated gear made the barriers to entry very high.

Today, you can purchase powerful high-definition digital cameras at a fraction of what greatly inferior cameras used to cost in the early years, and many personal computers, such as Apple's iMac, come with free editing software that is powerful enough to edit a feature film. These technologies have significantly lowered the barriers to entry. So now you have young people in their teens or early twenties shooting weddings and making a living (**FIGURE 2.1**).

We referred to the professionals of today as "cinematographers." I (Ron) have been in debates with more seasoned video professionals that would disregard the term cinematographer used in conjunction with anyone that is not shooting on film. Put aside the fact that "cinematography" is not a reference to the medium, but the science of light and composition. Put aside the fact that many of today's Hollywood cinematographers are themselves shooting in digital. The fact of the matter is that the most successful wedding video professionals today are as talented as any of the pros you'll find in Tinseltown. And many of them are shooting weddings with the same gear. (Ironically, a lot of them are shooting weddings on film, too, and being paid handsomely for it.)

FIGURE 2.1 Twenty-two-year-old Joshua Smith specializes in high-end destination weddings and model photography and has already been named one of the industry's 25 most influential producers 2 years in a row.

TODAY'S GEAR

Some of the equipment used today by the most gifted wedding cinematographers is the same equipment used to film your favorite episodic television programs and feature films. In order to achieve the level of cinematic excellence the artiste in them demands, many of today's wedding cinematographers are using Steadicams, jibs, 35 mm lens adapters, and high-quality HD cameras in order to create works of art that look and sound like feature films (**FIGURE 2.2**).

Then, there is another breed of cinematographer that has actually reverted to nostalgic technology. Old 8 mm and 16 mm film formats are being used creatively by some of today's artists, and they're getting top dollar for their work. In fact, it's ironic that in this age of high definition and Blu-ray, some of the highest-paid wedding film producers in the world—and some of those booking the most celebrity and royalty jobs—are shooting on camera gear that's older than the industry itself. Believe it or not, there are even some wedding studios that have shot weddings on actual 35 mm film—clearly an indication of our changing times.

FIGURE 2.2 Loyd Calomay of Red 5 Studios (www.red5studios.net) a professional Glidecam and vest setup. Photo by John Lauren Photography.

WEDDING VIDEO INDUSTRY RESOURCES

Great resources online and offline where the budding wedding video producer can learn everything about both the creative and business aspects include:

WEVA (Wedding and Event Videographers Association, www.weva.com). Established in the early '90s, WEVA is still the largest and oldest association committed to providing educational resources for the wedding and event videographer. In addition to their forum, each year WEVA holds a conference and trade show where between 1,000 and 2,000 video producers from around the globe converge to learn, network, and make new friends.

VU (Video University, www.videouniversity.com). Perhaps the largest online community of wedding and event video producers is located on VU. They have forums dedicated not only to weddings, but corporate shoots, photography, editing, and even a section for Mac users. This is a great place to start if you have questions about the industry and want fast and friendly feedback.

WedFACT (Wedding Filmmakers Alliance of Creative Talent, www.wedfact.net). A relative newcomer to the wedding cinematography forum world is WedFACT. Started and run by Canadian video producer Walter S. Chelliah, this community has deservedly earned an international reputation as the place to join to see the latest, most cutting-edge work in the business. The forum recently started an awards competition called WedFACTION that judges member videos submitted online.

Re: Frame (www.reframecollective.com). Started by a handful of leaders in the industry, Re: Frame is a boutique event produced twice a year in different locations. The events are designed to offer training in the latest creative trends to a small and intimate crowd.

In [Focus] (www.infocusvideoevent.com). The newest entry into the wedding and event video conference world is In [Focus]. Created by three of the original Re: Frame co-founders, In [Focus] offers business and creative training from world-renowned video producers in an intimate gathering. Not nearly as large as WEVA, but allowing significantly more attendees than Re: Frame—and with a different approach from both—In [Focus] effectively complements the existing shows.

EventDV (www.eventdv.net). *EventDV* is the trade magazine for the event video industry. Written primarily by videographers, it covers industry trends, business strategies, and event video gear, and features profiles of studios doing innovative work. *EventDV* hosts an annual awards competition called the EventDV 25 in which the magazine's 20,000 readers are invited to vote online for the 25 "hottest and most influential" studios in the world. They recently added an online TV site called EventDV-TV (www.eventdv-tv.com) that features some of the most successful studios in the business.

EDITING LIKE A FILMMAKER

Today's award-winning wedding movies are opening with panoramic vista shots, rich in color, and backed by Hans Zimmer-like soundtracks. The scenes are edited and juxtaposed with the audio in such a way that you feel like you're watching a scripted movie. The best man makes a joke about the groom's dancing ability (or lack thereof) and the scene cuts to a hilarious montage of the groom throughout the day, shaking his behind, tapping his feet, and grooving on the dance floor.

The popularity of "timeshifting" has also become a staple in the arsenal of the world's best wedding movie producers. In a timeshifted wedding movie, you rearrange the events of the day out of chronological order to tell the story of the day more effectively, just as directors do in contemporary feature films. Instead of a straight "A to Z" documentary of everything that happened on the wedding day, these timeshifted movies may start with the maid of honor's toast during the reception, then cut to the bride getting ready in the morning, then cut to the bride and groom dancing their first dance, and so on. The toast might even be used in voiceover with appropriate scenes of the wedding, such as the father of the bride talking about his daughter as the movie shows him walking her down the aisle or dancing at the reception. Like pieces to an emotional puzzle, the scenes of the day are gathered and aligned to tell a story that feels chronological on an emotional level, despite the events being presented in a different sequence.

BEYOND THE HIGHLIGHTS CLIP

If you plan to make wedding filmmaking a primary source of revenue for your business, you have a plethora of options to offer your potential clients. Part of the secret to success in the wedding filmmaking business is learning how to take concepts and ideas from other media sources and infuse them into your wedding movie production. These are all viable upsell opportunities for you to generate more revenue from your bridal client. Each one has its own unique benefit to the bride and groom. Determine what kinds of things they find important, then use that information to offer one or more of these options that meet their needs.

LOVE STORIES

One of the most popular side items from today's wedding movie menu is the "love story." This is a short documentary about the bride and groom that is most often shown during the reception. It is usually composed of interviews, photos, and perhaps some b-roll of the couple holding hands on a pier, kissing on a grassy meadow, or roller skating in the rink where they had their first date.

We suggest that when producing your love story, think about ways to make it as entertaining as possible. See how many aspects of the couple's dating life you can re-enact. Call up their friends and family to get them into the picture. Make sure to have fun on the set, too.

As we'll talk about later in our discussion on branding, the experience you create for your clients is a key aspect of building your brand, which is important in your sales and marketing. A big part of our brand for our wedding movie division is *fun*. When we're shooting a love story, our clients feel like they're on a movie set of a romantic comedy. We joke around, laugh, and create an atmosphere and a feeling of joy they take away with them long after the camera stops rolling.

Then, if you can transfer those feelings onto the screen, plus get the audience to cry at the end, you'll have a veritable blockbuster on your hands.

CONCEPT VIDEOS

Much like love stories, concept videos are short films starring the bride and the groom, and perhaps their friends and family. The main difference is that where the love story is in essence a short documentary, the concept video is a fictional narrative. Typically, the concept video will be a spoof on some pop-culture TV show or movie the bride and groom are fans of. Or, it could be a totally original piece meant to illustrate some aspect of their relationship in a unique way.

FIGURE 2.3 Scene from Cinematic Studios' award-winning "Bridal Boot Camp" concept video.

One of our first concept videos, for which we took first prize in an international contest, was "Bridal Boot Camp" (**FIGURE 2.3**), a comedy about a military-style boot camp where a bride and groom can learn how to be happily married. It was a perfect opportunity to play a series of visual pranks on the groom (all related to some marriage stereotype) while an overzealous sergeant puts him through the ringer.

The nice thing about concept videos is that, more than any other wedding movie option, they allow the Hollywood filmmaker in you to come out. Everything from writing a script, to creating a shot list, to yelling "action" and "cut" on the set, can be part of the process.

SAME-DAY EDITS

One increasingly popular addition to the wedding movie lineup is the "same-day edit." Only the bravest (or craziest) wedding filmmakers will try this one. Essentially, you take footage from the day of the wedding, hole yourself up in a room at the reception venue, and edit a three to seven minute highlight video of the day's events (**FIGURE 2.4**). If you thought shooting a live event like a wedding was pressure-filled, now try having to show the key events from the day to an anxiously awaiting audience. (Note that these are not rough cuts by any stretch, but stylized, carefully produced short movies.)

To make it work, it's best if you plan out your shots ahead of time. Lay out the video in your editing program, with slugs timed to the music, so that on the day of the wedding, you just have to replace the slugs with the shots. Sometimes we'll use text blocks describing the shot instead of slugs. If you can, hire a designated filmmaker to shoot just the shots needed for the same-day edit; otherwise, you'll have to remember to get the shots you need for the movie later even if you're tempted to pour all your energy into the same-day edit.

In the edited piece, make sure you save a spot for a clip from the first dance, which often occurs well into the reception. If you can show a highlights video from the day's events that also includes a shot from the dance the audience may have just witnessed an hour prior, the oohs and aahs from the guests and venue employees alike will be increased.

Same-day edits have become so popular, some studios are now offering only same-day edit packages. The advantages of this are obvious to any wedding filmmaker who's ever been buried under an editing backlog. But arguably the biggest advantage of doing a same-day edit is the exposure you get when you show your best work in front of an entire reception venue full of potential future clients. Be sure to have business cards ready after the applause subsides.

FIGURE 2.4 Daniel Boswell of DV Artistry (www.dvartistry.com) captures a first dance dip for his same-day edit.

WEDDING-DAY MUSIC VIDEOS

Perhaps equally crazy as shooting and editing a highlights video to be shown at the reception is getting the bride, groom, their wedding party, and other friends and family to participate in a music video shoot on the wedding day. You need a couple that is willing to dedicate a chunk of their wedding day to performing take after take as you film the various shots you need for the video. Again, a shot list is required. You'll also need a boom box with the song you plan to have the "stars" sing.

Naturally, the song should be one they know the words to so the lip sync looks convincing. Also make sure the bride and groom have recruited willing participants ahead of time. Good luck trying to coax a bunch of groomsmen, ready to start drinking at the bar, to spend what little time they have between the ceremony and the reception to shoot a music video. (The cocktail hour is usually the best time to shoot most of the shots. But you can get shots throughout the day as well, as long as everything is planned.)

What makes these shoots special is that you do them on the day of the wedding. It provides a fun spectacle for other guests to watch, and it adds to the experience of the day. Naturally, something like this isn't for everyone. But, the clients who do go for an option like this will be some of the most fun people you'll meet.

BRIDAL SPOTLIGHT VIDEOS

For the most part, brides will wear their dress only once. It's a shame to spend all that money on a dress and not get to wear it again. Well, give them the opportunity to not only wear it again, but to be filmed in a beautiful, stylized video. The bridal spotlight is essentially a music video starring the bride and her dress. These videos are usually filmed in various urban or nature settings, like back alleys, the beach, green pastures, and the like (FIGURE 2.5).

FIGURE 2.5 International award-winning wedding filmmaker Jeff Wright on his first-place bridal spotlight shoot.

TRASH THE DRESS

Perhaps the antithesis to the bridal spotlight video is the "Trash the Dress" (TTD) video. As with the bridal spotlight, you're giving the bride an opportunity to wear her dress again, and be filmed for posterity. But this time, she's going to do things in (and to) the dress that will essentially ruin it. This may include jumping in a public fountain, swimming under water in a swamp, getting into a mud-wrestling match with her new husband, or going dirt bike racing.

The idea is to create a shocking display and spectacle (and vaguely advance the idea that the marriage is for keeps, so she'll have no need for the dress again), while at the same time having a lot of fun (FIGURE 2.6).

FIGURE 2.6 Trash the Dress filming in the Nevada desert by Chris P. Jones using an 8 mm camera. *Image ©2007 John Michael Cooper, AltF.*

VIDEO INVITES/TRAILERS

In today's Web 2.0 age, the use of video online has grown tremendously. Even those of an older generation are familiar with sites like YouTube and Facebook. This means that most, if not all, of your clients' friends and family can enjoy additional creative services like video invites and trailers.

A video invite can be anything from just a headshot of the bride and groom talking to their guests and announcing the big day to a full-blown Hollywood-style movie trailer, complete with motion graphics, voice-over, and special effects. Your clients can then post it on YouTube, Facebook, or other video-sharing sites, and then send a link to all the wedding guests. In addition to giving your clients something their guests will talk about (more bragging points for the bride and groom), it gets your work in front of hundreds of friends and family well in advance of the wedding day. That's a great marketing opportunity.

PHOTO MONTAGES

No discussion of wedding movie side items would be complete without a discussion of the photo montage, aka the slideshow. More often than not, the bride and groom will take their photos and make their own slideshow using a program like iMovie or even PowerPoint. In cases like that, they're often very long, and not particularly interesting. But they're photos of friends and family, so guests will survive them.

If you get the opportunity to make a photo montage, it's your job to do something that looks significantly better than what the layperson would do. The rising popularity of Animoto (www.animoto.com), however, will make it more challenging for wedding movie producers to offer montages as a service.

Animoto is an online service that allows the user to upload photos, select a song, and get an advanced edited montage, timed to the music. What normally would have taken hours to edit traditionally in a nonlinear editing program takes just minutes with Animoto.

As you'll quickly gather as you read this book, the ability to evolve and adapt with the changing times is a necessity in this business. The latest trend in photomontages is the 3-D montage. Elements of the photos are cut out and placed on different layers in a program like Adobe Photoshop. They're then re-imported into the editing program, and manipulated to give the whole photo a 3-D look.

Successfully implementing these 3-D montages can take hours in Photoshop, your NLE, and often a designated motion effects program such as Adobe After Effects (which is, essentially, Photoshop on a timeline) or Apple's Motion. To be compensated fairly for the time needed to edit such a montage may require more funds than many brides will invest. But if you are able to market them successfully, they can be a lucrative product offering (**FIGURE 2.7**).

FIGURE 2.7 This is a screen shot from a 3-D photo montage by David Robin Films, produced primarily in Adobe After Effects. David's company has earned more than $26,000 (yes, twenty-six thousand dollars) for one of these montages.

SHOW WHAT YOU WANT TO SELL

Whether you offer one, some, or all of the options in this chapter, make sure you have samples to show on your Web site and on your demo DVD. If you don't have any to show, and if you're finding it difficult to sell them without an example, you should consider making one free of charge. Choose a client who will be an exceptional candidate, someone who will really get into it and make the whole process look like a lot of fun. If you can, always show outtakes. Anything that can illustrate what the experience is like working with you will go a long way toward convincing a prospect to add one of these options to their package. Once you have a solid portfolio of options, don't feel the need to continue offering them for free. One sample is enough in each category to show what you are capable of producing.

IN FOCUS:
DAVID ROBIN

A PIONEER CONTINUES TO PUSH THE ENVELOPE

One of the pioneers of the wedding video industry, with more than 25 years in the business, is David Robin of Boulevard Video Productions and david robin | films (www.davidrobinfilms.com). David's Encino, California, business has had the opportunity to produce wedding, event, and commercial video productions for Hollywood celebrities and the social elite of Los Angeles. Due to his celebrity clientele, he's had the opportunity to direct the likes of James Caan and Paris Hilton for client bar mitzvah videos.

For the past two years, David's studio has been selected to record the Oscars' Governors Ball, and the 2008 Emmys' Governors Ball. To add to that, for the fourth consecutive year, David was elected to the EventDV 25. The reason David has continued to remain at the top of his game is because he continues to adapt with the changing times.

It wasn't long after Canon released its EOS 5D Mark II (the DSLR that shoots high-quality HD video) that David was taking it with him and shooting weddings with it. He's also become a leading producer of 3D photo montages (**FIGURE 2.8**), and his bar and bat mitzvah concept videos are legendary. When you look at David's business, it seems fresh and young, keeping up with the changing times and current trends of both the video and Internet world.

FIGURE 2.8
Another screen shot from one of david robin | films' 3-D montages.

IN FOCUS: STILLMOTION

NEW KIDS ON THE BLOCK

A studio out of Toronto, Canada, is making a huge splash in the wedding filmmaking industry despite being on the scene for only a few years. StillMotion (www.stillmotion.ca) is a leader in producing cinematic works of art that boggle the mind. Video artists Patrick Moreau, Michael Wong, and Konrad Czystowski use Steadicams, 35 mm adapters (FIGURE 2.9), HD video cameras, and the new Canon 5D Mark II the way Picasso used a paint brush. Their work evokes emotion, tells stories, and looks like something you'd see on the big screen.

They are meticulous about their craft, but at the same time, are extremely savvy marketers and brand builders. Their Web site, blog, and printed collateral all come together to create a cohesive look and feel. Their studio also provides photography services, and the one-two punch is great for business.

FIGURE 2.9 Patrick Moreau of StillMotion demos the Canon EOS 5D Mark II on a Steadicam Flyer at one of the company's highly sought after Evolution Experiences, a 3-day in-studio workshop in Toronto, Canada.

IN FOCUS: LOYD CALOMAY

THE 'CULTURE CLUB'

Another producer who is making waves in the wedding cinematography world is Loyd Calomay out of Tustin, California. Loyd is living a filmmaker's dream. His studio, Red 5 Studios (www.red5studios.net), gets paid good money to shoot spoof concept videos for his clients. He's spoofed everything from *Mission: Impossible* and *The Matrix* to *Notting Hill* and *Napoleon Dynamite*.

When you see some of these productions, your jaw will drop at the detailed, choreographed fight sequences, dazzling visual effects, and high-energy soundtracks. The behind-the-scenes photos of these shoots look like Hollywood studio press images (**FIGURE 2.10**). Loyd has become so adept at producing these concept videos that he has a whole section of his Web site devoted to them. He does about a half-dozen a year and charges as much as he does for a full wedding—as well he should.

FIGURE 2.10 A behind-the-scenes look at the filming of Loyd Calomay's spoof production of the television show *Heroes*.

You'll also notice that in offering these concept videos, Loyd has tapped into a certain demographic that really likes them—young, professional Asian-Americans.

Tapping into a specific cultural community is a very smart marketing strategy when selling wedding video services. Close-knit communities with a common cultural background (whether based on race, religion, gender, etc.) tend to refer business to one another, and can be a source of loyal clientele. For David Robin, it's the strong Jewish community in Hollywood. For Loyd, it's the Asian-American community. Other savvy wedding videographers have tapped into the religious community of the Church of Latter-Day Saints (LDS); for years, award-winning Salt Lake City wedding filmmaker David Perry promoted his services using a demo that consisted almost entirely of LDS brides talking about the meaning of LDS marriage and the significance of Temple weddings. When you're seen as an expert in meeting the needs of a particular demographic, clients in that demographic will seek you out.

EVENT EMPORIUM

IN THIS CHAPTER, WE'LL DELVE into other avenues and sources of revenue in video production, specifically for the wedding and event videographer. Although the options are nearly limitless, it's important to remember not only what we've covered in the previous chapters about choosing your path, but also the title of this book: *ReFocus.*

We don't want you to look at this chapter as an instruction manual for what you should be doing, but more like a suggested playlist. It's something like the Genius button in iTunes. You choose a song and the Genius button offers you suggestions for other songs you might like. Sometimes the songs fit, and sometimes they don't, but only you can make the call.

Let us be your Genius for a moment and offer you some suggestions that might fit with where you are and where you want to be. As you go into this chapter, consider what "song" you're playing right now, and filter the following ideas through that lens.

EXPANDING YOUR REACH

How do you know when you're ready to add to your offerings as a video producer? Is there ever an ideal time to expand your services?

At the end of Chapter 2, we mentioned that you can generate revenue from targeting specific cultural communities. You can take this strategy to the next level when you start marketing specific event video services. With expertise in both religious and cultural events that are catered to very specific cultural communities, you can serve these communities more effectively and build new revenue streams for your business.

One of the questions we hear most frequently from video professionals who are considering adding to their current list of services is, "When is the time to make the move?" Similar to getting married, having your first child, or buying a home, there is never a perfect time.

However, there are some key issues to consider when making the change:

Are you current with your outstanding projects? You wouldn't want to start offering new services while in the middle of a backlog of editing projects that you can't see your way out of. The entrepreneurial and creative drive that is usually an asset can turn into a liability if you always focus on the next big idea when you haven't completed the last big idea.

Are you delivering projects on time and on budget? Adding anything else to your business mix will likely complicate your workflow, accounting, and sales and marketing efforts. Since current clients are considered the best source of referrals and future projects, make sure they are satisfied first before opening the door to other options.

Does your company need another revenue stream? This one question could potentially trump the other two. If your current revenue streams have dried up because of the economy or the season, getting another service or option to clients right away can mean the difference between keeping your doors open another year and leaving the business.

Take some time to answer these questions before moving on to the emporium of events listed in the rest of this chapter. If you have a mom-and-pop company, talk through them with your spouse or partner. If you're on your own, find another businessperson or mentor to help you answer them and do an honest assessment of where you are today.

From religious and cultural ceremonies to retirements and memorials, our lives are filled with events. The event video producer is poised to capture and share these events in a way that many people may not even know is possible. Your job is to find your niche, an event or area that inspires you, and "take that hill" for your business. Make it yours. Become the expert, the specialist. That's when the calls will start coming in.

RELIGIOUS AND CULTURAL EVENTS

According to Jean Chatzky of *Money Magazine*, many of today's teen celebrations have grown-up price tags. Shows like "My Super Sweet 16" on MTV surely aren't helping budget-conscious parents keep their teens' expectations modest. And Chatzky wonders if the infamous "bridezilla" is being replaced by "teenzilla."

Money Magazine, USA Today, and *The New York Times* have all written articles about the high cost of teen celebrations, with prices easily reaching six figures. Would the following price tags shock you?

- Sweet 16 party: $10,000
- Bar or bat mitzvah: $9,500
- Quinceañera: $8,000

Given those figures, I think it's worth taking a look at what's possible in these arenas for event video production.

BAR AND BAT MITZVAH

First up is the bar and bat mitzvah celebration, perhaps second only to weddings in the event video world with respect to popularity. Essentially the bar/bat mitzvah is the coming of age of a young Jewish boy or girl, which happens after completing years of Hebrew school. It is an extremely significant event in the life of a Jewish family. Entire families get involved, including grandparents, parents, and cousins. The bar/bat mitzvah celebrant will even invite a number of his or her friends from school. In many communities, the amount of time and money invested in a bar/bat mitzvah rivals that invested in weddings. In affluent communities in particular, it's not unheard of to have budgets in the five- or six-figure range. So this is definitely an area where you can make a great living.

One thing that's unique with bar/bat mitzvah events (FIGURE 3.1) is that you're really dealing with two clients, the parents and the teen. It's a positive in that you are also catering to a younger demographic, which gives you more creative freedom; bar/bat mitzvah's often present great opportunities for concept videos. You could also make a pitch to parents to do a fun video skit starring their teen as a superstar. It gives you an opportunity to create something unique and fun their parents will love seeing their son or daughter in. The teen will enjoy seeing themselves and show it to their friends, and maybe even get their friends involved in the process.

FIGURE 3.1 DVD cases from two of our first bat mitzvah productions—"VH1: Behind the Mitzvah and Mitzvah: Possible."

So in addition to doing concept videos, the event itself gives you many of the same shooting, editing, and storytelling opportunities that weddings give you. From the teen getting ready in the morning to going to the temple and the ceremony, you can do interviews with friends and family before the ceremony. As you transition to the party later on, it's similar to the wedding reception with food, dancing, cultural traditions, and toasts. Most likely there will be photos with a photographer. If you do end up creating a concept video or montage, it will be shown at the reception.

Something to keep in mind is that there are four types of Jewish temples: Orthodox, Conservative, Reform, and Reconstructionist. If you're not Jewish yourself, you will most likely not film Orthodox events.

If you are not familiar with the culture, it's vital that you learn those social mores prior to your first event. Be familiar with the appropriate things to do during the ceremony and at the temple. Knowing what to say and where to move will make a big impact in a sacred temple and should be taken into consideration when you're shooting.

Since a lot of the reading is done in Hebrew, find a way to incorporate the reading into your video in a way that makes sense. You may want to enlist the help of the parents and teens to translate and select key sections of the reading for the final production. Most clients will enjoy being part of the process, so get them involved early to make the video something they will treasure for years to come.

QUINCEAÑERA

Similar to the bar/bat mitzvah, the quinceañera or quince años (15 years), is a coming-of-age celebration in Latin American culture for girls turning 15. It's a significant event in the life of the family and the teen, and the budgets for these celebrations can be considerable. The dresses, planning, and decorations will often rival the formalities and elaborate plans of a wedding.

The celebration typically begins with a religious ceremony at a church. The young girl will affirm her faith and often receive religious gifts as part of the ceremony. From there, a reception, similar to a wedding reception, with music, food, dancing, and cultural traditions will take place.

FIGURE 3.2 Quinceañera celebrations can be as elaborate as any wedding celebration. (Photo © Carlos Garcia Photography)

References to quinceañera can be found in popular culture movies, television, and books, including a 2006 film (Richard Glatzer and Wash Westmoreland's *Quinceañera*), a soap opera, and TV series. It is important to note that quinceaños celebrated in the United States (**FIGURE 3.2**) often represent the family's economic and social status. This may be why we see rising budgets and so much attention paid to these teen celebrations.

BAPTISM AND CONFIRMATION

Baptism and confirmation take place in many Christian churches, including Catholic and Protestant (**FIGURE 3.3**). Traditionally, they may not be as elaborate as the above celebrations, but they are key moments in people's lives that can be shot and edited to create lasting memories. Because they are often smaller in scope, the shooting and editing requirements will also be more minimal. However, the size of the event doesn't preclude you from inserting your creative energy into these types of videos.

FIGURE 3.3 Lee Bakogiannakis of 2DG Style was awarded second place in a WedFACT competition for his Baptism video.

These types of family events are a way to ensure repeat business. When a couple gets married, you record their wedding and a few years later they have their first child and baptism. If you've maintained a relationship with the client, they'll call you because you built those strong connections around their wedding and engagement. This is the type of business that will keep you going in and out of season and in and out of recessions and economic downturns.

A key here is maintaining some type of periodic contact with your clients, with either a newsletter or blog, so that as events come up you are in the forefront of their minds. We will go into this in more detail in later chapters on sales and marketing.

CAPTURING MILESTONE MOMENTS

The next set of events are all related to milestone moments in an individual or family's life. "Milestone" is a key word to use in marketing and when talking to clients. It gives a sense of a moment passing that won't return.

BIRTHDAY PARTIES FOR MILESTONE YEARS

Sweet 16. 21 Forever. Over the Hill. The Golden Years. These are all phrases we're familiar with because they represent significant moments in our lives.

Former wedding clients may hire you when their parents reach these pivotal ages. The scope of the celebrations can vary widely, from a simple montage to the full production of a documentary, the possibilities are open.

A couple of years ago, we produced a 60th birthday event video for a mother of one of our early bridal clients. Her husband hired us to film the event and create a montage. The party was a grand affair that took place on a San Francisco Bay cruise ship.

ANNIVERSARIES

Anniversaries are big celebrations, particularly ones celebrating 25 years or more of marriage. They represent an opportunity for you to record the event (something like the reception at a wedding), but it's also a chance to do montage, love story, or documentary work as well.

We recently produced a 40-year anniversary video (**FIGURE 3.4**) that was 30 minutes long and included close to 100 photos, interviews with the husband and wife, soundtracks from the decade when they were dating, and romantic b-roll of the couple at their home. It was a huge success. People laughed. People cried. It was fun for the friends, children, and grandchildren to see old photos of the couple in their teens and early twenties looking young and full of life.

FIGURE 3.4 The DVD face from a 40th anniversary production. This is the couple on their wedding day in 1969.

It's fun to hear an anniversary couple's stories and it's also a great testament and example when you have a couple that has stayed together that long. Couples who have been married a long time will love to be able to pass that message along to their children and grandchildren.

Frequently, when potential clients are resistant to doing these types of projects, it's not that they don't want to do them; it's simply that they don't think about it. They may not know what is possible. That's why it's vital to have a monthly newsletter, a blog, and a place where you can show examples and keep your clients up to date on your latest products.

Be confident when you pitch these services. Remember that at the same time you are selling your services, you're also offering them the real gift of capturing the memories of these times in their lives. If you believe that, know that, and are confident in that, then you will be able to sell these services and grow and diversify your business by doing so.

RETIREMENT

Recording retirement events can be another big business. If you're able to do a number of retirement-related productions, you can market yourself as an expert in them.

When you're showing a retirement video to an executive, you may even find future business through the retiree's connections—perhaps corporate work via the company from which the person is retiring, fellow retirees, and personal work and events from friends and colleagues. It's an excellent way to get your work in front of a lot of high-income individuals who have a significant number of milestones happening in their lives.

If you're a wedding movie producer and you do a good job of keeping in contact with your wedding clients, a retirement video is likely a product or service you can sell to them for their parents. If this is something that interests you, now is the ideal time to get into it because of the baby boomers who are going to be hitting retirement. Retirement videos may not be very popular 20–30 years from now because much of today's generation will not have stayed at any one company for a significant length of time. This means there won't be the large corporate retirement parties that are still happening now.

MEMORIALS

Another event that is bittersweet is the passing of a loved one. Memorial videos are an opportunity to create a keepsake for the friends and family. You can record the memorial service itself, create a tribute video to show at the memorial service, or both. Tribute videos can be as simple as a montage of photos, or as complex as an A&E "Biography"-style documentary featuring interviews with friends and family.

If you're located near a large mortuary or funeral home, consider partnering with these companies to be the studio that creates these videos for their customers. It's an opportunity to create a high-volume, consistent business. But keep in mind that the day-to-day workflow of memorial video is very different from wedding video. If you build relationships with funeral homes, get your bookings through them, and produce photo montages to show at funerals, you'll typically have fewer than 72 hours to complete a project from booking and collection of assets to editing and delivery.

Alan Naumann is an expert in this area and writes a column called "Cradle to Grave" for *EventDV* magazine. In the May 2008 issue, Alan provided insight into why you might want to consider offering this service to your clients:

> Every time we produce a memorial tribute video, we gain acceptance with families whose lives have been impacted by our videos. As a result, we have never lacked for work. Whether it is doing a video biography, transferring home movies to DVD, or taping a wedding, it all stems from our work in funeral videography, and the way we have positioned our company as a media consultancy in the funeral market. Funeral videography is alive and well—and because of it, so is our business.

There are more detailed resources and training that you can find if this is an avenue you are interested in pursuing. It's a bit of an investment, but one resource is Naumann's *Complete Course in Funeral Videography*, available from www.memoryvision.tv.

CATCHING LIVE ACTION EVENTS

Live action events provide two possible avenues for your services. One is to create a video of the event itself for the organization. The second option is to produce a DVD of the event to sell.

Depending on whether the production is a stage event of someone else's written work, a musical containing copyrighted songs, or a concert, there will be varying licenses and rights you'll need to attain to record it and then sell it.

When negotiating the contract to create a DVD to sell, if possible, build into the contract a minimum fee or a sales guarantee so that all your hard work and labor is covered even if only a small number of people end up buying the DVD. For a recent DVD we produced that covered a photography seminar event, we negotiated a five-figure retainer (plus travel expenses) and we split the revenue from DVD sales 50-50. If you're not able to secure some sort of up-front payment, make sure the reward on the back-end is worth the risk (maybe it's a larger cut of sales or high-profile or wide exposure of your work with the right clientele).

SPORTS

High schools and colleges are great places to contact about offering sports documentaries or recap videos. From kids and parents vying for entrance and scholarships into colleges, to coaches wanting to improve their team performance through game analysis, the possibilities in this field are wide open.

Football has been and will probably continue to be one of the most popular and lucrative sports to cover. But don't let that discourage you from pursuing other sports such as lacrosse, gymnastics, tennis, or swimming. Each sport has a unique set of opportunities and participants with equal interest and enthusiasm.

FIGURE 3.5 Sporting event video is a growing business with plenty of live action to be captured.

Highlight reels for personal use or for academic scholarships are high on the list of priorities for families who have invested years of time, energy, and money into their children's sports success (**FIGURE 3.5**). Considering the money that can be saved with scholarships, an investment in a high-quality video can be well worth the effort—something to remind parents of when marketing this type of video.

Providing top-notch customer service and quality is key to getting repeat business and referrals. In an age in which many parents will have prosumer cameras and equipment, it's important to make your company and final product stand out. From clear audio to smooth shots, engaging soundtracks, and the best angles, paying attention to details will separate you from the pack.

Some videographers charge upwards of $7,000 for sports highlights reels, complete games, and interviews. Alternatively, general game DVDs can be sold individually for as low as $15 each. How you market yourself, what type of services you offer, and how much time and energy you invest, will all determine where your company will fit on the sliding scale of sports videographers.

DANCE RECITALS

Much like sporting events, for some families dance recitals (**FIGURE 3.6**) represent a huge investment of labor and love. Shawn Lam out of Vancouver, Canada (www.shawnlam.ca), is an international award-winning producer of dance recital videos.

FIGURE 3.6 HD video screen shot of a dance recital, featuring Emily Johnston from Vancouver's One Dance Creative Arts Centre.

Below is a high-level overview, in Lam's own words, for those interested in pursuing this type of event video.

> The dance recital market can be very lucrative and makes great strategic sense for a business owner who wants year-over-year growth. Unlike most social event video markets, such as the wedding video market, dance recitals happen every year so you are able to count on repeat annual sales. They also are a tight community, so if you do good work you can count on referrals.
>
> Most recitals are one to three hours per production and the deliverable is a one or two-disc DVD set. Set-up takes one to two hours before the show, mainly to work with the audio technicians to get a pair of XLR feeds from the sound board for the music and stage sounds (tap or vocals).
>
> There are also several related markets including dance competitions, video adjudication, and other stage events (plays, musicals, choir concerts, music acts). Some are more lucrative than others and the markets you go after should be a fit with your overall business strategy and model.

There are two ways to sell your work for these events. The first is to sell directly to students and parents with an order form. While this is the most common, Shawn takes a different approach in order to get his DVDs into the hands of more participants. By coordinating an agreement with the studio, the DVD is worked into the registration fee at a lower cost, so that each student automatically receives a copy. Although price per unit is significantly less, the volume approach of selling 200–300 DVDs versus 50 makes it worth creating such an agreement. Adding completed videos or short clips to your Web site is a great way to market your services and build traffic and buzz around your productions.

SPECIALIST VS. GENERALIST

In listing all of these types of events, in no way are we saying that you could or should incorporate all of them into your services. It really is an emporium, as the chapter title suggests. We are simply giving you an idea of the options. There may be some that interest you and others that you'd never want to cover, which is fine.

It's much more important that you are clear about what you want to do, what inspires you, and what energizes you. Equally important is clarity about what drains you and de-motivates you. Even though there may be great money in retirement videos, if it's something that causes you to sit at your editing desk and dread or procrastinate, that's not where you want to focus your energies. When reviewing business options, make sure you stay focused on what fits you, your brand, and where you want to be in the event video world.

Another point, which we addressed earlier, is specializing. As much as possible, you do want to specialize in an area of video production where you can be seen as an expert. Studies show that if you specialize in something, anyone who is looking for that particular type of product or service will go to the specialist first instead of a generalist. Be smart and strategic about how you market each of your services. Don't try to be all things to all people. Any one of these avenues could be a self-sustaining business by itself. But if you do pursue more than one, market them with different Web sites and company names. Yes, it does create a little more work, but from a branding and marketing perspective, it's a smarter approach.

IN FOCUS:
SHAWN LAM

UNPLANNED SUCCESS: AN INTERVIEW WITH SHAWN LAM

Q: How did you get started in dance recital productions?

My company's first contract was a dance recital. We didn't plan it that way; my brother and I started our first company to produce high school DVD yearbooks and later, wedding videos. When the dance teacher found out that we were already working in the school, she asked us if we could film her dance recital for the students. Because the dance recital was scheduled before the graduate dinner and commencement ceremony, this dance recital was actually our first video production, even though we had already booked several wedding clients for later in the summer. The videos were very well received.

Unfortunately, the following year the dance teacher was bumped from her teaching position due to union rules and we were unable to renew the contract.

Two years later I started Shawn Lam Video (**FIGURE 3.7**) and handpicked a few niche markets to build my business. I realized that previously I spent 90 percent of my time and marketing dollars on weddings and school clients, but they accounted for only 50 percent of my bookings. I found it much easier for me to book and retain clients from my other markets: primarily performance events, corporate events, and training DVDs. Dance recitals were one of my key performance event target markets.

Q: Is there any advice you would offer a video producer interested in targeting this market?

The dance recital season is concentrated in a busy mid-May-to-late-June end-of-school season, which means you can only handle so many recital contracts with a single two-person crew, and it isn't a market that can support you year-round.

FIGURE 3.7 Video producer Shawn Lam, in themed attire, filming the Kauhane School of Polynesian Dance year-end recital.

I decided to offer my services at dance competitions that happened much earlier in the year in order to get demo material that I could then show to prospective dance studios for their dance recital business. This is a great way to get your foot in the door.

Then I contacted participating studios one by one with the following generous offer: I would edit one of their competition routines for free in exchange for passing my order forms to their students. Once I got a commitment, I took the opportunity to ask them about their year-end dance recital video production and gained several contracts this way.

Q: What type of advertising have you done?

I had great success by taking out a small and very inexpensive ad in dance recital competition programs. For several years now I have reached my capacity in this short season and simply rely on my Web site and referrals to replace normal studio turnover.

COMMERCIAL SUCCESS

ONE OF THE MANY BENEFITS of being an independent video producer is the flexibility and adaptability of your business. While it's easy to get stuck in a rut shooting and editing the same types of projects, you don't have to stay there.

If you're ready to try something new and start exploring options outside of shooting personal events, this chapter is for you. We'll give you insight into the differences between commercial and personal event work as well as offer ideas for producing videos for more than just revenue—videos with a heart.

We'll also cover working with small companies to global entities and agencies. Once you're energized and excited about the possibilities, we'll reveal the sales process for commercial jobs, which differs quite a bit from personal events.

Let's get started.

CHANGING DIRECTION

We have always done commercial jobs, even from the beginning of our business. Prior to starting our company, Ron worked for Intuit as a business marketing manager. When he left that job in the summer of 2002 to pursue his dream of running his own video business, one of the first things he did was approach his colleagues at Intuit and ask if they had any work for a starving artist looking to spread his wings. And he got a job.

That first job was an internal concept video created to teach QuickBooks employees about the new version of QuickBooks 2003. We did a James Bond spoof that was written by one of the employees and directed by Ron. It was called "To Catch a Gecko" (**FIGURE 4.1**). (Like most technology companies, every year Intuit has secret code names for its latest product releases, and that year the code name was Gecko.)

FIGURE 4.1 Movie-like poster created for "To Catch a Gecko," featuring two of Intuit's employees as lead actors.

We went all out and got managers involved—even the vice president in charge of the QuickBooks division, who happened to be an avid James Bond fan. She was N in the spoof, which was a play on the character M in the James Bond series.

That project started us on the road to corporate work. Since then we've done corporate jobs for clients as a way to generate new business and keep revenue coming in as well as provide us with a diverse portfolio.

As you can tell from this example, there are incredible opportunities to stretch your creativity in corporate and commercial work. While some companies may be looking for a standard recording of their annual meeting, many other companies are ready to explore a more creative approach to training, marketing, and promotion. The more creativity and original ideas you bring to the negotiation, the better your chances are of getting to shoot and edit those types of productions.

In spring 2007, we made a strategic decision in our business, the first of many such moves that shifted our focus to commercial work. At the time, 65 percent of our revenue was coming from personal event work and 35 percent was from commercial work. All of the commercial work was simply from word of mouth. We decided to reverse that trend and change the direction from high-end weddings to corporate and commercial projects.

Up to that point, we had done everything to keep the two divisions separate. We had a separate name, brand, and Web site for each division. Cinematic Video Productions was the name for our commercial work, and Cinematic Studios was the name for our personal event work (**FIGURE 4.2**).

A tricky part of changing directions was that we wanted to keep the name Cinematic Studios, which meant we had to change what Cinematic Studios meant for our wedding clients.

The first reason we made the change is that to do the kind of work we wanted to do, we needed to go after larger corporate projects. We believed there would be greater upside potential for the company in the long term in making the switch.

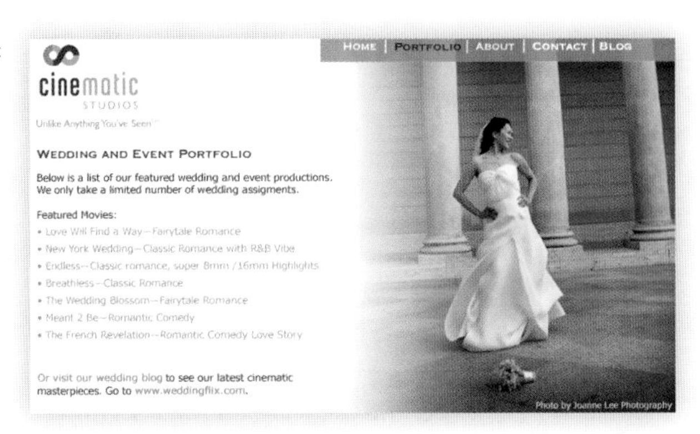

FIGURE 4.2 Cinematic Studios Web site portfolio page featuring a wedding image from Joanne Lee Photography.

At the time, Ron was engaged in a business coaching relationship with Kim Fulcher, a business and life coach and owner of Compass Life Designs. Kim laid it on the line and basically asked, "Why are you busting your butt for small personal jobs when the type of work you do should and could be bringing in significantly higher revenue in the commercial world? Clients who have the budgets to pay for the talent you have are who you should be pursuing."

Leave it to a coach to challenge your best intentions and your inclination to play it safe. Our coaching work with Kim is what inspired both of us to start coaching clients in our areas of expertise: branding, social media marketing, business development, blogging, writing, and life balance.

Another factor that nudged us in that direction was that 2007 was the year we produced a highlights video of the yearly conference for Wedding and Portrait Photographers International (WPPI), one of the largest, for-profit organizations for professional photographers (**FIGURE 4.3**).

FIGURE 4.3 WPPI 2009 hosted more than 12,000 attendees at the MGM Grand in Las Vegas. Photo © Kenny Kim Photography

When we first attended that conference, we did it ostensibly as a networking opportunity for the wedding business. More than 10,000 photographers attended the event. That sparked the idea that we had even more potential to reach those photographers and the companies that serve them.

Switching our focus to corporate work meant starting over with a new look and new positioning in the market. Clients were finding us through different avenues, and we were challenged to start marketing to a new clientele for the first time in our history. In the first year after making the switch, our ratio of corporate to personal events reversed.

Moving quickly, we formed strategic partnerships with other companies within the wedding and portrait world, including liveBooks, Pictage, and PDN Photo Plus Expo. In one year, we established ourselves as the leading provider of professional video services in the pro photographic industry. That was the niche for our commercial work.

UNLOCKING THE SALES PROCESS

A key to success in corporate video production is having a keen understanding of what goes into the process of luring and booking prospects. We want to share with you some tips and tools you can use—information we wish we had at the very beginning of our foray into this brave new world.

KNOWING YOUR CLIENT

There are some key differences between commercial and personal event work that affect the sales process.

Clientele. You're obviously dealing with a different clientele—rather than an individual or a family, you're dealing with a corporation or perhaps multiple individuals on a team. Understanding what makes these types of clients tick is crucial for success.

Mind-set. Another key difference is the demographic you're pursuing and mindset of your new client base. We think it's crucial that you have a separate Web site for commercial and wedding work. Having a splash page on your site with a link going to each site is not the same as having a separate Web site for each. In fact, it dilutes your message by casting you as a generalist rather than a specialist.

Focus. The reason to have a separate Web site for each division is to appear to have a clear focus. Whether it's deserved or not, many corporate clients have a negative impression of wedding videographers that will preclude them from selecting you for a job. It can be harder to sell yourself to corporate clients if you are also showing them Sally and Harry's wedding video.

Deadlines. Deadlines are going to be much stricter in the corporate world than in personal event work. It's not uncommon in the wedding world to miss deadlines and promised due dates. There are some wedding companies that promise turnaround times of six months, but then they take a year to deliver the final product. That will not work in the corporate world. You need to be able to hit the date that you give your client. If you're going to miss a deadline, communication throughout the process is critical.

A WALK THROUGH THE PROCESS

The process we're going to take you through is a generalized one that has worked for us. Take from it all the elements that fit best with *your* studio.

When you're in the process of submitting a bid to a client, many times the client will give you an RFP (request for proposal). This is a document that outlines the general objectives of the client, required deliverables, and a formal request to your company to submit a bid (**FIGURE 4.4**).

There are different schools of thought on submitting bids. Some video production companies will put together a detailed bid with line items for all the different aspects that go into the job. This strategy makes it easy for clients to pick and choose what they want if the budget is too high for them as submitted. We used this strategy for the first couple years.

In this arrangement, *Flyin' West* will serve as Project Lead and will have primary interaction with the client. At all appropriate times throughout the design and approval process, you will be asked to participate in meetings with the client. The great majority of these meetings will be facilitated via phone. Invoices will be submitted to *Flyin' West*. Please note if a deposit is necessary to commence work. *Flyin' West* allows for a 30-day window to remit payment upon receipt of payment from the client. Historically our turnaround of payment is within 5-8 business days but we allow for extended time away from the office for business or personal travel.

Description of Requested Services

A. Video production services to capture weekly Sunday morning services to be edited to 30 or 45 minutes at the direction of the client. May include a standard, or frequently changed intro and outro at your creative direction.

1. Concept development
2. Design and implementation of process flow
3. Videotaping and/or training of Cathedral resources to complete same [assume start up quantity of 13 videos]. Please provide your recommendation for implementation.
4. Editing
5. Music selection and application
6. Coordination with the Cathedral's webmaster/web designer for the uploading and placement of vides in the Media Center
7. Coordination with the StreamingFaith.com resources to ensure timely uploading of videos
8. Evaluation of video effectiveness with recommendations for improvement

B. Video production services to capture a minimum of 10 special event or ministry specific videos of no more than 10 minutes at the direction of the client.

1. Concept development
2. Design and implementation of process flow
3. Videotaping and/or training of Cathedral resources to complete same [assume start up quantity of 13 videos]. Please provide your recommendation for implementation.
4. Editing
5. Music selection and application
6. Coordination with the Cathedral's webmaster/web designer for the uploading and placement of vides in the Media Center
7. Coordination with the StreamingFaith.com resources to ensure timely uploading of videos
8. Evaluation of video effectiveness with recommendations for improvement

C. Design of the Streamingfaith.com "site" where the Cathedral's videos will be viewed. Please see www.streamingfaith.com for example.

FIGURE 4.4 Sample request for proposal.

Then, after some years of experience, looking at projects and keeping track of time and other factors, we revised our bid strategy. We shifted from having a line item for everything to having a detailed description of the project, including the number of people on the crew—anything that the client can physically see and quantify. What we don't include is the number of hours for editing or number of people involved in post-production. We also don't include hours allocated to the pre-production process. Instead of saying 20 hours of editing, we'll simply list motion graphic work along with the number of finished minutes for the project. The benefit of this is that if it takes you a shorter amount of time, you still receive the same amount of money originally agreed upon. Likewise, if it takes longer, you cannot charge for more hours unless the client requests additional work after seeing your first round.

If you go this route, we strongly suggest you create an internal line item bid so that you know how long it will take you. Then transcribe it into a written proposal with one grand total at the bottom.

SETTING YOUR PRICE

When determining how much to charge for a corporate or commercial project, the process should be the same one you use to determine how much to charge for an event video. Figure out how much time is required for each aspect of the project and apply your hourly rate. An important thing to keep in mind is that you should not necessarily strive to be the lowest bidder. In fact, in many cases, being the lowest bidder may lose you the job.

The first five-figure corporate gig we ever produced was one we almost lost because we were prepared to bid significantly less than what was eventually awarded. Up to that point we were accustomed to smaller, sub-$5,000 projects for local nonprofits. When presented with this opportunity, our preliminary bid was a little more than double what we'd earned for our highest-paying corporate job prior to that. The point of contact in charge liked our work, and since he was referred to me from a friend, he let me see some of the other bids. They were all more than double what we were about to bid. It's generally not common to see bids from other companies, so we were fortunate in this situation.

This client provided a service to Fortune 100 companies. They were close to awarding the job to a major university whose bid was more than twice as high as ours. Had we gone in with that original bid, we would have been perceived as too inexperienced to handle this caliber of job. We revised our bid by making two significant changes:

1. Charging a higher rate per hour than what we were accustomed to (a rate we had always aspired to charge but felt hesitant to charge).
2. Itemizing aspects of the job we never considered one could charge for (such as concept design, producer fee, and professional makeup.)

In the end, we were awarded the job based on our work, and it was for an amount exactly double what we were originally prepared to bid. It was a terrific lesson in corporate bidding we learned. And it changed our whole outlook on the process.

CONTRACT TERMS TO INCLUDE

Several key items must be included in any contract proposal. Regardless of the job, the proposal is not complete until it includes the following:

1. Expected turnaround time
2. Payment process
3. Copyright usage
4. Breakdown of what client will get (length and style of final product, not number of hours of editing)
5. Revision process, number of revisions, or revision hours included
6. Hourly rate for revisions, any extra cost for revisions beyond complimentary time
7. Your use of completed project for marketing purposes
8. Indemnity clause
9. Place for initials by key components, including payment process, revision process, turnaround time, and your use of final product
10. Corporate ID number

The last point to make about the sales process is that with corporate clients, the payment cycle is often much longer, sometimes as long as 60 days. So arrange your payment structure so that you get much of the fee up front (or at least prior to editing). Then, when you invoice for the final payment, send the invoice as early as possible.

DOUBLE INDEMNITY

Indemnity paragraphs are meant to provide a shield of protection from events that may occur during the production process that could cause one or both parties to become the subject of a lawsuit. Particularly when it comes to corporate jobs, which may be more public and reach a wider audience, the liability exposure is greater. Below is the indemnity paragraph we use in all of our contracts:

INDEMNIFICATION: Client warrants that it has the full legal rights to any and all photographic, film, or video images supplied by the Client to Studio for use in the Video. Client agrees to indemnify, defend and hold Studio and its officers, directors, agents, employees, representatives, associates and affiliates and each of them, harmless from and against any and all losses, costs, damage, liability and expense, including reasonable attorneys' fees, arising out of any claim whatsoever, directly or indirectly, from the use of copyright images supplied to Studio by Client.

PROJECT MANAGEMENT

Once you have the job, we suggest setting up a good project management system. Ideally, it will be a centralized, online depository where you can upload files, leave messages, track progress, have a calendar, and so forth. You'll want a system where you can track everyone who is assigned to the job, including everyone from your team and everyone from the client's team. That makes it easier for collaboration and communication with one another about the status of certain projects' due dates and the like. A good project management system (**FIGURE 4.5**) shows a strong level of professionalism to the client, so they can see that you have your act together. You have a great way of tracking the project and keeping all the t's crossed and i's dotted.

THE VIDEO BRIEF

One of the primary sources of frustration and potential client dissatisfaction on any project is unmet expectations. To avoid this pitfall, we strongly recommend you have the client write a video brief. This is a short document (usually a page or less) that outlines exactly what the client is looking for. Much of this information may be on the RFP if one was submitted. The brief should include the following:

Client objective (e.g., sales, education, etc.)

Aesthetic description (style, type of music, approximate length, etc.)

Required delivery date

Point of contact

List of client representatives on team

Any other special instructions related to the project

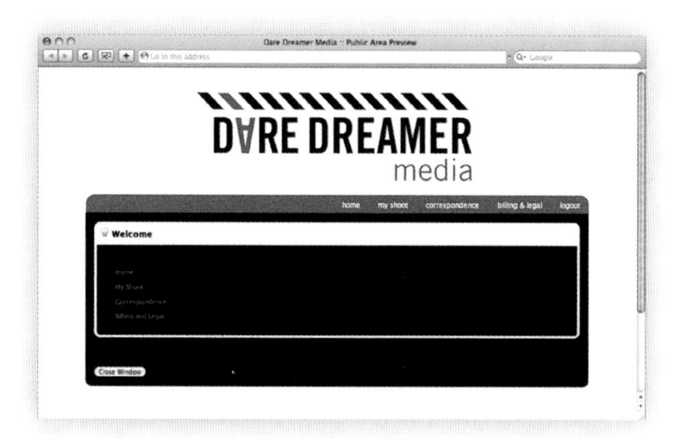

FIGURE 4.5 ShootQ (www.shootq.com), a project management system, allows up to three brands so you can customize the logo and colors for the public page clients use.

EXPLORING THE RANGE OF COMMERCIAL WORK

Now that we've gone over marketing, sales, and contracts, let's talk about the different types of commercial work that you might have and how to approach the projects you book.

CORPORATE VIDEO WITH A HEART—NONPROFIT WORK

The first type of commercial jobs we got were relatively small gigs for local nonprofit organizations (**FIGURE 4.6**). Keep in mind that doing work for a nonprofit doesn't mean *non paid*. Nonprofit is just a tax status that an organization has, allowing it certain tax benefits. Some of the largest companies in the world are nonprofit organizations. There will be times when you'll be approached by a nonprofit that really does have a very limited budget, so in certain circumstances, as a way to give back to your community, you may want to offer pro bono work. In addition to using your talents to help the community, oftentimes these organizations have donors with deep pockets, either high net-worth individuals or large corporations.

FIGURE 4.6 Girls for a Change (GFC) is one of our long-standing nonprofit clients. It has grown to a nationwide organization since we first started working with them.

From a marketing perspective, working for a nonprofit is a great way to get your work in front of prospects. These types of projects are a great way to break into corporate video production, especially if you are a wedding and event videographer looking to make the transition.

SMALL- TO MID-SIZED COMPANIES

Next are small- to mid-sized companies. These may include companies you are already working with if you are a wedding and event video producer (for example, photographers, coordinators, venues, and so on). If you do a wedding or event video, give a copy to the key vendors with a note telling them you have a corporate video division that could produce a promotional video for them. Promotional videos are a great way to get your name out and market your business.

Another source of work for companies in this range is local businesses that want to run a commercial on the local cable station. Contact the cable provider in your area to see if there's an opportunity to provide your services to their advertising clients. You could collaborate with the cable provider to have them offer the service (with their branding), but the video itself will be produced by (that is, "powered by") your company. The downside is that the cable company gets the credit for the work, but the volume and consistency of work may be worth that trade.

THE BIG 'APPLE'

The title of this section is inspired by the work we did for Apple Computer when they hired us to produce a string of customer testimonial videos. When you start working on high-profile videos for a client with a global brand, it's a whole new ballgame. Let's talk about some of the general issues you will face.

Because you are dealing with a global brand, there are going to be strict rules and regulations you may have to abide by in how you represent that brand in your video. The corporation will most likely insist on tight control over everything from the fonts you use to the color scheme to how you display the logo onscreen. If you want to save yourself a lot of headaches during the process, make sure at the start to get a representative from every department of the company that will have a say—legal, marketing, product management, and the advertising or PR agency if applicable. Most large companies have entire manuals dedicated solely to how the various company branding elements must be utilized in ads and other types of media. Get a PDF of that manual and make sure your shooters and editors are familiar with the rules.

With respect to creating the team of client and studio representatives, it's a good idea to have one primary point of contact on the client team. You don't want to have to communicate with 15 different people in order to get something done.

FINAL THOUGHTS

The last thing we'll say about commercial work is that it represents one of the best forms of repeat business. Due to the time and energy involved in finding a video vendor a company can entrust with its brand, once you're on board, as long as you deliver quality and consistent work on time (and on budget), you'll most likely have that client for life.

IN FOCUS:
PIXELPOPS DESIGN

A company that has enjoyed one of the most successful transitions from wedding to corporate that we have seen is: PixelPops Design of Dallas/Fort Worth, owned by Lance Gray and Brian Gunn (**FIGURE 4.7**).

FIGURE 4.7 PixelPops Design is owned by Lance Gray and Brian Gunn.

The company was formed in 1999 from the merger of successful and independent wedding and event studios owned by Gray and Gunn. They went from doing high-end weddings to doing corporate work. Their primary reason for the change involved a similar frustration we had—finding bridal clients willing to invest the amount of money required for the level of work they provided. The progression was slow for a few years as they honed their skills in serving the corporate video market, but once they hit their stride, success was huge.

Their corporate client list reads like a "Who's Who" of well-known and respected brands: Google, Intuit, Fossil Watches, MBNA, Charles Schwab, Expedia.com, Cisco Systems, Hotels.com, and many, many more local and regional companies (**FIGURE 4.8**). Besides video production, their suite of services also includes rich e-mail and Web site design, DVD authoring, interactive Flash projects, film transfer, and mass disc duplication.

FIGURE 4.8 Screen shot of PixelPops video production work.

They have even kept a toe in the wedding and event video market by targeting some of their testing and design services to the wedding videography community. Lance is also a master of Adobe Photoshop (he writes a monthly series of Photoshop tutorials for *EventDV* magazine called "Graphic Thoughts"), and the company sells a line of Photoshop educational DVDs. Their 2008 revenues were nearly $1 million. Not bad for a couple of ex-wedding videographers.

IN FOCUS: KRIS SIMMONS

Like many professional videographers, Kris Simmons (www.mindyourvideobusiness.com) found that the easiest way to break into the video industry and the fastest way to start receiving income was to offer his services as a wedding videographer (**FIGURE 4.9**). After several years of shooting and/or editing 40+ weddings a year and making just enough money to get by, he realized it was time to make a major change in his video business. It was time for him to go corporate or to go home.

FIGURE 4.9
Kris Simmons manning a jib on the set of a corporate shoot.

He shared his experience with us...

I believe the straw that broke the camel's back for me was the first time I was hired to videotape a grand opening of a new business that was followed by a reception.

The finished product was a 10-minute highlight reel of the event and my total time investment for both shooting and editing was 8 hours. The rate for that corporate job was $1600. At the time, $1600 was more than I was averaging per wedding package and those shoots/edits easily took anywhere from 20 to 40 hours to complete. I've never been a math genius, but it didn't take long for me to figure out which project paid more and with less hassle.

After this realization, I started spending more time cultivating leads with local businesses and organizations, and less time marketing my wedding services. My main corporate service offering at the time included meeting & event videotaping/editing services and duplication services. That list of services has since grown to include just about every video, webcasting, interactive media and/or audiovisual service imaginable.

In 2004, I officially stopped taking orders for wedding videos and eliminated it altogether from our service offering. From that point, we have been a full-blown corporate video production agency and have built a client list of over 200 companies.

Since making the transition from weddings to corporate, my business revenue has increased over 1000% and my personal income has increased by more than 400% and continues to improve each year.

II

SALES AND MARKETING

YOUR CURRENT ASSESSMENT

BEFORE YOU CAN DEVELOP YOUR company into the type of business you imagine, it's important to know where you currently stand. In order to facilitate that understanding, we've created a Sales and Marketing Assessment Tool, which you'll find in this chapter.

Once you know where you are, you can easily identify strengths and weaknesses. Knowing this vital information will move you ahead of the pack when it comes to selecting the right sales and marketing mix for transforming your company.

The fast-moving, digi-flat world in which we are operating requires a clear understanding of whether our strategies are in line with today's rapidly changing marketplace.

This is *not* a pass-or-fail test. It is a tool, a litmus test of sorts telling you where you are. Without insight into where you are, there is little room for moving into a more productive, successful future.

So let's get on with the assessment.

SALES AND MARKETING ASSESSMENT TOOL

Answer the following questions to the best of your ability. Your first response is likely the most honest. Don't answer the way you think you should or by what you know you ought to be doing. Answer based on reality. What are you really doing today? That's the correct response.

If you prefer to take the test online or print a copy, visit www.bladeronner.com and click REFOCUS at the top of the page. Just make sure to come back here to decode your results.

WEB SITE PRESENCE

1. What kind of Web site do you currently have?

a. HTML

b. Flash

c. Template

d. Custom site, personally designed

e. Custom site, professionally designed

2. Have you implemented SEO (search engine optimization)?

a. Yes

b. No

c. I don't have time

3. How does your site compare to those of your competitors? Is it different?

a. Yes

b. No

c. I don't have time to compare

4. How easy is it to navigate your site?

a. A 10-year-old could navigate easily

b. It takes a little work

c. I sometimes get lost on it

5. Do you have white text on a dark background?

a. Yes

b. No

6. Do you have music playing when the site opens? Is it royalty-free music?

a. Copyrighted music

b. Royalty-free music

c. No music

d. Music is optional, but doesn't start right away

CLIENT MAINTENANCE

7. Are you meeting your deadlines? If not, how late are you?

a. Always meet contracted deadlines

b. Usually a few weeks late

c. Generally a few months late

d. I have productions over a year or more late

8. What percent of your jobs are late?

a. 0%

b. 25%

c. 50%

d. 75%

e. 100%

9. Do you acknowledge client birthdays and anniversaries?
   a. Never
   b. Rarely
   c. Often
   d. Always
10. How long does it take you to respond to emails and phone calls from current clients?
   a. 24 hours is my standard policy
   b. Within a week
   c. When I get around to it
11. Is that response time longer or shorter for potential clients?
   a. Shorter response time for potential clients; I need new gigs
   b. Same response time for both
   c. Longer response time for potential clients; I respond to my current clients first

ADVERTISING

12. Where are you advertising?
   a. Magazines
   b. Newspapers
   c. Yellow Pages
   d. Online
   e. Facebook
   f. Google
   g. All of the above
   h. None of the above

13. How are you getting your message out to your prospects?

a. Advertising

b. Direct mail

c. Social media marketing

d. Web site (build it and they will come philosophy)

e. All of the above

f. Other

14. Do you use direct mail for advertising?

a. Yes

b. No

BRANDING

15. Do you have a brand? If so, define it in one sentence.

16. Is it unique?

a. I'm not sure. I saw another company with something similar.

b. It's a mix of a few sources of inspiration that I pulled together.

c. It's the result of a detailed business plan and meeting where I deliberately went in a direction different from my competitors.

17. Is your brand simply a logo, or have you aligned all aspects of your branding to a cohesive unit?

a. Right now it's just a logo and/or typeface

b. I've been meaning to incorporate it into other aspects

c. I have aligned everything into one cohesive brand unit

MARKETING: E-MAIL, NEWSLETTER, SOCIAL MEDIA

18. Are you using social media such as Facebook, MySpace, Twitter, and blogging to market your business?

a. I blog

b. I have a MySpace and/or Facebook account

c. I have a LinkedIn account

d. I'm on Twitter

e. All of the above

f. None of the above

19. If you are blogging, how often do you blog about business?

a. Twice a week or more

b. A few times a month

c. I started one a few months ago but haven't touched it since

d. What's a blog?

e. I don't have time to blog

20. How often do you communicate to your current list of clients (through e-mail marketing, postcards, etc.)?

a. Once a week

b. Once a month

c. Once a year during the holidays

d. When they contact me

e. As little as possible since I'm late on their project

SALES TRACKING

21. Do you have a sales and marketing plan?

a. I know what I want to do, I just need to find time to do it

b. I'm an artiste and believe that if I do good work, people will come

c. I've implemented some ideas, but need to do more

d. I've written down my sales and marketing plan and am working on implementing it

22. Are you tracking where your leads are coming from?

a. Yes, but I'm not sure what to do with the information

b. Yes, and I customize my response based on results

c. No

23. If you're doing any kind of marketing campaign, are you tracking the return on that investment?

a. I'm doing marketing but don't have time to track return on investment (ROI)

b. Yes, I keep all the numbers in my head

c. Yes, I crunch all the numbers and keep the data

d. Yes, I have an intern/assistant who does the tracking

e. No

24. Are you recording how many people are clicking through to your site from e-mail ads and Web site ads??

a. Yes, but I'm not sure what to do with the information

b. Yes, and I customize my response based on results

c. No

25. Are you recording how many people are calling to inquire?

a. I know how many people call, but not the referral source

b. I know how many call, when they call, and where they are from

c. With my backlog, answering the phone is the most I can do

PRICING

26. How have you developed your pricing?

a. I picked a number out of a hat

b. As a beginner, I set my price low since I didn't think my prices should equal that of someone with more experience

c. I looked at what my competitors were charging and charged more

d. I looked at what my competitors were charging and charged less

e. I did a thorough analysis of my costs and built in the kind of profit I wanted

DECODING YOUR RESULTS

Now that you've answered the questions to get an idea of where you stand, let's figure out what your answers mean.

WEB SITE PRESENCE (1–6)

A strong Web presence is critical in today's world. Particularly for wedding work, you're likely dealing with a younger generation raised on MTV that expects their video producers to be hip and savvy in all aspects of their online presence. If you don't have the time or skills to bring your Web site up to date, hire someone who does. There are so many options available that there isn't any reason not to have a Web site presence you can be proud to show any prospective client.

If you're choosing to use a template-driven site, we strongly suggest choosing a less popular theme or template. Ask the owners of the template site which themes are most popular—particularly for video production companies—and then go in the opposite direction. Same thing goes for your competition. Look at what they are doing and don't do it.

White text on a dark background has been proven over and over again deter people from reading. They will spend less time on your site simply because of that one factor.

Music. Get rid of any copyrighted music on your site. Triple Scoop Music (www.triplescoopmusic.com) and Digital Juice (www.digitaljuice.com) both offer an extensive collection of music that is royalty-free and will appeal to any client base. Once you've got royalty free music, make sure that you are not setting the music to start automatically when the site is opened. Especially for wedding video producers, your clients will often be searching for your services at work and may immediately close any window that starts playing music right away.

Navigation. Navigation on your site is almost as important as the aesthetic appeal. Sites that have convoluted or complicated navigation menus frustrate clients. In Chapter 6, "Building Your Brand," we address the importance of creating an amazing experience for your prospective clients. You'll hamper that experience if prospects find it hard to locate the information for which they're searching. A well-designed Web site is both aesthetically pleasing (conforming to your brand), and functionally effective.

SEO. Lastly, make sure you've taken Search Engine Optimization (SEO) into consideration when designing your Web site(s). This involves ensuring that the keyword meta tags, the Web page titles, *and* the main body of your site all have words and phrases that will help your Web site rank high on search engines. Keep in mind that the "robots" and "spiders" used by popular search engines such as Google and Yahoo to crawl through your Web site to look for these keywords have gotten smarter. They're designed to ignore the tricks that Web site developers have commonly used to dupe the spiders and boost rankings. For instance, one trick is to write a long paragraph laced with keywords and put it on your home page, making the text the same color as your background; effectively rendering it invisible. Search engines now know to ignore any text on a Web page whose color is set to the same color as the background.

CLIENT MAINTENANCE (7–11)

A backlog of projects in the event video world is so common that people are more surprised by someone who delivers on time than they are by someone delivering a year late. That has to change, for our industry, our businesses, and our peace of mind. It's time to regain our integrity in our contracts and our word. Avoid over-promising or over-committing. Maintain relationships with your clients that are positive and your business will reap the rewards.

Acknowledging special events, such as birthdays and anniversaries, means more than you might imagine. Use a client database system such as ShootQ or Highrise (www.highrisehq.com). Once it's set up, the maintenance is easy. You can hire an intern or even a high school student to come in once a month and prepare all the birthday and anniversary cards for that month. A small-time commitment will pay off in the long run as you nurture the low-hanging fruit of your current clientele.

Don't favor potential clients versus current clients. It may seem more important to respond to prospects, and it is important to respond in a timely manner, but not more important than responding to current clients. As mentioned previously, the nurturing of your current client base is key to your success.

ADVERTISING (12–14)

There is no magic advertising mix that will bring clients rushing to your front door. Your advertising mix will depend on your target market, your services, and your goals. Make sure that your advertising fits all of those aspects. For example, don't advertise high-end video production in the Yellow Pages. Clients looking to invest a significant amount in a wedding video will most likely find their videographer through another vendor, a friend or colleague, or online. Yellow Pages are better suited for services geared to a more budget-conscious consumer.

Your advertising mix should also include an online component. Whether it's the online version of a magazine, Google or Facebook ads, or banner ads on a targeted Web site, you need to have some form of online ad presence in your mix. The number of consumers from both younger and older generations who are online is too substantial to ignore.

BRANDING (15–17)

Having a brand and being able to define it in one sentence is powerful. It keeps you and your company focused. If you have employees or interns, make sure they know who you are and what you stand for. Make it clear to your prospects and clients as well.

If you started the branding process with a logo and typeface, make it consistent throughout everything that your clients touch in relation to your company. From your Web site to your Twitter page, from envelopes to business cards, everything should look and feel cohesive (FIGURE 5.1).

FIGURE 5.1 Cohesive brand identity for the Cinematic Studios wedding division created by Special Modern Design (www.specialmoderndesign.com).

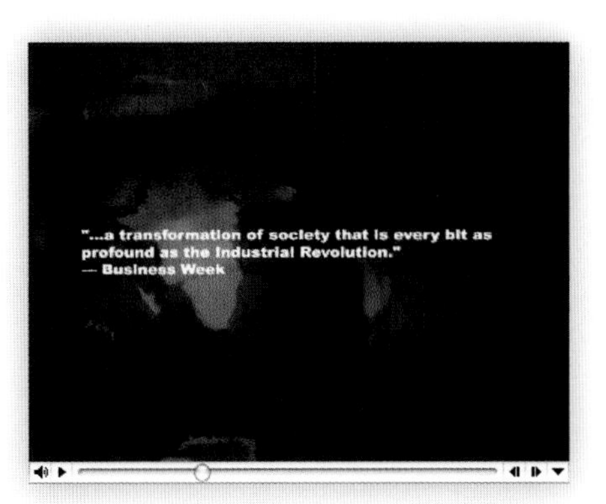

FIGURE 5.2 Screenshot from "Invasion of the Blog," a video teaser for our popular presentation on blogging.

MARKETING: E-MAIL, NEWSLETTER, SOCIAL MEDIA (18–20)

We've said it again and again (and will probably continue to say it throughout the book): social media marketing is where it's at. It's not going away, and companies who become early adopters of new technology will win. If you haven't taken the plunge into Facebook, Twitter, blogging, or any other platform of social media marketing, choose *one* to explore each month. At the end of the year, choose your favorite services with the best ROI and make them work for you.

We started talking about blogging and its critical importance more than three years ago (**FIGURE 5.2**). Many in the video world took the challenge and started their blogs with fantastic results including, increased Web traffic, higher sales, and more press. You need only two to three blog posts per week at about 500 words per post to keep your audience coming back. It's worth the time and energy invested and will keep you in contact with your current and potential clients (for more detail, see Chapter 8, "Leveraging Technology").

SALES TRACKING (21–25)

You must have a sales and marketing plan to survive. If you don't, make sure to check out the following SMART goals section to get one started. It's OK to start small, but be deliberate and stay focused.

Once you have a plan, you can start tracking against that plan. Are you meeting your goals? There are enough resources online to help you keep track. Make it as simple or complex as you want, but make it happen. Without knowing what's happening, how will you ever feel in control of your sales and marketing—or even your company? Counting on just "word of mouth" to do your marketing for you won't help you build your business. Industry veteran John Goolsby once wrote in *EventDV*, "Many business people toss around the phrase 'word-of-mouth' because, in truth, they do not really know how they're getting their business." Don't let that be you.

PRICING (26)

The bottom line on pricing is that you need to do a thorough analysis of your costs and build in the kind of profit you want. Any other form of pricing may not get you the rates you need or want. We'll cover this more in Chapter 9, "Getting Paid What You're Worth."

That's the breakdown. Now let's move on so that we can get you where you want to be.

DEFINING MARKETING AND SALES

Marketing and sales are often grouped together, just like they were at the beginning of this chapter. But really they are two very distinct aspects of your business and it makes sense to understand the differences between them and how each will impact your bottom line.

Marketing is broad in scope. It's the overall collection of activities that you do in your business to discover what your product or service should be, price your product correctly, and promote it. Marketing is the larger picture and consists of a wide range of activities, including public relations, branding, viral marketing, e-mail marketing, and the like.

Sales is just one aspect of the marketing process. Sales has a very specific objective. It is all about persuading and compelling your prospects to make the leap and invest in your service.

Ed King is the director of the Small Business Services and Professional Development Division of Wayne State University's School of Business Administration. He created a very compelling video in early 2009 that says, "I don't understand why everyone is complaining about the economy. The answer is very simple. You provide a solution to someone's problem. Find the solution, put the solution in front of your client, and make the sale." In essence, the sales process is about problem solving.

When you are talking about sales and marketing, though they are often grouped together, it is a good idea to think about them separately. To illustrate the difference, let's look at the fictional company, VP Video.

THE MARKETING CAMPAIGN

Even though VP Video already has a video business, in creating a marketing campaign, they first need to determine the path they want to follow, the type of business they want, and the kind of product they want to sell. For VP Video, this means producing wedding videos.

Now that they've decided they want to produce wedding videos, they need to figure out what kind of wedding videos they want to make. Do they want to make short-form cinematic or long-form documentary? Do they want to do same-day-edit only videos?

Once that is decided, then they figure out what kind of client they want to have. Do they want to go after high-end or mid-range clientele, or do they want a volume approach? To determine this, they'll need to ask questions and research their target client to uncover their needs and get clear ideas about how they can fulfill those needs. Once they've chosen a target, they need to determine what the competitive landscape looks like in their market: How many companies are in each tier and how successful are they? How can VP Video enter the marketplace and offer something unique?

Based on those decisions, the next step is deciding on branding that fits their company, suits the service and product they offer, and appeals to their specific target clientele. A key question to ask is, "What feeling do I want to invoke in my prospects when they think about VP Video, hear our name, see our Web site, or see our company?"

THE SELLING PROCESS

The next step is to get the word out in the marketplace. Think about which selling avenues will work best for your product or service.

The selling process comes down to actually getting the client to buy your service. Part of the sales process is helping the client solve a problem and providing a solution to that problem. It's also about engaging with the client and having all the decision-making, branding, and marketing efforts come to fruition.

During a sales call, you focus on the person or event. Identify whether their answers to your questions fit into what you have determined as the service you are offering. From that point, it is simply a matter of getting the client to see that you offer the solution to the problem they have.

This process, if effectively implemented, will save you countless hours by ensuring that you are clear about who you are and about your target market. It will also save you from potential client nightmares by making sure that the jobs you book are a good match, rather than taking any job that walks in the door.

TRACKING SUCCESS

Peter Drucker, author of over 30 business and management books, wrote, "If you can't measure it, you can't manage it."

Another aphorism that applies to the sales-tracking process comes from Charles Coonradt: "You have to measure what you want more of."

Going back even further, the Renaissance astronomer Rheticus suggested that if you can measure something, then you have some control over it.

Variations on this notion abound, but the message doesn't change. If we want to succeed in any given area, we need to track for success. Isn't that what we want: more success and more control?

One of the important aspects of an effective marketing campaign is being able to track your success (**FIGURE 5.3**). You need to figure what's working and what isn't, and adapt your strategy accordingly. That's the only way you'll be able to deliberately grow sales and evolve your business. Not to say you couldn't grow a business without tracking, but it may be more luck than through a solid plan.

There are numerous ways you can track your sales and marketing efforts:

E-mail marketing campaigns. For e-mail marketing, just about every major e-mail marketing service has some way of being able to track people who click through or read the e-mail. That is one way of being able to track your success. Tracking results will show you which days more people open their e-mails (we've had success on Mondays and Tuesdays). Tracking results keeps you aware of which links are most popular, whether those links are to your Web site, special deals, or blog. We go in more depth about e-mail marketing in the "In Focus" section of Chapter 8.

FIGURE 5.3 Most online marketing services offer a view of your results, similar to ShootQ's charts and analytics.

Advertising. If you have any kind of advertising, you can probably get ad results from the company with whom you are advertising. If it's online advertising, there should be some way of tracking how many people click through. Services such as Google Analytics or Facebook allow you to track the number of click-throughs that you get from a particular online ad campaign. Remember that there is a vast difference between knowing this information and actually scheduling time to check it, evaluate the results, and make adjustments based on those results.

Codes. The other way you can track the effectiveness of a sales and marketing program is to include some sort of code that will allow you to track where a client heard about you (**FIGURE 5.4**). You can use one ad but use different codes in different sources. You can include a call to action—for example, "Mention this code for a discount." That way when potential clients mention the code, you can begin to see where your ads are succeeding the most. This is especially helpful for printed ads and direct mail where there is no way to click through.

FIGURE 5.4 Sample advertisement with unique code for tracking leads.

Surveys. Using surveys with your current client base or when a client does hire you is a quick and easy way to pull referral data. Ask them where they heard about you and then use a customer relationship management program to track those leads and find out where they are coming from.

Using a database to track all this information is very important so that you can quickly look up how many people found you through one particular ad or aspect of your sales and marketing.

Using a system such as ShootQ (**FIGURE 5.5**), which has been designed with photographers and videographers in mind, saves you time and energy that can be dedicated to other parts of the business or even to just enjoying life out from behind the camera and computer. ShootQ's motto is, "What will you be doing while ShootQ is working for you?" It's a pretty nice system to have working for you.

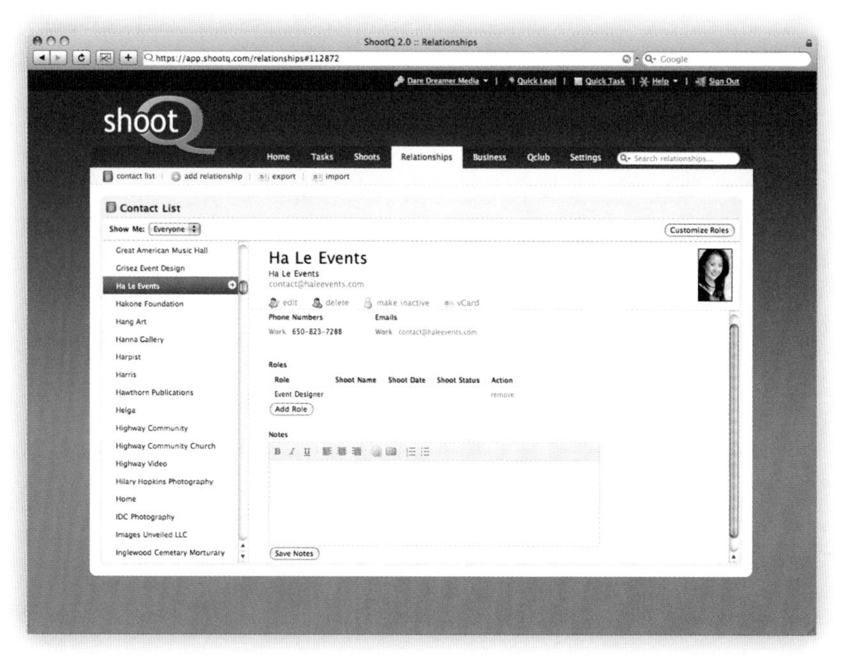

FIGURE 5.5 ShootQ simplifies relationship management for small businesses.

THE CHANGING MARKETPLACE

Earlier this year on one of my (Ron's) blog posts, a question arose about the relative importance of having a unique Web site within a local market. I was addressing the proliferation of template sites in the industry and how so many videographer Web sites look alike. I mentioned that a bride shopping for a videographer would find them all blending together, making it difficult for anyone to stand out.

However, since many of the lookalike sites were for studios in different geographic locations, some made the argument that it didn't matter if the Web site of one videographer, say in New York, looked like the Web site of another studio that was based in Los Angeles. (You can read the entire blog post at: http://bladeronner.com/?p=375.)

I contend that because of the Internet and other media, or technology as it is today, even though you are in New York, you *are* competing with people who live across the country. It's not uncommon for clients (in both the personal event space and the corporate market) to pay travel and lodging costs for their videographer if they find a studio they really want to use. That means it *is* important for you to stand out and be distinct, because that client in your backyard may opt to fly in a videographer who is 3,000 miles away because *your* company didn't stand apart. So, the reality is that our world is "flat," and in essence, *everybody* is a competitor.

Keeping that in mind is very important when figuring out where your business currently stands. Reviewing your current assessment, how do you stand up in a digi-flat world? Is your marketing focused just on your geographic location, or could it appeal to people who may not be in your vicinity?

We're not saying that you have to market outside your vicinity. If you have a nice business that is reaching people just in your market and a lot of your business comes from your area, chances are you should focus on that. That's what we call low-hanging fruit. But being mindful of the digi-flat world means leaving the door open for opportunities that may come from *outside* your geographic location and then being prepared to handle them.

There are different marketing tactics that you can employ to survive in the digi-flat world. Some of them include having a strong social media marketing campaign (including Facebook, Twitter, MySpace, and blogging); these are all ways to put your shingle out for the global community to see. Another useful tactic is building a network of videographers in other areas to assist if you get a job outside of your geographical area.

We've spent time building a national network of talented filmmakers and video producers that we can tap in just about every major metropolitan area in the country. So if it's not in the client's budget to fly me (Ron) specifically to the job, then we can generally find a videographer in our network who meets our qualifications in order to serve the client. To be able to say "we can do that" is part of the marketing of Dare Dreamer Media. And it keeps us mindful of the digi-flat world.

Same thing goes for editing. To keep costs down, you may *not* want to have a formal studio, especially if you are one of those mid-sized companies we talked about in Chapter 1. But you may still be working with five or six different editors, some of whom may live in your area or 3,000 miles away.

One of our top motion graphic editors lives in California while we are in Atlanta. But, again, today's technology (including broadband Internet and online project management) makes it easy for us to share work, look at files, review videos, and so on. And with our FedEx account, we can ship hard drives (the cost of media is so low, you can get a 500 GB hard drive for less than $100). So it's very easy to essentially have a global studio. The money you save by not having the space or overhead is money you can put toward things like FedEx rates and hard drives. That becomes a part of your marketing strategy—you are building your business in such a way that you can offer your service to global clientele.

GET S.M.A.R.T.

"One of the most important things we can do in pursuit of success is set clear, explicit goals about what we want to accomplish," wrote anthropologist Dustin W. Max. "Most of us have a bunch of vague goals, like 'lose weight' or 'write a novel.' We want 'someday' to do x, y, and z, but without clear goals, we don't seem to make any progress. We chug along, picking at our big life projects now and again, rarely coming any closer to finishing, and we feel horrible about ourselves. If you don't set strong goals, you won't achieve them."

Do a search on SMART goals and you will quickly find many different iterations of the acronym. While the wording may change, the general principle of getting clear about your goals, writing them down, and reviewing them is solid. It even came up in Tasra's days working for Apple in the Employee Development department.

For our purposes, we will use the acronym in this way (**FIGURE 5.6**). You should create goals that are...

Specific

Measurable

Attainable

Relevant

Time-bound

Don't cringe when we tell you about goal setting. Even though you've heard it before, the power isn't in the hearing, it's in the action. So take action this time and make your goals work for you.

Let's look at each goal attribute as it relates to your sales and marketing.

Specific. It's hard to hit a moving target, or a blurry target. Goals are no different. Your goal must be clear and specific. No generalities. When setting your marketing goals, consider your target market, what you are selling, and your location.

Not SMART: I want to sell videos!

SMART: I want to create and sell short form cinematic wedding videos, targeted toward a high-end clientele.

FIGURE 5.6 SMART goals will point you in the direction of success.

Measurable. We talked earlier about being able to measure the success of sales and marketing campaigns. You need to put systems in place that can measure the effectiveness of your goal. If your goal is 20 jobs on the books by June 1, then keep a running tally in plain sight that you can refer to frequently to see how you are progressing toward that goal.

Not SMART: I want to sell a lot of videos!

SMART: In my first year of business, I want to sell 20 wedding videos at an average price of $3,000 per video.

Attainable. You want to have a goal that stretches you. At the same time, you need to have a goal that is realistic. If you know you can't achieve it or it is virtually impossible, that will affect your overall business.

Working toward something that you cannot achieve sets you up for discouragement and failure.

Not SMART: In my first year of business, I want to make a million dollars selling wedding videos.

SMART: Within five years, I want to create a business that can generate a million dollars in sales, comprised of high-end corporate work and DVD duplication.

Relevant. Create a goal that is relevant to the kind of business you are doing and the service you want to provide. Don't set a goal that you think you should achieve. Don't copy other people's goals just to prove you can do what they can. Make sure that whatever goals you have are relevant to you and your business.

Not SMART: I want to create video services that appeal to every kind of bride.

SMART: I want to create a suite of video services that fits my brand, which will be marketed toward a high-end clientele.

Time-Bound. We all work better with deadlines. They create a sense of urgency and focus that doesn't happen without a clearly defined timeline. Once all the smart elements are in place for your goals, you can really focus on reaching them. Having a specific number and date is important!

Not SMART: I eventually want to have a million dollars in revenue.

SMART: In five years I want to have a million dollars in revenue, or in the first year I want to generate $60,000 in revenue, or I want to be able to sell X number of videos in the first year of business.

SETTING S.M.A.R.T. GOALS

Now it's your turn. Visit us online at www.bladeronner.com. In the REFOCUS section, download a worksheet for writing your S.M.A.R.T. goals today. Don't put it off.

As Tony Robbins, the "master motivator," likes to say, "Don't leave the site of a breakthrough without taking some action."

Get the worksheet, write down five goals, and post them where you will see them every single day—in front of your computer, on your bathroom mirror, on a poster in your office, or wherever you think they will become a part of your daily routine. Whatever it takes to remind you where you are going is key, and it will condition and prepare you to forge the path you want to follow (**FIGURE 5.7**).

Even better, write a mini-version to keep in your pocket or purse at all times.

Ready to see some change? Go one step further and share your goals with a colleague or trusted friend who can help you be accountable. You can make it happen. It all depends on how much you want it and what you are willing to do to achieve it. Go forth and conquer!

FIGURE 5.7 Keep your goals somewhere close where you can see them every day.

BUILDING A BRAND

IN THE BUSINESS WORLD, particularly among small business owners, misconceptions abound about what branding really is. When many people think of branding, they think of the various elements that comprise a brand: business cards, collateral, Web site, etc. These elements are important, but effective branding is much more than the sum of its parts.

WHAT IS A BRAND?

Branding is the overall experience and feeling that a client or prospect has when they think about your company or hear your company name.

According to Matchstic, a brand identity house, "Branding is all about mindset. It's what people think, feel, and say about you. It's why they will or won't do business with you." The team at Matchstic defines brand strategy as "the process of aligning internal strategy with external brand communications. Making sure that the two are working together is incredibly important, and before we begin work on any external brand communications, we must first understand the internal strategy and personality."

Basically, you can't create a brand until you know who you are and what makes you and your business remarkable. If you've read this far in the book, we hope that picture is starting to become clearer for you. If not, you may want to review the earlier chapters on choosing your path and assessing your sales and marketing.

Our experience has shown that in the video world, particularly on the event video side, branding is one of the weakest areas for many studios. However, we are excited about the opportunity to share with you what we have learned about shaping our brand and being able to create something that has meaning for our clients and our business.

We'll cover some of the key areas video producers—and any small businesses—can focus on in order to make quick and substantial changes. These areas include:

1. Touchpoints that convey your focus and area of expertise in a succinct and brand-relevant way.
2. Web sites that communicate a clear message with use of color, fonts, text, imagery, and layout.
3. Business cards that leave an impression with striking visuals, well-chosen text, and a consistent look and feel.

According to Marty Neumeier, president of brand consultancy Neutron and best-selling author of *Zag*, *The Brand Gap*, and *The Dictionary of Brand*, "A brand is not what you say it is, it is what the client says it is. All you have is the power to influence it." (**FIGURE 6.1**)

FIGURE 6.1
Marty Neumeier's best-selling book on branding, *Zag*

This maxim is often repeated in the branding world because it holds true. When it comes to how your brand plays to your audience, you have the power to influence through your choices, presentation, and creativity. That's it.

What it really comes down to is this: You may say that your brand is one thing (such as high-end and reaching out to luxury brides), but what you say doesn't really matter if that is not what you're communicating to the client.

The impression they get when they see you, hear your name, or visit your Web site will determine the true message of your brand. If you want people to say and believe what you intend, the best way to make that happen is to be consistent in how you represent your brand visually, emotionally, verbally, and physically. You have to see it from an outside perspective. Get out of your own world and into theirs to understand where your prospects are coming from.

THE BRANDING EXPERIENCE

What is the experience that your clients have when they work with you? Have you ever thought through the experience—from start to finish—that your clients have?

In his book, *The Starbucks Experience*, Dr. Joseph Michelli talks about *touchpoints*. Touchpoints are the various points in your business that a prospect or a client will come in contact with when doing business with you: from the point when they first see your Web site to sending out an e-mail inquiry and your response to that inquiry, to the people who answer the phone to talk about your business, to the consultation you have with a prospect or client, to the experience you have on the shoot, whether it is a wedding shoot, corporate shoot, or other event. How do you deliver the final product? What kind of packaging are you using? Are you doing anything extra?

DESIGN VERSUS ART

Art is aesthetic and subjective.

Design is functional.

All these different touchpoints are the experience-builders clients have when dealing with you. It's important for you to look at every touchpoint you have in your business and make sure that it maximizes the brand experience you want to create for your client.

Take a few minutes and walk yourself through from the first point of contact you have with a client via Web site or phone—all the way to final delivery of the finished product. Make some notes to yourself about the feelings you have along the way.

GETTING BRANDED

Now that we've defined *brand*, your next question should be obvious: "How do I get one?"

Perhaps the most efficient way is to hire a professional. In the event video world, nearly every video producer has encountered the bride or client planning to get their "Uncle Charlie" to shoot and edit their video. As a professional, you know the value you bring to the table in terms of your experience. Branding is no different.

Unless you come from a design, branding, or marketing background, there are many elements that go into a brand you probably don't have the experience with—but a professional branding consultant does. For example, the understanding of market demographics, psychographics, how people respond to colors and shapes, what is currently in style and what is not, and the importance of design versus art.

All these elements along with experience go into being able to create a brand that will speak to your prospects. Hiring a professional who has experience dealing with these components will be an incredible and effective investment in your business.

Consider your investment in a brand similar to the way you describe your services to a client. The investment will appreciate in value. Done right, it will stand the test of time. Done wrong, it will leave you constantly changing and tweaking what you've done, which essentially causes you to start over every time in building brand recognition and value.

That said, we do understand the reality that small businesses may not be able to invest in a solid branding or design company. It's not unheard of to spend $5,000–$20,000 on a branding experience, from Web sites to business cards to creating a positioning statement and logo (**FIGURE 6.2**). Even at the $5,000 level, many small businesses don't have the financial wherewithal to make that happen.

DARE DREAMER
media

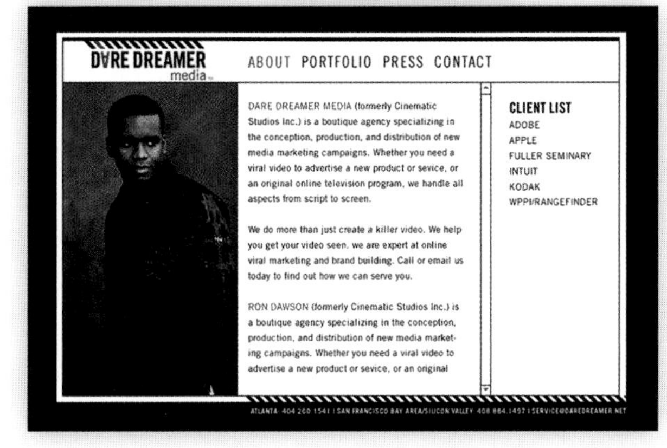

FIGURE 6.2 The Dare Dreamer brand's logo, business cards, and Web site. Brand designed by Navata Design (www.navatadesign.com).

So the next question becomes, "What can I do now?"

First, do your homework. Identify the kind of client you want to attract and the kind of companies that you know are successfully attracting that type of client. If you are in the wedding and event business and you are looking to attract high-end brides, find local photographers, coordinators, and florists who are successful in reaching those brides and look at their branding. Look at their Web sites, collateral, and position statements. See if you can have lunch with one of them to talk about the touchpoints they go through.

(Note: There are some companies that are successful *despite* their branding, rather than *because* of it, so you want to make sure that you are talking with someone who is successful in their business and their field, and also has a strong sense of branding.)

Second, look for workshops and seminars that have professionals who address the issue of branding. You may not have five grand or more to spend on a branding campaign, but maybe you do have $750 or even $1,000 to spend on a one- or two-day workshop with a vendor who has expertise in that field.

Third, do market research. One assignment Ron gives to his business coaching clients is to have them go to the mall and look at companies that are reaching the kind of demographic his coaching clients want to reach. He has them look at their logo designs and typeface usage, and the experiences they are creating in their stores for the clients they serve. It seems like a simple assignment, but it gives you an idea of what that clientele expects and will be looking for.

Fourth, read. As Charles Jones said, "You will be the same person in five years as you are today except for the people you meet and the books you read." Too many small business owners don't take advantage of the vast wealth of knowledge on every topic imaginable. Branding is no different.

Do a search for some of the bestselling branding books, buy some, and set aside reading time. If you're reading this book, you're already one of a unique group of go-getters, willing to invest in your learning and education. Your business will be transformed because of the investment of time. Don't like reading? Get audio or video versions of popular books. The information is so widely available, in so many formats, there is really no excuse not to get it.

Start with Seth Godin's *Purple Cow*.

ARE YOU A PURPLE COW?

If you haven't read *Purple Cow* by best-selling author and marketer Seth Godin, you're missing out. In his signature style, Godin says, "You're either a Purple Cow or you're not. You're either remarkable or you're invisible. Make your choice."

Thousands of brown cows can be seen driving up I-5 from Los Angeles to San Francisco. You pass through a patch of hills literally covered in the sights and smells of cow—nothing exciting, nothing out of the ordinary.

But if you inserted a Purple Cow in that mix, people would stop and stare. Or at least do a double take. It would get people talking, wondering, questioning, even telling their friends. The next time you drive up that interstate, you'd be looking for that Purple Cow. You might even have your camera ready. Wouldn't you like to *be* that Purple Cow that everyone is looking for? You can.

RECOMMENDED READING LIST

A few books we recommend that have valuable information and insight on branding include:

The Anatomy of Buzz Revisited: Real Life Lessons in Word-of-Mouth Marketing, Emanuel Rosen

Building Brandwidth: Closing the Sale Online, Sergio Zyman and Scott Miller

Designing Brand Identity: A Complete Guide to Creating, Building, and Maintaining Strong Brands, Alina Wheeler

Fast Track Photographer: The Definitive New Approach to Successful Wedding Photography, Dane Sanders

Lovemarks: The Future Beyond Brands, Kevin Roberts

Love is the Killer App: How to Win Business and Influence Friends, Tim Sanders

Made to Stick: Why Some Ideas Survive and Others Die, Chip Heath and Dan Heath

Outliers: The Story of Success, Malcolm Gladwell

Purple Cow: Transform Your Business by Being Remarkable, Seth Godin

Reality Check: The Irreverent Guide to Outsmarting, Outmanaging, and Outmarketing Your Competition, Guy Kawasaki

The Starbucks Experience: 5 Principles for Turning Ordinary into Extraordinary, Dr. Joseph Michelli

The Tipping Point: How Little Things Can Make a Big Difference, Malcolm Gladwell

Your Marketing Sucks, Mark Stevens

Zag: The #1 Strategy of High-Performance Brands, Marty Neumeier

Here's how:

Do great work. Simple and obvious, we know. But look at it from the standpoint of the consumer seeing hundreds of samples (or at least 20 or 30 samples). Are you just another brown cow getting lost in the masses? Or is your work the Purple Cow—the one that makes people sit up straighter, watch it again, send it to their friends, and then talk to them about it over drinks?

Be remarkable. Seth Godin also talks about being remarkable so people can remark about you, saying, "Be obsessed with remarkable." Remarkable, again, can be the work that you provide, the customer service you give, the experience of working with you as an artist, or a combination of all of those things. Focus on the word "experience," creating an overall experience that makes people want to remark about you.

Create a signature brand. In Dane Sanders' first book, *Fast Track Photographer*, he introduces the concept of a signature brand photographer (although the target for the book is aspiring photographers, the concepts transcend industry). In a signature brand, the *photographer* is more important than the *photography*. You, as a video producer, are in a similar situation. No matter how good your work or business is, some aspect of it can always be mimicked by somebody else—with one exception. You.

To become a signature brand, or a Purple Cow, find out what aspect of your personality, or your character, can be fused into the fabric of your business to make you stand out. When you've succeeded, clients will want to hire your business because of the opportunity to work with *you*.

The branding process brings those unique qualities to the surface, much like mining. You've got to do some digging to bring the shiny stuff out into the marketplace.

LEAVING A MARK

In his book *Love is the Killer App*, Tim Sanders writes, "Those of us who use love as a point of differentiation in business will separate ourselves from our competitors just as world-class distance runners separate themselves from the rest of the pack trailing behind them."

Sanders, who also wrote *The Likeability Factor*, has got this strategy down, and teaches others how to do it in his bestselling books. Likeability can be learned. You can become a "lovecat" by increasing your knowledge, expanding your network, and sharing your compassion.

Once you've got that down, you'll start leaving a trail of "lovemarks" as Kevin Roberts describes in *Lovemarks: The Future Beyond Brands*. Kevin Roberts, CEO worldwide of Saatchi & Saatchi, shows that by building respect and inspiring love, businesses can change the world. Wouldn't you like your business to do that? More than just paying the bills, wouldn't you like to change the world, your industry, and the world of your clients?

Companies that get it right don't just have loyal followings—they have fanatic followings. One of the most popular lovemarks in the world of technology is Apple, Inc. It consistently posts record increases in profits, even when competitors are posting losses. Apple is definitely high-end in the technology field. You may pay three times more for an Apple computer than a brand that runs Windows. And people are willing to pay because of the love that they have for the brand.

Fanatical fan bases support companies with powerful word of mouth. Customers become evangelists. Think about the Mac-versus-PC battles on popular video discussion boards. People are passionate and willing to defend the brands they love. The emotional connection people make with your brand will differentiate you from every competitor in your marketplace.

While you may have heard or read about some of these ideas before, are you doing them? Have you taken action on the things you know would make a difference to your brand experience—and likewise to your bottom line?

While writing this book, we admit we've been reminded of things we've let slip—ideas we know we should be implementing or may have started on, but then let go in the busyness of owning and operating a company. Let this moment be your restart. Don't wait until you've got all the answers or have worked everything out—just get started.

Here are seven things you can do today to start leaving your mark:

1. **Deliver quality.** Don't let anything out the door that isn't up to the highest standards. If it's going to be late because it doesn't meet QA standards, let the client know. Chances are they'll be thrilled you are going to such great lengths to give them an exceptional product.

2. **Offer service.** Even though you're busy and your e-mail box is overflowing, take the time to respond to requests with consideration. Remember that you're building relationships and creating fans. That won't happen if you ignore legitimate requests.

   Think about the scene in *Miracle on 34th Street* in which Kris Kringle is working at Macy's but directing customers to other stores because he knew a certain store was the best place to get a particular toy. The unexpected result? Customers felt so good about the fact that he was offering such exemplary service that they became more loyal to Macy's and profits increased. Those kinds of things will make you stand out in people's minds: going against the grain.

3. **Build (or rebuild) trust.** If you're late on a project, communicate clearly with the client without excuse. Give them a new deadline you can meet and make that deadline no matter what. Keep your word and commitments by under-promising and over-delivering. It's better to say that you will have a turnaround time of two months and deliver in six weeks, than it is to say that you will have a turnaround time of four weeks and deliver in six weeks. Set an expectation and then exceed that expectation.

4. **Be honest.** Mistakes happen. Equipment malfunctions. Audio gets garbled. Tapes get lost. It's a reality of doing business after any amount of time. Expect it. Be prepared for it. Be honest about it with your client.

5. **Be open.** If you haven't been asking for honest feedback from your clients, now is the time to start. Send a survey in exchange for a gift card. Ask the hard questions even if you're afraid of the

answers. Find out where you really stand. If you know the truth of how you are perceived, you can set out on a new path.

6. **Educate and inform.** Offer your clients and prospects relevant and timely information through your blog. Post links to articles, special deals, and items of interest to them. Give them something for nothing. Share your knowledge. The more you give, the more you'll get back. It's a principle that never changes.
7. **Create a community.** Use social media such as Twitter, Facebook, and newsletters to keep in contact with your client base. Connect them to you with timely information and connect them to each other with common ideas and solutions to their problems.

RESOURCES FOR SURVEY CREATION

The following companies offer the ability to create and send online surveys:

- **Constant Contact:** Easily create surveys from 40 unique templates. A 60-day free trial is available. www.constantcontact.com
- **Survey Monkey:** This revolutionary tool lets you create and publish custom surveys in minutes, and then view results graphically and in real time. www.surveymonkey.com
- **Zoomerang:** This survey tool allows you to create online surveys while providing powerful reporting and advanced survey logic. www.zoomerang.com

Next, let's talk about some of the things that make up your branding experience. However, remember that these things by themselves are not your brand—they're aspects of your brand. Each one needs to communicate a consistent message about who your company is and what it is all about.

WEB SITES

We'll start with your Web site because it is often the first touchpoint your prospects have when they come across your business. Since much searching for your service will be done online the way you present your portfolio and brand online is extremely important. Ron has written extensively about this on his blog at www.bladeronner.com.

We touched on this a bit earlier when talking about the digi-flat world. But it bears repeating that your Web site must stand out as something that communicates a unique brand. When prospects visit your Web site, you don't want them to have the feeling they've been there before—because your site looks like every other site they've seen.

We understand that you may not have the financial resources for a professionally designed Web site. In that case, consider using a template—a predesigned starting place—for your site. If you decide to go the template route, be sure to choose a lesser-used template from the dozens if not hundreds of templates you can choose from. If you've done your research, you'll no doubt see that a few templates seem to be the most popular. Using a template isn't a bad idea, as long as you put some time and energy into customizing it and you create a truly unique site.

However, if you have the financial capability to invest in a Web site designer, that can be very beneficial. With respect to branding, the biggest advantage of a custom site is that it is unique and you can create it in a way that suits your needs.

Showit Sites, started by photographer and entrepreneur David Jay, is a Web site creation service that allows you to easily publish a dynamic, media-rich Web site with no coding (**FIGURE 6.3**).

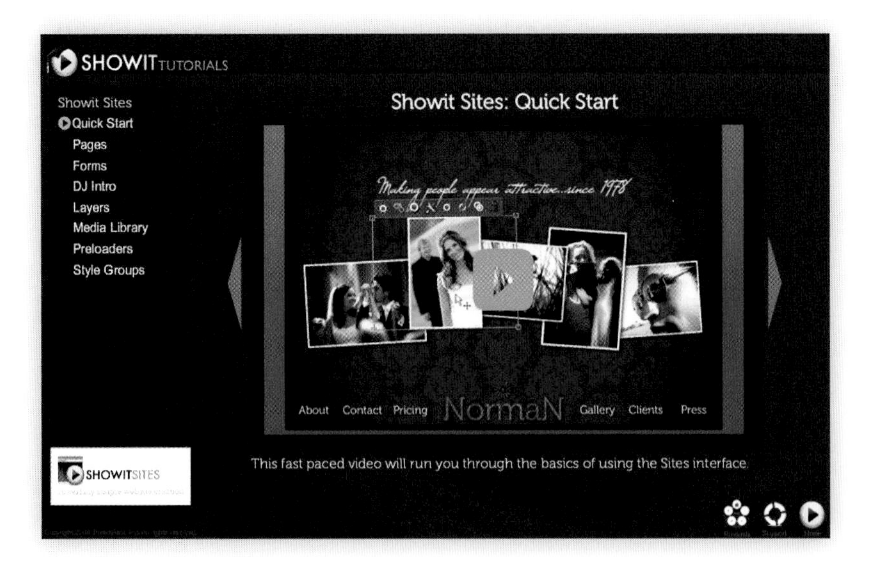

FIGURE 6.3
The Showit Sites design tutorial.

FIGURE 6.4 We've received significant praise and positive feedback on the Showit Site we created for our photography company, Teen Identity Portraits (www.teenidentity.com).

It's an ideal blending of the two options, a middle-ground between template-based and professionally designed. It gives you the flexibility and freedom to completely change your site any time, custom design your pages, and set yourself apart from your competition (**FIGURE 6.4**). You can download a free trial at www.showitfast.com. Mention *ReFocus* and get the equivalent of two months free when you sign up for one year.

When planning your Web site, remember to consider design and functionality. Things that diminish the effectiveness of a Web site include being too hard to navigate, being too cluttered, and providing a negative user experience. Simplicity, straightforward navigation, adequate white space, and colors and shapes consistent with your brand are all important considerations.

Look outside the photo and video world and see what companies in other industries are doing, such as graphic designers, computer companies, and even bookstores. For example, the Apple site is good to look at because it is clean and makes use of white space. You can see the minimal use of words and text—and the focus on the graphics—because that's what draws people in and catches their eye.

Which Web sites draw your attention? Which do you enjoy visiting and return to again and again? Draw some inspiration from those sites instead of limiting yourself to only other videographers or people in your industry or vicinity.

Back in the early days of Cinematic Studios, Inc., we actually made it a point not to look at other videographers' sites. The main reason we avoided them was because we believed many of them were not targeting their market correctly. They had pictures of the videographer smiling in his tuxedo with the camera on his shoulder, or had images of camera gear spinning. Intuitively, we knew that these sites were not designed to attract the market clientele we were going after, which in our case was high-end brides.

The inspiration we got early on was from photographers who were designing their sites like online fashion magazines, in terms of the photos they used and the way they wrote the copy. You never saw a picture of a Hasselblad or other equipment on a photographer's Web site. It was always stunning imagery telling the story.

When you are adding images to your site, don't feel like you always have to use video stills. Feel free to work with local or non-local photographers to produce images for your Web site. On our first Web site, when our focus was high-end wedding videography, we made a point to only use video stills. We believed our work was just as good as photographers' work and there was no reason why we shouldn't have video stills instead of photos.

As we worked on reaching a higher clientele, we received feedback from other designers who said our video grabs were poor quality because of the full size we were blowing them up to on the site. It was at that point we reached out to photographers in our network.

This worked for two reasons. We had clean, crisp images from photographers to improve the aesthetic of our site. And we communicated to our prospects what type of vendors we worked with. If they saw their photographer's photos on our site, it built a level of trust in their mind that we were on par with that vendor, and gave us credibility by association. It doesn't take away from your art as a filmmaker or video producer when you have photographs as opposed to video stills.

Prospects will still see your portfolio and your work, but it will be the photographs (and the branding the images help to create) that draw them in.

BUSINESS CARDS

Business cards are another aspect of the branding experience that you provide to clients. Again, you need to ask yourself, "What kind of client am I going after?" If you're pursuing a high-end client, then you need a business card that suggests that.

If you're going after a high-end client that has an eye for design and quality and then give them a flimsy, cheap business card—or, worse yet, you hand them a business card that you created from one of those perforated sheets that you get from an office supply store—that will send the wrong message about who you are and the quality of service you offer.

If you've seen the movie *Hitch*, you'll remember Will Smith's distinctive black business card. It was a high-quality, completely black, square card with minimal text on one side. It set him apart, and differentiated his service and company. How could you adapt that idea for your own business cards?

Back in our first year in business I (Ron) met Tim Sudall (www.videoone.tv), who is an extremely successful event video producer out of Philadelphia. I was in line with him at an industry event and was sharing with him my business cards, which I had created using those perforated office supply store cards and my inkjet printer.

He made a point to tell me that the quality wasn't there and that I needed to get business cards that reflect the quality of the business that I was trying to put forth. With regard to business cards, it doesn't really have to be that expensive, and he gave me some resources that I could pursue.

That's exactly what I did and have never looked back (**FIGURE 6.5**).

FIGURE 6.5 This is our business card today. Notice the upside down "A." It caused a lot of controversy and discussion among colleagues who reviewed it. The debate it started convinced us to use the design. It makes the card a Purple Cow.

PACKAGING

A similar event happened when I met Trisha Von Lanken for the first time, just after she gave a presentation. I was new in the business and was excited to meet her and give her a demo DVD of my work to get her feedback. The DVD I gave her was packaged in one of those cheap plastic CD cases. She immediately told me that the packaging didn't work. If I wanted to grab the high-end bride, that wasn't going to happen with my current packaging (**FIGURE 6.6**). (It's funny how I had a knack for getting feedback on things I didn't ask for. But I'm so thankful I did.)

FIGURE 6.6 What *not* to do when packaging your demo DVDs.

FIGURE 6.7 Our movie-like DVD packaging delivered in standard Amaray cases.

When I returned to our studio, we immediately worked on putting our DVDs in custom-made cards. It made a huge difference in the way we presented ourselves. From there, we moved to traditional cases and designed custom covers that looked like real movies. Our clients loved them and it fit the brand we were selling, which was about having the experience of starring in your own movie (**FIGURE 6.7**).

As we became more educated in branding and the importance of standing out, we decided to move away from using traditional Amaray cases. Instead, we purchased tin cases with clear covers. They looked and felt like film cans (**FIGURE 6.8**). They were round and had a cool, retro look, which fit perfectly with the fun, creative style that the Cinematic Studios brand represented.

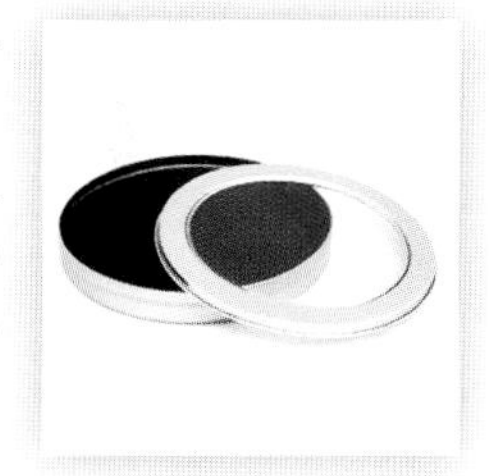

FIGURE 6.8 The cases we chose had a real film-can look.

They say that necessity is the mother of invention, and our colleague and friend, Joshua Smith of CinematicBride (www.cinematicbride.com), created an entire company around the need for inspired packaging. Loktah (www.loktah.com) is a natural media packaging company, "inspired by the natural beauty of the earth, featuring products that recall the planet's majestic form" (**FIGURE 6.9**).

FIGURE 6.9
"Natural" DVD packaging from Joshua Smith's Loktah.com.

Josh's desire to be creative and present something different to his clients inspired him to undertake this venture. In his search, he found a need within the video and photography industries and aimed to meet that need with Loktah.

This packaging solution won't fit every brand, but it is a clear example of how being tuned in to your brand will force you to get creative with every aspect of your business and every touchpoint for your clients.

I (Ron) remember a conversation on one of the popular videography boards about whether it made sense or was worth investing in these cases because of their higher price point. For our brand, it was an easy decision: Yes. When you're marketing to high-end clientele, standing out among the crowd and presenting a high-quality product in high-quality packaging are worth the extra investment. And if you are charging the right kind of money for your work, then having a compelling presentation for your DVDs will be a cost you can bear.

Taking it a step further, consider Starbucks' business and branding model. It has been shown that for each unit they sell, they spend the least amount of money on coffee beans, which is what they are supposedly selling. More money is spent on all the other things the company creates for the client.

The power and the value of packaging should not be lost on many of you, particularly because of one of the "lovemarks" we talked about earlier—Apple. Many envy Apple's packaging and design because the company creates an amazing experience. People enjoy opening their iPod or iPhone box because it is so cool. Apple has even received reports that after people open a package, they will put it all back together, so they can show their friends and family what it was like to experience opening it. That is a lovemark.

Think about creative ways in which your final presentation can be used to communicate and continue to advertise your company—even when the product is sitting on your client's coffee table or shelf.

FINAL THOUGHTS

Having a consistent look and feel throughout your Web site that matches your collateral (business cards, stationery, brochures) and continues through your packaging is critical. All these elements contribute to the brand that reaches the clients you want.

Branding isn't just for studios pursuing high-end clients. Even if you are going after volume and clients who are more budget conscious, it does not mean that you can ignore branding. In many ways it is just as important on the low end because you are going to be dealing with clients who are easily moved by price. You need to have something that they can grab onto and develop an affinity for. If you are competing on price, it is going to be harder for you to stand out in the crowd because competitors can always undercut you. So having a unique brand will be that much more important.

Whether you are going after a high-end clientele or a more budget-conscious customer, your brand and the branding experience you provide can make or break your company and determine your impact on everyone who encounters you.

IN FOCUS:
THE STARBUCKS EXPERIENCE

If you haven't already figured it out, a running theme in this chapter has been *experience*. Above everything else, experience will determine how a client or prospect interprets your brand. One of the best books written about the client experience is *The Starbucks Experience: 5 Principles for Turning Ordinary into Extraordinary*, by Dr. Joseph Michelli.

We had an opportunity to see Michelli speak at an event we filmed in January 2009. During the event, he talked about how raw coffee beans cost about four cents per cup. But by adding hot water and filtering those coffee beans through a thin sheet of paper, you can sell it for one dollar per cup. Moving up, if you package it right, you can sell it in the store for two dollars per cup. But if you add an experience to it—say, sitting in a nice lounge area (**FIGURE 6.10**) with good music, good food, good smell, and the opportunity to get online and do some work—you can sell those coffee beans for *four* dollars per cup.

FIGURE 6.10 Consider the customer experience you provide to your clientele.

The Starbucks branding experience has become such a lovemark that you don't even have to have the experience to still pay that amount per cup. There are people who use Starbucks drive-throughs or who quickly run in and run out, yet still spend the same amount of money for what many coffee connoisseurs say isn't a remarkable cup of coffee in and of itself.

Starbucks is, for all of its ups and downs, a great example of what can be done when a brand really focuses on the experience. In his book, Michelli reveals how you can follow the Starbucks strategy to reach out to communities, listen to employees and consumers, seize growth opportunities, and custom design a satisfying experience that benefits everyone involved.

So let's think about the Starbucks experience and the touchpoints that you might typically go through from the time you see a Starbucks while driving down the freeway to the time you leave.

Touchpoint 1: You're driving down the freeway and craving that rich, grande Caramel Macchiato with light whip. You see the familiar green circle with the siren. You have now experienced your first touchpoint. It's the logo and brand experience that other companies have tried to mimic and that Starbucks relentlessly protects and preserves.

Touchpoint 2: You drive up, walk in the door, and are hit with three things that engage your senses: sight, smell, and sound. The sight is a cool, hip, comfortable lounge area that invites you to stay. The smell is fresh-brewed coffee. That signature smell is strong enough that you can leave the store after just five minutes and still smell the coffee on your clothing. (There have even been rumors that Starbucks is considering stopping the sale of breakfast sandwiches because the smell of the sandwich is overpowering the coffee smell that people know and love.) Finally, there's the distinctive sound: How many other coffee companies have their own music label? There are CDs playing and showing that music is for sale. Touchpoint 2, you are engaged and invited in.

Touchpoint 3: Once you order, whether your server is young or old, he or she probably looks hip, friendly, and energetic—and has the ability to scream out those long complicated orders for individual coffee drinks. Part of the experience is saying your order right. It has become so much of a pop culture mainstay that in the Tom Hanks and

Meg Ryan movie, *You've Got Mail,* Hanks' character poked fun at it: "The whole purpose of places like Starbucks is for people...who don't know what the hell they're doing or who on earth they are, can, for only $2.95, get not just a cup of coffee but an absolutely defining sense of self: Tall! Decaf! Cappuccino!" That's how powerful the Starbucks experience has become.

Touchpoint 4: We finally get to taste the coffee itself. But it's still the experience that engulfs the tasting: Taking a newspaper or magazine and your cup of coffee, and finding a space to sit and relax. Slowing down in a busy world. Connecting with friends over a cuppa joe. Doing some work on the free Wi-Fi. These are the relaxing and inviting experiences that typify the Starbucks experience.

So, with all that in mind, what experience do you give your clients? When they see your logo, are they drawn to it or repelled by it?

When they enter your studio, are they blasted with rock music and the smell of leftovers for lunch? Or are you deliberate with the music you choose and the smells that visitors experience when they enter your place of business? Is there an inviting atmosphere with comfortable chairs, familiar decorations, and customer-focused staff?

Is it *just* about the experience? Of course not. You need to deliver a great product, too. But the difference between creating an unforgettable experience and just delivering the product is the difference between four cents per cup and four dollars per cup.

Which would you prefer?

THE RIGHT AD MIX

THE NEXT STAGE IN YOUR sales and marketing process is advertising. Advertising is the process of getting your message out and in the front of those you want to invest in your services. Having a good advertising mix is essential and should be part of your overall strategy for marketing your business.

In this chapter we'll cover traditional advertising methods, as well as more contemporary options you can explore in order to get your message out.

MAKING THE MOST OF MAGAZINES

For event and video producers, magazines can be a very effective way to get your name seen. One thing to keep in mind when you're advertising is that part of its purpose is to get your message in front of people, so that when they think of the service you offer, your name and your brand come to mind. The purpose of print advertising is not necessarily to get people to act right at the moment of seeing your ad. Having a clear goal for your advertising will help you track the success of each different campaign and advertising outlet.

Most sales and marketing professionals will agree that a new prospect needs to get an impression from a business at least a half-dozen times before they decide to choose that particular service. So when you're pursuing your first clients, the more places they see you, the better the chances of them investing in your services.

A host of magazines exist for you to advertise in, particularly if you are an event video producer (**FIGURE 7.1**). The important thing to keep in mind when you're selecting a magazine is, "Does the demographic of the magazine match the demographic of the ideal client for my brand?"

FIGURE 7.1 This is one of the early ads we placed in *RangeFinder* magazine for our promotional video services. *RangeFinder* reaches 50,000 professional photographers.

If you're going for a more budget-conscious, volume-based clientele, make sure the magazine you select is reaching the numbers necessary for you to reach that volume of clients.

Some critical elements to consider when creating a magazine ad include:

1. What is your purpose? Is it exposure, brand recognition, and impressions on prospects? Do you have a specific call to action, giving prospects a reason to pick up the phone and call you, or send you an e-mail?

   Here are some sample calls to action:

   - "Call now to get info about our special offer!"
   - "E-mail us today to find out how we can create a unique video for your company."
   - "Call now for a 20% discount on our new product offerings."

2. Are the look, feel, and design of the ad consistent with your brand? Depending on the outlet, you may want to consider having a professional design the ad or at least bring in someone with a good eye for design.

   Major corporations spend a considerable amount of money on advertising itself—and on professionals to create the advertising. Think about ads that stick with you. Someone or a team of people spent hours, days, weeks, maybe even months crafting everything from the text to the color scheme to the images in order to leave a lasting impression. Since you are in a particularly creative field, you probably have access to many people who can give you some input on creating an ad that will work and fit your brand.

3. Is your message singular and focused? If you have too much going on or the ad has too many messages being communicated, it will quickly lose its effectiveness.

4. Is your message provocative and different? Will it stand out in a magazine full of other ads from companies similar to yours? How can you design something that will evoke an emotion or controversy, or leave an impression long after they've stopped reading the magazine?

Going back to the Purple Cow effect we discussed in Chapter 6, are you going to create an ad that looks like every other ad in the magazine, or will you design something that makes people stop and think?

TARGETING WITH DIRECT MAIL

Another advertising option is direct mail. Direct mail can be postcards, letters, or e-mail, and there is a lot of discussion and debate about how effective it is. If you get a good list that is targeted to your clientele and is big enough to give you an appreciable response, it can be an effective marketing venue.

Back in the '90s when I (Ron) worked for Screenplay Systems (a small software company serving the film and TV industry), direct mail was a significant part of our marketing program. We mailed a campaign three times a year, and those combined campaigns accounted for at least half of our yearly revenue. They were usually huge sales, as much as 50 percent off the software (which retailed as high as $990). We also spent huge amounts of money on expanding our mailing list and adding to the clients we already had, and it always paid off.

Again, when you're doing direct mail, you want to think about design, content, and having a call to action. For direct mail, the call to action is even more important than in a magazine. A magazine can be just about getting your name out there. But direct mail is almost always associated with some action you want the recipient to take, whether it is picking up the phone, e-mailing, filling out a form, or taking a survey.

E-MAIL VERSUS POSTAL MAIL

For the past few years, e-mail has become a popular form of direct mail. It allows for interactivity, it makes it possible for the reader to respond immediately, and it can be significantly less expensive than a postal mail campaign to the same number of people. The irony is that now, with how bad e-mail spam is, direct mail may have reclaimed its former status as the more effective direct mail solution compared to e-mail. A well-designed direct mail piece may actually have a greater chance of being read than an e-mail–based campaign.

Here are some tips to keep in mind when creating an e-mail or postal mail campaign:

1. For e-mail, keep it short. If your readers have to do a lot of scrolling, they're much less likely to read the entire message. If you must write a longer e-mail, consider adding a short table of contents at the beginning. That way they can quickly surmise if it's worth reviewing.
2. For either type of campaign, consider low-hanging fruit. In other words, instead of investing lots of money in acquiring lists, first try reaching out to your current client base.
3. Make sure there is some way to track the effectiveness of your approach. With e-mail, most services provide some form of online tracking software to calculate your open rates, see how many click-throughs there were, and so forth. For a postal campaign, you may need to include a code system. When clients contact you, have them provide their code, then track the codes in a database. You can use the codes to track overall responses from the campaign, effectiveness of certain parts of the list, geographic location of repliers, and so on (**FIGURE 7.2**).

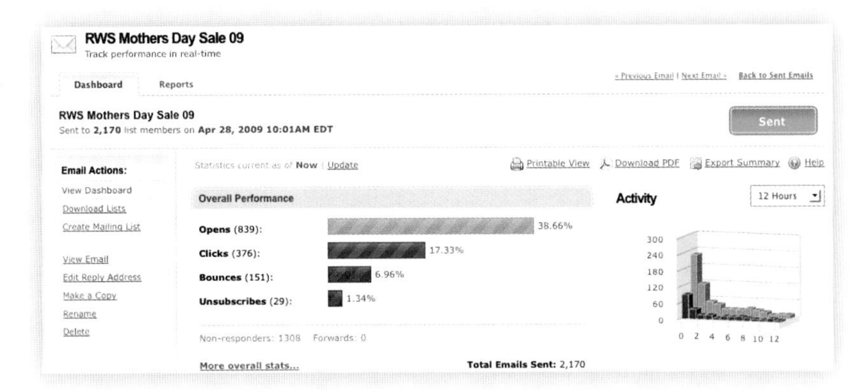

FIGURE 7.2 Results for one e-mail campaign we did for Tasra's book, *Real Women Scrap*.

OTHER AD OPTIONS: FACEBOOK AND GOOGLE

You have many options for advertising online, including digital magazines, podcasts, and traditional banner ads. Two venues that have proven successful for many videographers are Facebook ads and Google ads. With Google and Facebook ads, you're able to set a certain number of impressions (the number of times an ad is displayed) and click-throughs (the number of times someone actually clicks on your ad). You can even set a price that you pay per click. Generally speaking, the higher the price that you are willing to pay, the better exposure your ad will get (although price is now only one factor in Google relevancy rankings).

Once your advertising has reached the preset limit, the ads will cease to be delivered, limiting your risk.

One reason Google and Facebook have been very effective in the online advertising space is because they have created a way to deliver contextual ads. The ads that display are specifically related to the content on the rest of the page.

These services also have sophisticated tracking features to evaluate metrics, including how often and when ads are displayed and clicked.

START WITH A CLEAN SLATE

A few years ago, browsing through Barnes & Noble, we came across a book on an endcap titled *Your Marketing Sucks*. This title hit us hard. Who the heck did this Mark Stevens think he was, telling us that our marketing sucked? He didn't even know us. We had to pick up the book and see what he was talking about. (Lesson #1: Be provocative in your advertising.)

After only a few minutes of skimming the table of contents and a few chapters, we knew we had to buy it. It turns out that our marketing *did* suck! Our business was still relatively young and the concepts covered in the book really hit home.

One of our favorite chapters is Chapter 3, "Start with a Blank Page." In it, Stevens talks about the importance of ignoring what your competition is doing in their advertising and create something from scratch. If you start by looking at your competition, you could be setting the bar really low if their advertising is bad, or you could run the risk of mimicking them (and therefore blending in and not standing out).

It can be very tempting when creating an advertisement (whether for print, video, or audio) to start by researching what your competitors have done. Skim through all the ads in a magazine and see what you like and don't like—that's how we'd done it in the past. It seems natural. Right?

But Stevens is on to something here. What if you create a new ad in a vacuum? That is, take your understanding of your target market and craft a message that speaks specifically to them, in such a way that really makes you unique. Studying your competitors' ads can lead you to think that if you do anything too different, that it might be wrong. In truth, it's probably the rightest thing you can do.

Without the subconscious constraints you may put on yourself by studying other ads, you open up all sorts of possibilities. Stevens gives a great example of Albert Einstein as someone who valued the importance of imagination. Instead of sitting down and picking apart Newtonian physics, he started fresh and dreamt up big "what if?" scenarios. He then used his knowledge of physics to bring those scenarios into reality.

We had our own experience with this idea of starting from scratch. In 2006, when we were publishing Tasra's first book, *Real Women Scrap: Create the Life and Layouts You've Always Wanted*, we hired an expert designer to produce the cover. The designer had worked on covers for some major publishers and authors. Tasra's book took 12 basic scrapbooking lessons and paired them with analogous life lessons. Our designer had never worked on a scrapbooking book before, so we gave him a bunch of ideas from the covers of other books about scrapbooking. We also gave him some of Tasra's scrapbook designs for inspiration.

His first few passes were OK, but they were not hitting the mark. Frankly, they looked like every other scrapbooking book. We knew that wasn't what we wanted. So we told him to forget about everything we had given him, and just create something on his own, based on our description of the book. We encouraged him to go all out, and feel no obligation to conform to any predetermined ideas about what a "scrapbooking" book should look like (**FIGURE 7.3**). What he came up with was brilliant.

FIGURE 7.3 Here's the cover of *Real Women Scrap (www.realwomenscrap.com)*. We liked the design so much, we used the image of the woman and the three scrap decals above as the logo, too.

It expressed the fun and whimsical essence of the brand and of living the life you wanted. It targeted women. And it incorporated, ever so subtly, elements of scrapbooking. This book cover stood out in the sea of scrapbooking book covers, all of which were filled with typical scrapbook layout designs.

This is another example of why hiring a professional to help you with your sales and marketing can be so effective. But whether you hire a pro or play the ad designer yourself, it behooves you to consider starting with a clean slate.

IN FOCUS:
ME RA KOH

Earlier we mentioned the valuable lesson we learned from Mark Stevens' book, *Your Marketing Sucks*. Stevens writes, "You will never jump ahead of the pack if you accept the conventional wisdom. Healthy skepticism is a good thing. Question every single thing you have heard about the 'right way' to market."

A few years ago, we found a great example of this by a successful wedding and portrait photographer in the Pacific Northwest: Me Ra Koh.

We first saw Me Ra's ad in the *Grace Ormonde Wedding Style* magazine, an extremely high-end and exclusive magazine that not just anyone can advertise in. Once you're approved to be in the magazine, a full-page ad costs upwards of $15,000. Me Ra had a full-page ad unlike any in the magazine.

What would you expect a traditional wedding photographer's ad to look like? Most likely, some beautiful portrait of the bride silhouetted against a bay window. Or the bride in a long veil descending a circular stairway. Another common shot is the bride peeking out from behind her colorful bouquet. In all of these cases, your natural reaction may well be, "Been there. Done that." As beautiful as the photos may be, and as clever as the copy may be, in and of themselves, they're not unique.

Me Ra's ad, on the other hand, was completely unconventional. It was a photo of *her*. That's right, instead of a photo *by* Me Ra, she used a photo *of* herself—one in which she was laughing a big, hearty laugh (FIGURE 7.4). Our immediate thought was, "Why on earth would she put a picture of herself on a full-page ad—especially an expensive one?"

Later, when we met Me Ra in person, we understood the brilliance behind the ad. She was giving a talk at a photography convention we were filming, and she told the story of this ad. She also said how successful it's been for her—how she even had one bride call her up and say, "Oh my gosh! You totally get me." This was a bride who had never met Me Ra, but got that feeling all from that photo. Me Ra continues to use and pay for that ad as of the writing of this book.

FIG. 7.4 Me Ra Koh Photography's *Grace Ormonde* Wedding Style magazine ad: a stark contrast to the traditional wedding photographer ad.

We believe the ad is successful for two reasons. First, it stands out. While every other ad is a bride in a dress, this ad makes you stop and take notice. Even now, this ad is the only photographer's print ad that we can recall (and we've seen a lot of ads). Second, the photo captures the essence of Me Ra's fun-loving personality. She is able to convey the uniqueness of herself, and her brand, in a photo—and most remarkably, a photo *of* her, not *by* her.

Now this doesn't mean that you should just go out and take a picture of yourself laughing and having fun. The point is that you should stretch yourself and think outside the box in different ways. Grab your audience. Just like the title of Mark Stevens' book grabbed *us*.

LEVERAGING TECHNOLOGY

ON TUESDAY, JANUARY 20, 2009, history was made. CNN, one of the largest media and television conglomerates in the world, joined forces with a *little* technology company in Silicon Valley called Facebook.

Their goal? To help viewers share the experience of another history-making event that day—the inauguration of the first African-American President of the United States.

Can you leverage technology? Yes you can.

ADOPTING NEW MEDIA TECHNOLOGIES

The use of video on the Internet is evolving at an incredible pace. The way we watch television programming is changing so much that major corporations are taking notice and taking advantage.

In five years, many predict that all new TVs will have some kind of Internet connection to access entertainment. Already, companies such as Apple, Netflix, and Hulu are posting content that can be viewed online via special hardware devices. In ten years, the primary source for viewing television content may be online, with the content delivered to these special devices.

Changing times will play a role in how you deliver your content and, more importantly, these changes will shape how you market your services. As video producers, we need to keep up with the changes. The way your clients typically watch television or video content will largely determine how they will want your services to be delivered. The reason event videographers eventually had to switch from VHS to DVD was because all their clients were buying DVD players. A similar change is happening now. If you haven't already done so, you will need to start shooting exclusively in high-def. Why? Because every TV made will be HD, and that's what your clients will want.

You also need to become familiar with "new media." Wikipedia describes new media as a term meant to encompass the emergence of digital, computerized, or networked information and communication technologies in the later part of the 20th century. Blogs, social networking sites such as Facebook and MySpace, cell phone and iPod-compatible videos, and podcasts are all examples of new media. The 21st-century video producer will be an expert in the use of new media. Here's how.

POWER MARKETING WITH PODCASTS

A podcast is simply one method of distributing a multimedia file via the Internet for playback online, on your computer, and/or on a mobile device. Most podcasts are delivered in audio formats such as MP3, downloaded from Apple's iTunes store, or listened to online. However, video-based podcasts are growing rapidly and online video in general is continuing to increase in popularity.

It is estimated that by 2012, more than 40 percent of all video will be viewed outside of a television set. As a video producer, you're in a unique position to take advantage of your everyday tools of the trade to vastly improve your marketing and position yourself at the forefront of emerging trends.

Creating an audio or video podcast is a great way to establish yourself as an expert, as well as create a recurring audience. At Dare Dreamer Media, we've been very successful at using both the audio and video flavors of our photography podcasts, *F-Stop Beyond* (**FIGURE 8.1**) and *F-Stop Beyond: In Living Color* (**FIGURE 8.2**), to establish a strong name and brand recognition in the professional photography industry, which is where we focus much of our commercial video work.

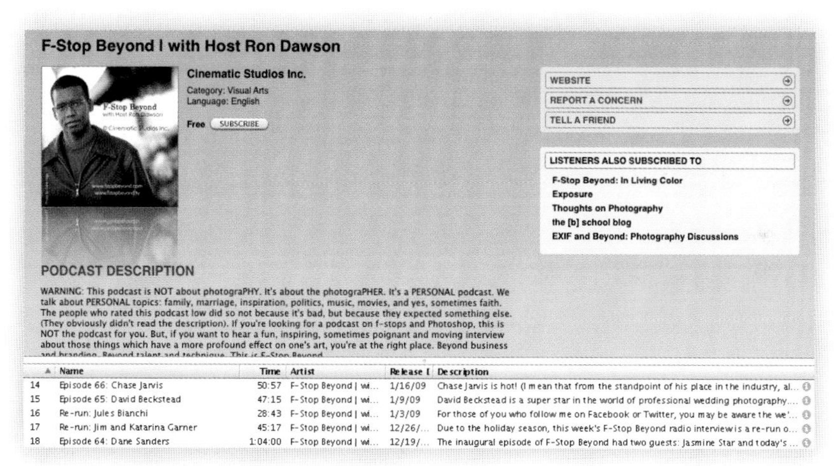

FIGURE 8.1 The F-Stop Beyond iTunes page.

FIGURE 8.2 Video thumbnail of "F-Stop Beyond TV" live at Brooks Institute with celebrity wedding photographer, Mike Colón.

Robert Allen of New Jersey is a veteran of wedding and event videography, and arguably one of the highest-paid professionals in that industry. He has successfully used his audio podcasts, "The Wedding Podcast Network" (FIGURE 8.3), to grow perhaps the largest podcast network of its kind aimed at brides. His network comprises ten different programs ranging from fitness to fashion. He's had some of the most elite wedding vendors in the nation on the show.

Forget about the exposure his brand is getting to thousands of brides (who all could potentially be clients). And forget about the networking opportunities he's created as a host and producer of such a show. More importantly, Allen has developed an entirely new segment of his business that could grow to be bigger than even his video revenue.

Other successful videographers who've taken the podcast plunge include veterans Al and Kathy Ritondo of "WedVidTalk," Steve Yankee of the Video Business Advisor, Brian Alves of the widely popular "The DV Show," and corporate video producer Kris Simmons.

Early in our podcast strategy, we used the video podcast "Me2WeTV" as a way to network with high-end coordinators (who were guests on our show), and bring a recurring audience of viewers to our Web site.

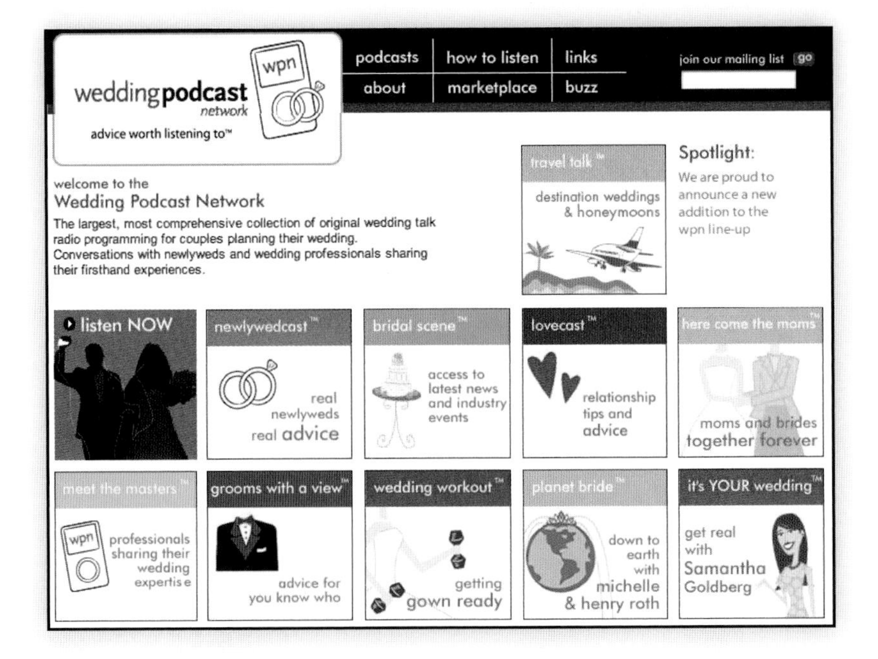

FIGURE 8.3
The "Wedding Podcast Network."

If you decide to take the podcast plunge, here are a few things to keep in mind while developing your strategy:

Know your target. Determine ahead of time precisely what market you will target and what you hope to gain by exposing your brand to that market.

Be unique. There are thousands of podcasts on the Internet. What will set yours apart from the pack?

Keep branding in mind. Develop a short and catchy bumper intro and outro; create an on-air personality. Develop a signature style that will entice your audience to return.

Create a system. It's very important to systemize your podcasting process. You should know when the podcast will be recorded, how it will be edited, what service you'll use, and other important details.

Keep costs low. Don't start off too grand. Keep it simple. Let the information be the main draw. There are plenty of free and low-cost hosting sites.

Promote it with a press release. Once you've launched your podcast, write a press release and send it to any offline or online periodicals read by your target audience.

Use iTunes. A presence in iTunes is a must if you want your podcast to be taken seriously. All the major video and audio podcast hosting services have some form of iTunes distribution feature. Use it.

Be consistent. Once you start publishing, establish a set time when the podcast will air periodically and stick to the frequency you promise your audience. Weekly or bi-weekly is a good interval.

Whether you want to market yourself to brides, large corporations, or fellow video producers, the possibilities are endless for how you can use either video or audio podcasts to market your brand and grow your business.

BLIP.TV

There are many solutions for creating a video podcast. We'll cover the details of the one we use, Blip.tv. Blip.tv makes it very easy to syndicate your content. It has a long list of social networking sites it can easily integrate with. It also makes it easy to list your podcast in iTunes (FIGURE 8.4).

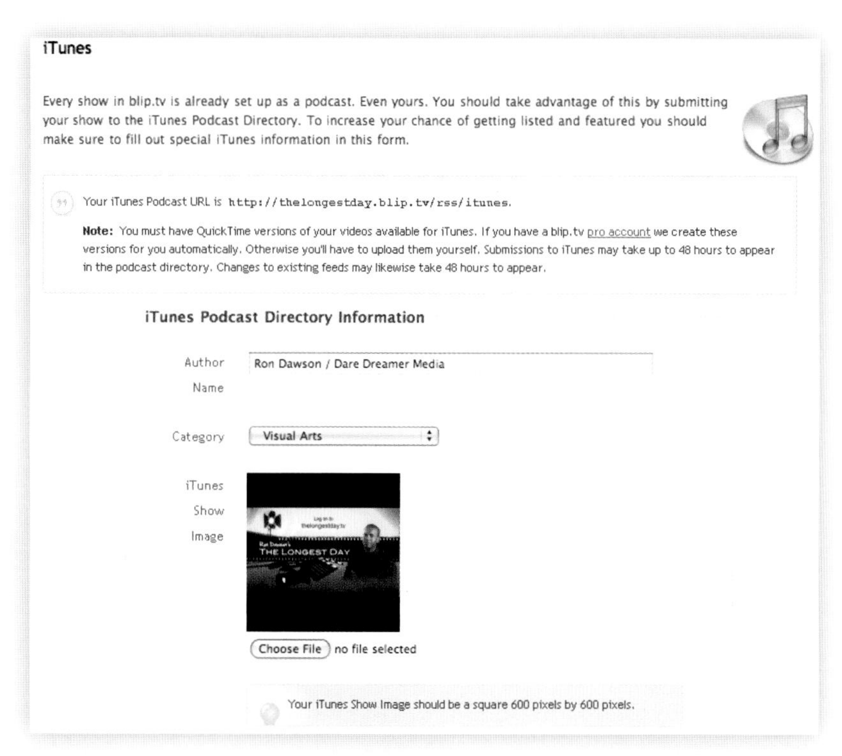

FIGURE 8.4 Prepping your podcast for iTunes is as simple as filling out a form.

Note that all videos you upload to Blip.tv can be downloaded in iTunes using the auto-generated iTunes feed. If you want to have your podcast searchable in the iTunes store, follow Blip.tv's easy directions for registering the feed. This is a step you must take if you want people to be able to log onto iTunes and find your videos without knowing your specific iTunes RSS feed.

Every video you upload can be downloaded via iTunes. However, unless your video is iPod-compatible, it won't be able to be viewed by an iPod/iPhone or synced to the user's device. If you've uploaded such a file (for example, an .flv video), but you want an iPod-compatible video to be added to your iTunes feed, make sure you select the "Add additional format" link, which will give you the option to upload additional videos. Select "iPod" as the role, then, in that field, upload an iPod-compatible video.

WOW YOUR CLIENTS WITH MICROMEDIA

There once was a time when a bride could say that a key difference between her wedding photos and her wedding video was that she could take her photos with her. That's all changed.

Devices such as iPods, iPhones, and other video-compatible mobile media players, PDAs, and cell phones make it possible for brides to take their wedding videos wherever they go. Corporate clients can pull out a Blackberry Storm and show a potential customer their latest promo video (produced by you, of course). If you're not using *micromedia* in your marketing mix, you're missing a great opportunity.

Here are some simple ways to use micromedia in your business:

FREE iPod versions of client videos. We've seen many event video producers add iPod versions of client videos to their repertoire. That's great. If you do this, we advise that you provide them for free. The incremental dollars you gain selling an iPod version is small in comparison to (1) the experience you give your client by giving them something for no additional cost and (2) the exposure you'll get as your clients excitedly shares their videos with friends and colleagues.

iPod version of your best work on *your* cell phone. Make sure you have iPod versions of your best work on your mobile device as well. You never know when you might be in a position to share it with a potential client.

iPod versions. Chances are, you've been to a number of movie trailer Web sites where an iPod-compatible version of the trailer is included for download. Where appropriate, you should do the same. Make sure you add a visible watermark and/or credit information and URL to the clips you post as a deterrent to piracy. You could also add these versions to a password-protected client site if piracy is a concern. (One note about the fear of piracy: Don't lose out on the opportunity to get your work in front of hundreds of people due to your fear of a handful of dishonest people who may steal your work. Unless you're a national or international brand, chances are that even if someone pirated your work, it would not affect your bottom line. Pirates will always find a way to steal. Don't let fear of them prevent you from getting your work out there.)

Podcasts. If you decide to produce a video podcast, make sure you make downloadable episodes compatible with iPods.

It is a good idea to always have some form of contact information at the end of any clips you make into iPod versions. In most cases, this will be a URL where the viewer can find out more information. Even if you create an iPod version of a client's wedding video (or portion thereof), take the time to add your URL. If you use a low-opacity watermark in the lower-right corner, add your URL at the same time and you'll have covered yourself two ways.

SOCIAL NETWORKING

Social networks are online communities of people who share common interests or activities, or who are interested in exploring the interests and activities of others. Most social networks are personal in nature. However, businesses have found that social networks represent a viable avenue for marketing and business networking. Social networking sites are particularly effective for the video producer due to the viral nature of sharing your work on these sites.

Way too many social network sites exist to even consider discussing all of them, and one could write an entire book on the topic. Our hope is to cover a few of the more prominent ones to give you an idea of how to work them into your marketing efforts.

GOING VIRAL WITH FACEBOOK

The relative importance of a site such as Facebook was mentioned at the beginning of this chapter when we referenced the historical inaugural address televised by CNN and broadcast online via a Facebook collaboration. Note that when looking for a partner, CNN went to Facebook, not MySpace. With more than 175 million members, Facebook has dethroned MySpace and become the undisputed social network leader, with MySpace and Twitter as No. 2 and No. 3, respectively. This isn't to say that you should totally discount the value that a presence on MySpace can have. MySpace is still particularly popular within the music scene. For purposes of this book, we chose to stick with Facebook, Twitter, and LinkedIn. The concepts we'll discuss are applicable to most, if not all, social network sites, even though each has its own unique method of implementation.

GETTING STARTED WITH FACEBOOK

The single greatest benefit to using Facebook (as with other social networks) is its viral nature. Obviously, networking is a key aspect of it. But the way your network can grow is what's so amazing. As a visual artist, you're poised to use that viral power to get your work seen by thousands of individuals. Let's take a look at how this viral marketing works.

Everyone on Facebook has a main "feed" where they can see all of the activities of their Friends. That's the first important thing to know. You grow your network by requesting to be friends with people on Facebook, and by confirming friend requests from others. The more friends you have, the more viral the site can be for you (**FIGURE 8.5**).

FIGURE 8.5 This Facebook home page displays the news feed for Ron Dawson. A posted video is playing.

Let's say you have 100 Facebook friends. Anytime any of these friends posts a photo or a video, makes a comment, or takes a similar action, you'll see that activity in your feed, with a link back to the photo, video, comment, or whatever it may be. And, as a friend of yours, anytime you do the same, it'll show up in their feeds.

Now, let's say you post an amazing video. Five of your friends see it, watch it, and comment. Now, everyone who is a friend of those five people will see that they made a comment on your video—plus, they'll have a link to watch the video on which they commented.

Here's the beauty—even if the other people are not friends of yours, they can see the video since one of their friends made a comment on it (so long as when you posted the video, you tagged it so that "Everyone" can see it).

Now, let's say one of the people who commented on your video happens to be a very popular person on Facebook and has 3,000 friends. All 3,000 of those friends will have that comment appear in their respective Facebook feeds (**FIGURE 8.6**). See the potential?

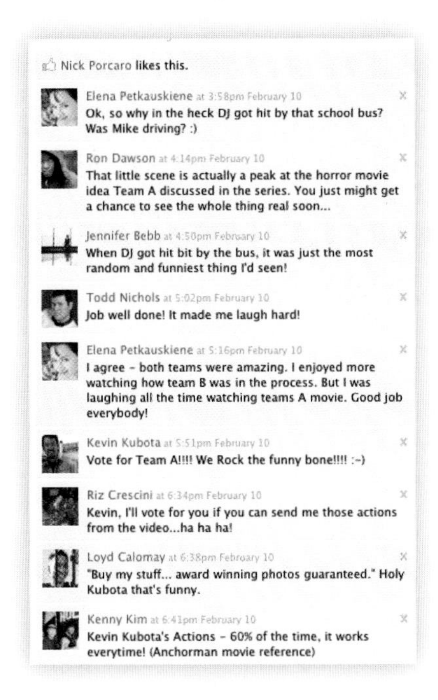

FIGURE 8.6 This screen shot shows only a portion of a thread of comments on one of the videos Ron posted on Facebook. All the friends of these people will see that comments were made.

And it doesn't stop there. Any Facebook members who see that video can share it with their friends, or post it to their Facebook page. The network and its possibilities are endless.

TAGGING AND USING VIDEOS ON FACEBOOK

Sharing videos on Facebook is extremely easy, and as we've mentioned previously, it has great viral capabilities. You can upload all the common video formats (including .mov, .wmv, .mp4, .m4v, and even .flv) as long as the file size is less than 1 GB and the video length is 20 minutes or less. As the video is uploading, you can add a title and description. Best of all, once the video is finished uploading, you can begin tagging.

Tagging is an important viral feature in Facebook. Any of your Facebook friends that appear in the video can be tagged. And, as you guessed, anyone else who is a friend of those particular people will see in their Facebook news feeds that a friend was tagged in a video. Your video will appear alongside that news feed item. Instant exposure. This is where having more friends becomes helpful. You must be friends with someone to be able to tag them (**FIGURE 8.7**).

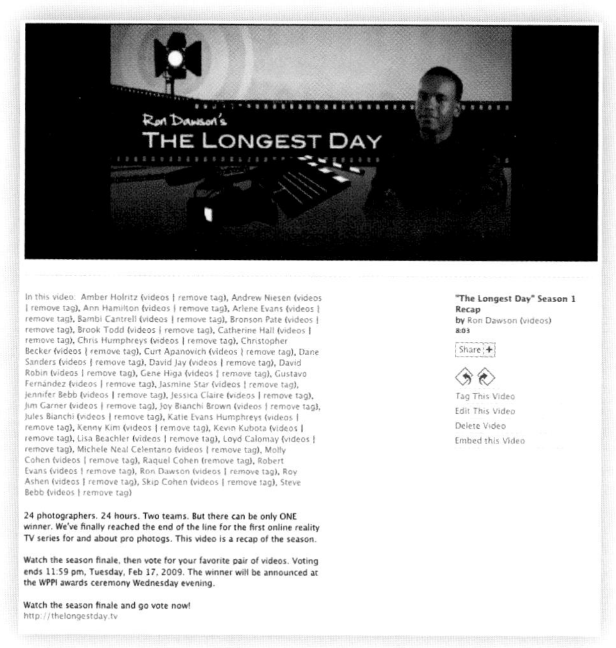

FIGURE 8.7 This is a screen shot of a video page on Facebook. You can see all the individuals tagged, alerting everyone who follows those people that they've been tagged. A few of the people tagged here have more than 3,000 friends each.

Sharing videos within and outside of Facebook is similar to doing so on other video sharing sites. As the owner of the video, you will have access to embed codes for your blog or Web site. From within Facebook, other viewers can e-mail the video to a friend, or post the video to their news feed, thereby allowing everyone who follows them to access it. One key difference though is that Facebook videos embedded outside of Facebook do not give viewers access to any kind of viral features. You can watch the video, adjust volume, and toggle full screen—that's about it.

THE CONTENT OWNERSHIP CONTROVERSY

In February 2009, Facebook posted a change to its terms of service (TOS) stating that Facebook owned any content you posted to its site. As of the writing of this book, the aspect of the TOS is changing. Facebook's intent in adding that point was not to take ownership of the content posted. The company is now in the process of reviewing user feedback to help craft something that everyone can live with. However, even if Facebook re-instates the same stringent term, its implications and limitations are worth considering.

First, most of you reading this are producing commissioned work on behalf of a client. Maybe it's a wedding video. Or perhaps a local company has hired you to film their holiday party. Do you honestly believe Facebook is looking to make money off these videos? Don't let fear and paranoia stand in the way of you using what could be an excellent way to market your brand.

PERSONAL PROFILES VS. PAGES AND GROUPS

There are two more aspects of Facebook you should consider as you build your social network: Pages and Groups. These are more commercial in nature, as they are designed to be viewable by the public at large (personal profile pages are limited to your friends).

Groups and Pages work relatively the same as personal profiles. But instead of friends, there are Fans for Pages (**FIGURE 8.8**) and Members for Groups (**FIGURE 8.9**). Here are a few benefits of the two options.

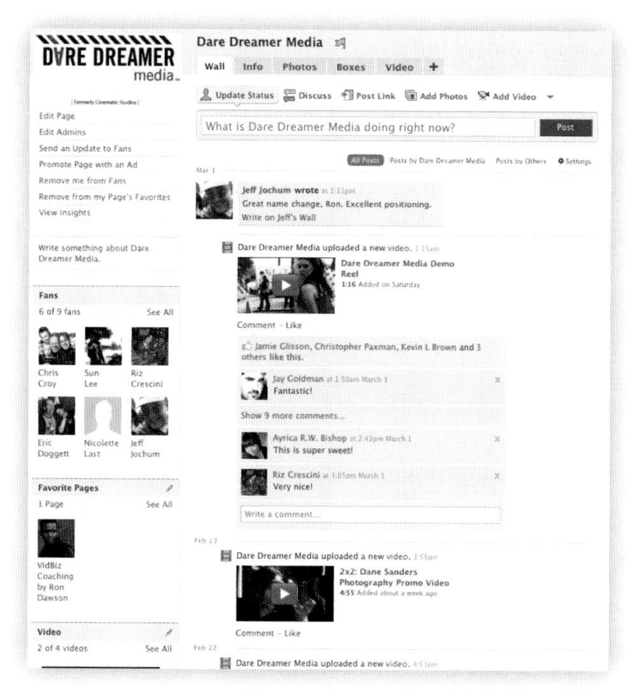

FIGURE 8.8 The Dare Dreamer Media Fan Page, now redesigned by Facebook to look more like personal pages.

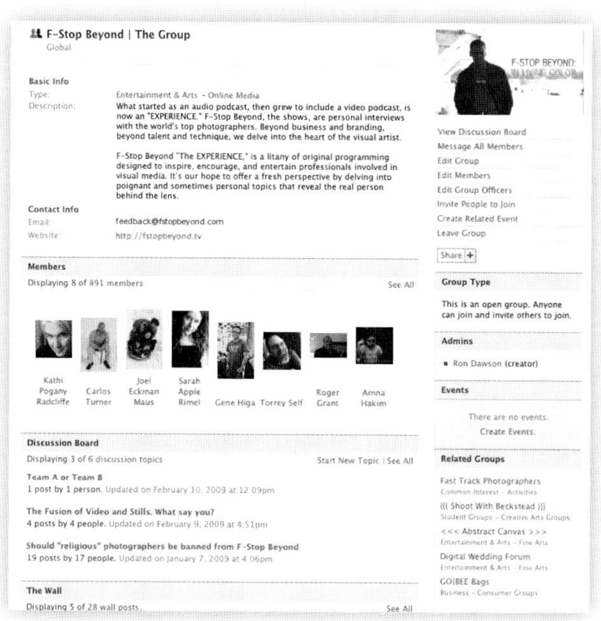

FIGURE 8.9 The F-Stop Beyond Group.

Indefinite number of members or fans. A personal profile is only allowed to have 5,000 friends. If you happen to have a large following, or are planning to build one, a Page will allow you unlimited fans.

Sending large mailings. If you want to e-mail a large number of people from your personal profile, you have to add the recipients' e-mail addresses one at a time. With Groups and Pages, you can send one e-mail to your entire base.

Sales and marketing tools. Facebook provides tools to help drive traffic to your Page and lets you check statistics like the number of page views. You can even track the number of cumulative video views for all the videos uploaded to your page.

To access the Pages feature, click on the advertising link at the bottom of your Facebook profile page.

STRICT POLICIES

Facebook has extremely strict policies when it comes to copyrighted music. The site will take down videos with copyrighted music and disable the accounts of repeat offenders.

Also, there is a no-spamming policy and anything that looks like spam will elicit a warning.

The last item to take note of when joining Facebook and uploading professional content is the Terms of Service (mentioned previously). There has been significant controversy recently and it is important to make sure you are fully aware of the Terms of Service before joining.

TWITTER DEE, OR TWITTER DUMB

I (Ron) remember one summer evening trying to explain the concept of Twitter to my father-in-law. The conversation went something like this:

"Well, basically, it's a way for people to tell other people what they're doing at any given time. For instance, here's a Tweet I'm reading on my iPhone now from Sarah. 'On my way to the restaurant.'"

My father-in-law replies, "Who the hell cares what I'm doing at this given instant! Do people really need to know I'm using the bathroom now?"

Well, his response was actually a bit more colorful, but you get the idea.

When you first hear about the purpose, it's not unusual to wonder why anyone would waste their time sharing such minutiae. But, like Facebook, there's a viral nature to Twitter that makes it a valuable networking tool.

SHORT AND SWEET

The crux of Twitter is that each Twitter entry can be no longer than 140 characters, including spaces. That forces you to be creative and to cut to the chase. This is why it's called microblogging. But, don't be misled into thinking it's all just a great big waste of time. Here are some popular uses of Twitter:

- Important announcements
- Soliciting advice or expert help
- Engaging in public conversation (there's a good reason for this we'll address later)
- Keeping clients or colleagues updated on the status of a project

CONNECTING TWITTER TO FACEBOOK

A key aspect of Facebook is your Facebook status. You can manually update it whenever you like. Again, every time you do, all the people who follow you will see that you updated your status. It was only natural that Facebook created a way for you to have your Twitter status update your Facebook status. Here's how. (We're assuming you have both a Facebook and Twitter account. If not, create them now.)

Go to the URL http://apps.new.facebook.com/twitter/. Or, do a search in Facebook for "Twitter," then click on the first application you see listed in the results.

When you come to the "Allow Access?" screen, click Allow.

Log into Twitter via the Twitter app in Facebook. After you test out the Facebook-to-Twitter functionality by typing a message and clicking on "Update," click on "Allow Twitter to Update Your Facebook Status."

On the following screen—"Allow Status Updates from Twitter?"—click the "Allow Status Updates" button.

Log into Twitter.com and test it out.

BLOGGING

Picture a newly engaged bride sitting at her desktop watching one of the finest videos you've ever produced. When it ends, she grabs a tissue, wipes her eyes, and sends you a personal note about how much she loved your work.

Or imagine a businessman searching online for "corporate videos" and stumbling upon your work. He clicks play, watches the first 30 seconds, and knows he's found the right person for the job—you. He immediately picks up the phone and gives you a call to find out if you're available.

The biggest battle for most small business owners is getting enough people to see your work. Often that battle is won or lost online, without you even knowing. Not very encouraging news. Here's the solution: Add a blog to your marketing mix and maximize its effectiveness. Doing so will help you reach your target market in ways you never imagined. And despite what you may think, entering the blogosphere to build your business doesn't have to be painful or time-consuming.

TOP THREE REASONS TO BLOG

There are three main reasons you should blog:

1. **Name Recognition.** Just like participating in forums, when you frequent a blog and comment often, your name becomes recognized. This builds community and trust among other readers of the blogs. By hanging around blogs that share common interests, you'll build a readership and learn the language of that group. You can find groups by looking in blog directories or Technorati (see the following pages).
2. **Increased Traffic and Visitation.** Most blogs will allow you to link back to your blog (or any Web site you like) when you leave a comment. That increases the number of URLs linking back to your Web site and subsequently the number of visitors. For example, if you visit the top photographers or wedding coordinators in your area, become well-known on the blog, and link back to your site, you will be reaching the clients of those ideal vendors. There aren't many other avenues for reaching your target market that quickly and efficiently.
3. **Reciprocity.** The more you comment on others' blogs, the more they'll comment on yours (it's part of blog etiquette). The more comments you get on your blog, the more visitors will be intrigued to stay and read, which in turn will help you gain traffic and readership. Remember to announce your new blog content, including videos, to people you meet in person and online, in your e-mail signature, and in your comments.

WHAT IS THE BLOGOSPHERE?

It may sound like a place you'd hear about in a *Star Trek* episode, but the blogosphere is just a fancy way of describing the mass of millions of blogs floating around the World Wide Web. (Is it any wonder this topic can seem overwhelming?) The truth is that only a fraction of those blogs are being updated frequently. An even smaller portion are used effectively as marketing tools.

Part of effective blogging is participating in the blogosphere and being a good blog citizen. Depending on your business goals, you may only need to focus on a handful of highly trafficked and effective communities of blogs.

FIGURE 8.10 Ron's WordPress blog, www.bladeronner.com.

IT'S ALL ABOUT THE AUDIENCE

The biggest battle for most small businesses is getting people in the door. Whether it's a product or service, reaching critical mass is an elusive and seemingly impossible feat. However, this is where businesses succeed or fail. For a videographer, it is critical that people see what you can do. In an industry that is competitive and visual, you must define, find, and connect with your audience. Building a blog (**FIGURE 8.10**) is your key to opening that door.

Audience Defined: Know your audience. Establish an image of your ideal client or customer. The better you know your customers, the more you know about how to reach them. You can tailor your content and images to meet their needs and wants. If you haven't defined the ideal audience for your business, do it now.

Audience Found: Once you have clearly defined an audience, find them online through blogs, forums, carnivals, and other social networking sites. (A "blog carnival" is akin to an online magazine of links to blogs that all relate to a similar topic). Listen to the words they use, familiar catchphrases, and needs they express. Begin providing a solution to those needs. If all the engaged women in a blog carnival are talking about cheesy or boring wedding videos, you can respond with a blog post highlighting your most compelling video clips and bill it as the antidote to cheesy wedding videos.

Audience Connection: With a blog, you have the unique advantage of dealing directly with your clients and potential customers. Direct customer contact provides increased opportunities to showcase your work, build trust, and eventually make the sale or book the gig. That interactivity is core to the popularity and success of blogging as a marketing platform.

RULES OF THE ROAD

The number one way to participate in the blogosphere is to read other blogs and comment. That's it. Think of the blogosphere as one giant forum, where every blog is a different post. Find the posts you like to read the most, read them, read the comments people make on them, then post yourself. You already have the time and the talent it takes. You just have to apply that time and talent to blogging.

THE 'GOOGLE' OF THE BLOGOSPHERE

Technorati (www.technorati.com) is a massive search engine that exists to index all blogs in existence. Your first task after starting a blog is to claim it on Technorati so it can start ranking you. Your Technorati ranking is one more tool for determining the popularity and effectiveness of your blog. The more sites that link to your blog, the higher authority and level of trust you establish in the blogosphere.

When bloggers want to find other people talking about an area of interest, they frequently go to Technorati first. There is a sense of community and trust in blogs that doesn't exist for Web sites. The reason is that Web sites are considered "corporate" or biased, whereas blogs are generally regarded as more friendly, real, and honest. The validity of these assumptions isn't important for our discussion—it's simply the reality of the perception.

You want your page to show up in Technorati when someone searches for your niche, whether it is weddings, events, corporate work, or commercial work. You need to tag your posts, include keywords in your writing, and ping Technorati. Here's how:

Add Technorati Tags. Tags (**FIGURE 8.11**) are keywords that label the contents of your post to make it visible to search engines. Tagging your posts identifies the most relevant terms for search engines. This increases your visibility and rankings for those specific keywords. An automatic HTML code for adding tags can be found with a quick online search on "how to add Technorati tags."

Include Keywords. Each post you write and create should be keyword-rich—even if you're just posting the latest video you've completed and didn't plan on writing anything. Think again. Just a few short sentences with the right keywords can multiply your return on the time invested. Try to include words that are being searched for by your target audience. One way to find out what people are searching for is to use a search engine watch-site such as Google Trends, Yahoo Buzz Index, or AOL Hot Searches.

Ping Technorati. The concept of pinging oftentimes confuses new bloggers. Do they have to do it? How often? Is it important? The answers are "no," "anytime you update your blog," and "yes," respectively. You don't have to do it, but it helps build traffic. It's like raising the red flag on your mailbox when you put something in it. The mail carrier knows to pick it up and deliver it. The ping notifies sites such as Technorati that you've updated your blog and they can deliver that information to the blogosphere. Every time you post something new, it helps to ping. You wouldn't leave the red flag down and just hope the mail carrier stops by, so why do it on your blog? (WordPress blogs automatically ping Technorati and other major blog trackers when updated.)

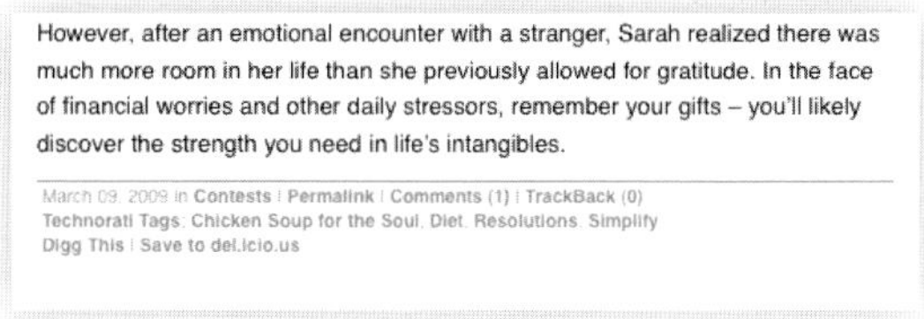

However, after an emotional encounter with a stranger, Sarah realized there was much more room in her life than she previously allowed for gratitude. In the face of financial worries and other daily stressors, remember your gifts – you'll likely discover the strength you need in life's intangibles.

March 09, 2009 in Contests | Permalink | Comments (1) | TrackBack (0)
Technorati Tags: Chicken Soup for the Soul, Diet, Resolutions, Simplify
Digg This | Save to del.icio.us

FIGURE 8.11 Technorati tags will help your blog post be found on Technorati.

SUGGESTED BLOGGING SOFTWARE

So, now that you realized it's important to have a blog, where do you get one? Perhaps Blogger, since it's free and you know many people who have one? Or, how about WordPress? That's a popular blogging service too. As you might expect, there are significantly more resources for getting a blog than room to write about them. We'll pick four that are worth discussing: Blogger, TypePad, WordPress, and customized.

Blogger. Google's popular blogging solution is used by millions of people, primarily because it's relatively simple to set up and it's free. Blogger is great for personal blogs, but when it comes to establishing a blog for your business, we don't recommend it. It has a less-professional feel. All Blogger sites have the blogger.com domain as part of the URL. So, your site would be http://myblognamehere.blogger.com. In marketing, it's considered a good idea to have a blog that is a subset of your company's domain name. Technically, it is possible to forward a domain to a blogger site, but the result is the same, a blogger.com URL. If you really wanted to, you could incorporate a Blogger blog into your Web site, or map your company's domain name to a Blogger blog, but that level of technical expertise is usually beyond most people, particularly the ones who decide to have Blogger blogs.

WordPress. There are actually two "flavors" of WordPress: WordPress.com, and the WordPress blogging software (found at WordPress.org) that requires installation into a Web site. WordPress.com is an online blogging service, similar to Blogger and TypePad. Like both of those services, if you use a WordPress.com blog, WordPress.com will be part of the domain. However, WordPress.com does make it easier to map a vanity URL to the domain. WordPress.com also has access to hundreds of themes (FIGURE 8.12). These are stylistic designs of blogs that allow for different looks. Think of it as your blog's uniform. WordPress sites tend to have a more streamlined look and feel. So, for design aesthetics, they feel more professional.

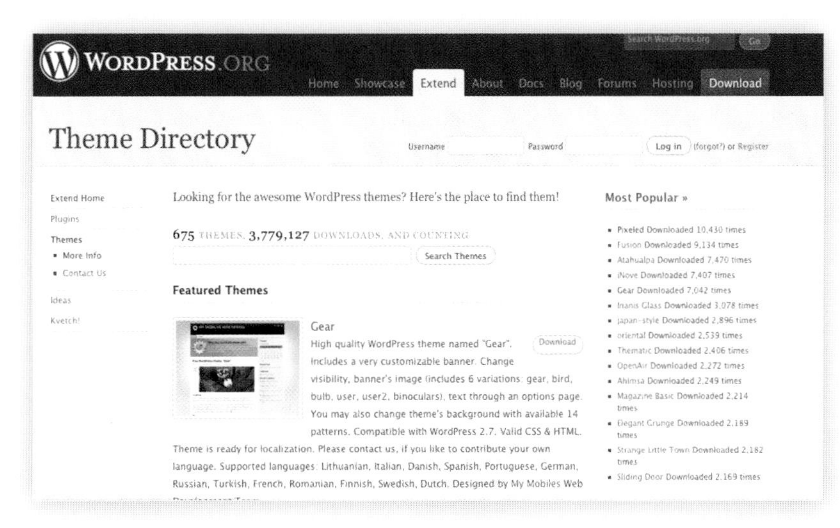

FIGURE 8.12 Use WordPress' Theme Directory to choose a visual style for your blog.

However, there is one significant drawback to WordPress.com blogs. To minimize the ability of hackers to affect WordPress.com, the site does not allow the use of "embed" or "object" HTML tags. To put it in layman's terms, you aren't able to use typical embed codes for these blogs. You have to use special one-line codes (as mentioned previously in the Blip.tv section). WordPress.com has instructions on how you can embed videos from popular sites such as YouTube, and more and more video sharing sites are creating connections to WordPress.com via these one-liners. However, the players created by these codes typically only have player controls (for instance, audio, scrubber, and so forth) and not the useful viral sharing features. WordPress.com is free.

WordPress Installed. The other version of WordPress, and the one we'd recommend of the two, is the installed version. This version gives you the ability to add video from any sharing site, and the blog will naturally be a subset of your domain (for example, www.mywebsite.com/blog). It's safe to say that a large majority of high-profile visual artists, social media experts, and technology reporters use installed WordPress blogs.

The downside of WordPress installed blogs is that they require more technical expertise. Installing the software can be frustrating for the less technically savvy. However, most popular Web hosting companies have some form of "1-click" WordPress installation. Once installed, it's very easy to pick a theme, activate it, and be ready to go. An installed

WordPress blog is free, but you'll need to install it onto a hosted Web site, which usually is not free.

TypePad. We like to think of TypePad as a great combination of the flexibility and professional credibility of WordPress and the ease of use of Blogger. TypePad has numerous features that allow for customization and designing an engaging user experience. Installing videos into a TypePad blog (FIGURE 8.13) is similar to working with an installed WordPress blog. You can add embedding codes, or if applicable, many video sharing sites have TypePad embed buttons from within the administration panel. Upload the video and click the button on the right, and that video automatically gets embedded into a new TypePad blog post. Like WordPress.com and Blogger, with TypePad your blog will have a typepad.com domain. But all the TypePad pricing plans, except for the cheapest, come with the ability to map a vanity domain to your blog (that is, mydomain.typepad.com becomes www.mydomain.com). As mentioned, TypePad does have a price tag. Plans range from just under $5 per month up to $90 per month. If you want a professional-looking blog that is relatively inexpensive and easy to use, TypePad is an excellent choice.

FIGURE 8.13
Tasra's TypePad blog, www.realwomenscrap.typepad.com.

Custom blog. For many, blogging is such an integral part of their business that they decide to invest in a custom-created blog. Just as you can get a Web designer to create a custom Web site for you, you can do the same for a blog. This will obviously give you the utmost flexibility in design and usage. The cost for such a blog could be in the thousands, though. If you go this route, make sure your designer gives you complete instructions on how to update and change the blog. If you have the budget, and the need for a unique implementation of blogging software, a custom blog may not be a bad idea. However, with the wide variety of established blog services and their extensive functionality, you'll more than likely be able to find what you need without having to invest a lot of (or any) additional money.

CONTINUING EDUCATION

It's always good to stay knowledgeable about new media, marketing, and effective ways to promote your business. When you're ready to learn more about effective blogging, we strongly suggest the following sites: www.copyblogger.com and www.problogger.net.

LINKEDIN

On the surface, LinkedIn (LI) is a professional social network site. There are more than 36 million members from over 170 industries in over 200 countries. But it goes so much further than just a networking resource or great viral marketing tool like Facebook. Rather, think of it as a great way to increase productivity. You can use your LI profile (**FIGURE 8.14**) and your network of trusted connections to point you in the right direction when looking for a job, recruiting for your business, looking for investors, and so on. Here are a few of the most effective uses of LI for your video business.

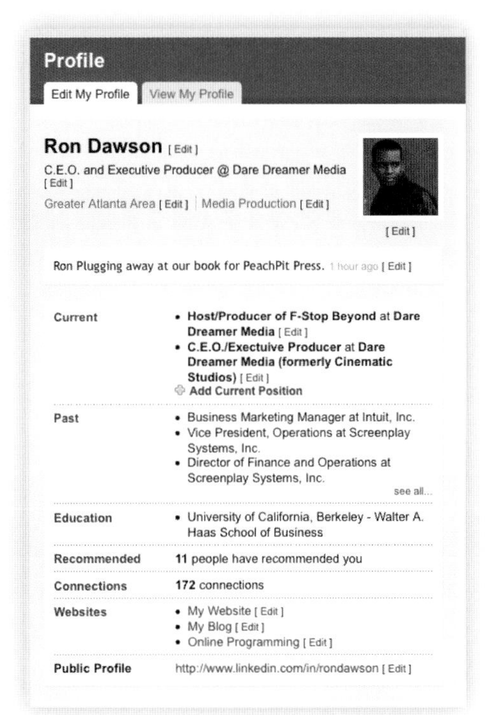

FIGURE 8.14 Ron's LinkedIn profile shows work history and includes links to Web sites.

Get recommendations. One of the best benefits of LI is the ability to get recommendations on your work from people in your network. When a recommendation gets posted, everyone in your network will see in their "latest LI updates" feed (**FIGURE 8.15**) that you've been recommended. This is an aspect of the viral nature of LI that is similar to Facebook. Recommendations can come from clients, colleagues, and past employers. What's more, they can also be attached to a specific job you had in the past. So, don't feel like you can only get recommendations for your current video business. If, in a previous position, you demonstrated a particular trait or skill set that would be appealing to potential clients now, get a past employer to write a recommendation based on his or her experience with you.

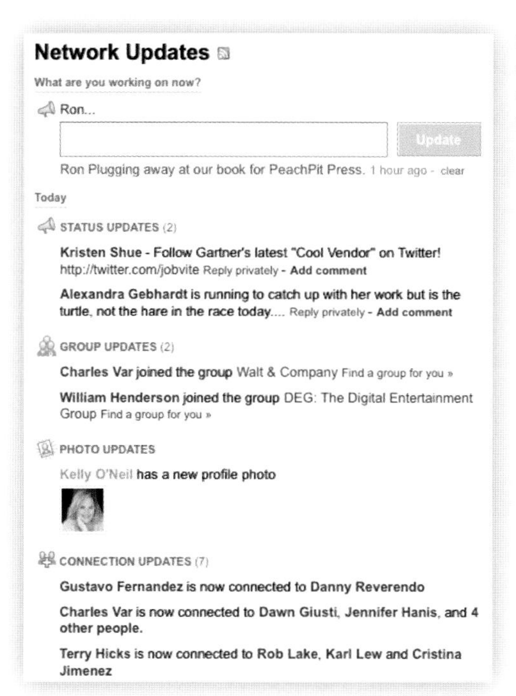

FIGURE 8.15 LinkedIn updates show you the activity happening within your network of connected professionals.

An online resume. LI gives you the ability to list your entire work history, including descriptions, time at the past job, and any recommendations you have related to that position. Rather than posting a copy of your resume online, provide a link to your LI profile instead. It is also a good idea to include a link to your LI profile in your e-mail signature.

Market your services and recruit. Through LI's question system, you can pose questions to people in your network who are looking for services you may offer. Or use your connection to one individual to get connected to another in your network, thereby promoting your services. Use the same system to recruit for personnel, contractors, and vendors for services you may need.

E-NEWSLETTERS

In the past, periodic paper newsletters were used by companies to update their clients and customers about what was happening with the company (for example, products sales, new releases, new employees, and other announcements). Today, the outdated and expensive method of sending paper newsletters has largely been replaced by electronic newsletters (e-newsletters).

Many terrific companies specialize in e-mail newsletter creation and management. Again, there are too many to try to name and describe in this book. Two of the best known are Vertical Response and Constant Contact. They share many of the same features, but have different payment options.

Vertical Response is a pay-as-you-go model. You pay only for the e-mails you send. Constant Contact has a monthly subscription model. The number of subscribers you have and how often you e-mail them will determine what is more cost-efficient.

Here are some helpful tips in the effective use of e-newsletters in your marketing mix:

Pick the lowest-hanging fruit. A common phrase used in successful business marketing is "pick the low-hanging fruit." It's a metaphor that describes the act of marketing your services to current and past clients. These are people and companies who already have invested in you and (hopefully) already had great experiences working with you. It therefore stands to reason that these clients are more likely to buy from you again. E-newsletters are a great way to keep these clients updated on any new services you have available, and to keep your company in the forefront of their minds.

Keep subject headings short, yet enticing. A good subject heading can make or break an e-mail newsletter campaign. That one line may be the only chance you get to have the recipient open the e-mail and take a look. Pick one or two items to highlight in your subject that you believe will have the most impact.

Be mindful of anti-spam laws. There are some specific laws that you need to be mindful of when sending e-mail newsletters. The most important law is that anyone you send an e-newsletter to needs to have opted into your e-mail list. What's more, each newsletter you send must give the recipient a means to opt-out of the list (that is, no longer receive e-newsletters from you). All of the major e-newsletter services will have this feature. Check to see if they also give you the option to ask the user why they are opting out. In addition, e-newsletters must have a physical company address somewhere conspicuous in the body of the e-mail.

Track the performance. Whichever system you decide to use, make sure you have the ability to track the performance of each e-mail campaign. Metrics that are important to know include how many people opened the e-mail; how many clicked through to your Web site; which links in your e-newsletter received the most clicks; how many recipients opted-out; which e-mail addresses opened, clicked, opted-out, purchased, and so on. It's imperative for you to know what's working and what isn't so that you can continue to improve future e-mail marketing performance.

Keep them frequent, but not too frequent. If you're going to have an e-newsletter campaign, it's important to make them frequent enough for clients to remember you're out there. Marketing experts all agree that a prospective buyer of a service needs to see an impression numerous times before any action will be taken. If you send one newsletter and stop at that, you risk the chance of many subscribers missing it. However, if you do it too frequently, then you risk being an annoyance and significantly increasing your opt-out percentage. We believe a good safe interval is once a month or bi-monthly.

Allow for multiple opportunities to subscribe. Make sure you have plenty of opportunities for people to sign up for your e-newsletter. In addition to the contact page of your Web site, other strategic locations include a link at the footer of each Web page, your e-mail signature, and your blog.

Offer incentives. To entice visitors to visit your site and subscribe to your e-mail newsletter, offer something for free in exchange for them signing up. You want it to be something that's easy to give them, doesn't cost you much (or anything), but is still valuable to them. For our e-mail newsletter aimed at professional photographers, we offer a free audio download from our CD on "Getting Paid What You're Worth." We put a link to the download in the auto-responder the subscriber gets to confirm their subscription request. Another good example that may be useful for wedding videographers is a free e-book on wedding planning tips. Perhaps contact a local wedding planner to write it, thereby giving you an opportunity to collaborate with a vendor who can refer business to you. You help the planner by getting his or her name out to brides, and the planner helps you by providing you a valuable asset to give prospective clients.

IN FOCUS:
JULIAN SMITH

Perhaps the best example of the convergence of new media marketing and how it can be successfully used to market oneself is found in the story of a director of photography from Nashville, Tennessee. Julian Smith already had a decent following of viewers to his periodic comedy video shorts. Then, in March of 2009, he struck viral marketing gold. He created a video called "25 Things I Hate About Facebook"—a four-minute clip that poked fun at 25 popular aspects of Facebook that can be annoying at times. It was simple—just Julian, a few actor friends, a black background, some royalty-free music, and a few clever graphics. But it was extremely funny and within a week of posting, it grew to become, at one point, the No. 1 watched video on YouTube that week. In less than a month from its mid-February posting, it garnered more than a half-million views on YouTube alone. Who knows how many other views it got on Facebook?

In four days, I watched Smith's Facebook friends count go from somewhere in the low 2,000 range (already a big list), to the 5,000 friend maximum. He then created a Fan page to accommodate all the extra people, and that quickly grew to more than 4,000 fans. By the end of March 2009, he had over 12,000 subscribers to his YouTube channel.

But, there's more. Facebook loved the video and invited him out to Palo Alto, California, to make another comedy video about the new Facebook design. That same week, Smith had meetings with Google. Later, he met with companies in Los Angeles as well. Keep in mind, his "day job" is probably the same as yours: if you're reading this book, shooting video.

We use Julian Smith as a case study primarily because he is in the same business as you. He's a visual artist who leveraged his other artistic talents and the popularity of Facebook to generate such wild buzz that one of the largest companies in Silicon Valley brought him out to "take a meeting."

Now, we understand that you won't necessarily go out and become the next Julian Smith. But what if you could achieve even a fraction of his success? What if you created the kind of buzz that got that many people visiting your Web site, or your blog, or your YouTube channel, or our Facebook page? What if your work was being seen by thousands of people every day? Heck, what if only hundreds of people were seeing your work every day? Do you think your work is good enough that a small percentage of them might reach out to hire you?

IN FOCUS:
THE LONGEST DAY

So, maybe you feel that the Julian Smith example is so far out, you can never see yourself doing that. Well, we can bring it down to earth. In early 2009, we produced the first online reality TV program for and about professional photographers called "The Longest Day". Through leveraging connections we built in the professional photography community (connections we made in large part to the weekly podcast we produce, F-Stop Beyond), we were able to raise $17,000 (**FIGURE 8.16**) to produce the show and release it as nine short episodes and two trailers.

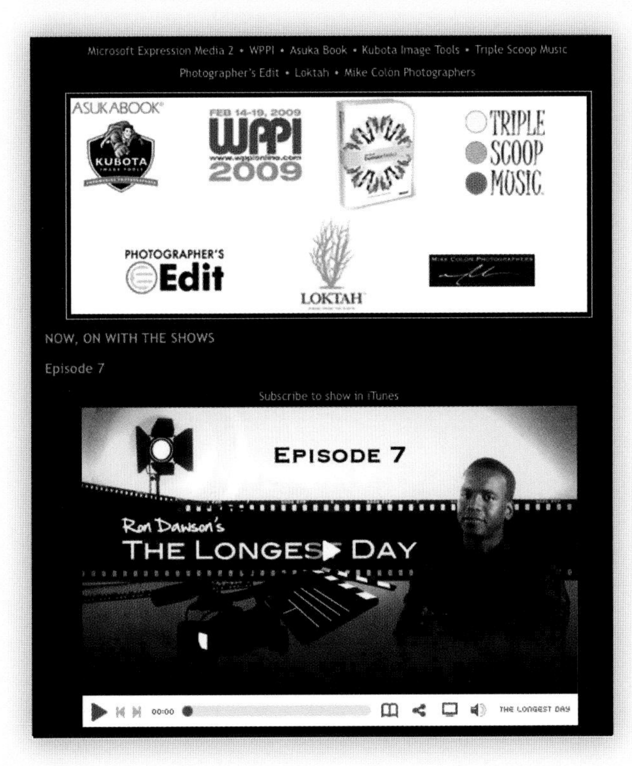

FIGURE 8.16 Screen shot from "The Longest Day" blog that displays the show's sponsors.

In a couple of months, they aggregated more than 40,000 views via Blip.tv alone. Who knows how many other views were attained via Facebook, as many of the 24 photographers in the show have followings of 2,000 friends and more. These numbers pale in comparison to our aforementioned DP friend Julian. But the buzz we created attracted the attention of the PR company for Microsoft's photography division. That, in turn, led to talks with them to produce a series of additional programs to help highlight Microsoft's Icons of Imaging high-profile professional photographers sponsored by Microsoft, in much the same way that sports athletes are sponsored by shoe and clothing companies. By using a creative idea, having the chutzpah to pitch it to large corporate sponsors, and using a new media marketing strategy that included Twitter, Facebook, blogging, Blip.tv, and iTunes, our small two-person, boutique marketing agency/video production company was able to create a high-profile working relationship with one of the biggest companies on the planet.

GETTING PAID WHAT YOU'RE WORTH

THE QUANDARY OF HOW MUCH to charge for your services, and how to find clients willing to pay the rates you choose, is perhaps the most serious issue for small- to mid-sized production companies.

We recently discovered a production company that offered a litany of services at rates that seemed not only too good to be true, but financially unrealistic to maintain. I conducted an informal survey of similar companies on a few online forums, listing all the services and asking people to estimate what they would charge for the same list of services. On average, everyone surveyed would charge minimally three to five times what this other company was charging.

The hard labor costs alone associated with the work involved (that is, the amount of money one would need to charge just to pay the shooters and editors) was more than what this particular company was charging. Yet, this company was located in one of the largest metropolitan areas in the country and served by an airport that is an international hub. I was baffled. This type of pricing can only result in burnout and an inability to maintain quality standards.

The price you charge for your work has real financial consequences for your business and your way of life. There's also a psychological component to pricing that affects self-esteem, which affects confidence, which in turn affects the kind of rates you can command. It's a vicious cycle.

It is now time to end that cycle.

DEFINING WHAT YOUR SERVICES ARE WORTH

You may be under the impression that it's our goal to show you how to charge a lot for your work, or how to successfully market to land jobs from clients willing to pay you top dollar (the elusive high-end bride or six-figure corporate gig). But getting paid what you're worth isn't about that.

Rather, it's about recognizing the true value of what you do, and charging rates that allow you to have the lifestyle you want while building a business that can sustain itself and grow. That may or may not mean charging a high rate or holding out for high-end bookings.

Let's compare the business models of two companies we'll call Company A and Company B. Company A makes $10,000 per gig and Company B averages $1,500 per gig. Which company would you prefer to be? Your gut reaction may be Company A. But what if you found out that Company A does only three gigs per year and Company B does 3,000 gigs per year?

Now which company do you want to be? The correct answer is still "It depends." Three gigs at $10,000 each is fantastic yearly revenue if you're a high school student who happens to be an exceptional videographer and happens to get hired by three high-end clients.

Don't be starstruck or amazed by numbers like these without seeing the whole picture. How much a company makes per year or per gig is often seen as a bragging point. You'll also hear volume-based studios boasting about their number of bookings per year. However, unless you know the expenses, level of debt, the systems in place, and any number of other factors, those numbers don't mean anything.

This is an import point because we have found that it is easy for people to get caught up on numbers and think, "Oooh, VP Video makes $1 million per year. I wish my company could do that." What you may not know is that VP Video's expenses are $1.1 million and their debt ratio is killing their business.

The moral of this exercise is, don't dismiss a low-priced studio just because their rates are low, and don't assume a high-priced one is better or more successful just because its rates are high.

A PROPER PERSPECTIVE

Where we would like you to put your focus is on *your* company. What is your company charging for the level of service it's providing? Are you generating the income you need to grow the business, cover costs, make a profit, and pay yourself a salary that can sustain your lifestyle (or, at least contribute enough to your household to maintain the lifestyle you want)?

We believe many video producers are not getting paid what they are truly worth: colleagues we know who are struggling under massive workloads, huge backlogs, and low self-esteem, barely making ends meet.

The first step in getting paid what you're worth is believing in yourself. How can you convince someone to invest any amount of money in your services if, deep down inside, you don't believe you're worth it?

This is not the same as being able to *afford* your own services. Many people find it hard to charge an amount higher than what they think they can afford or would be willing to spend. That's a mistake.

Do you think most Mercedes car salespeople can afford the cars they sell? Do you think the clerk behind the counter at Rolex has the financial wherewithal to afford most, if any, of the watches for sale under that glass? The answer to both questions is most likely "no." Likewise, don't be handicapped by the reality that for the services you provide, your rates may be higher than even you can afford. That's perfectly OK.

Let's uncover what it is most of you do. Once you have an accurate picture of what it is you provide, you should have the confidence to know you may be worth significantly more than you're currently charging (**FIGURE 9.1**).

As a video production company, chances are you are filling most, if not all, of the following roles:

- Camera operator
- Director of photography
- Director
- Producer
- Audio technician
- Writer
- Editor
- Motion graphics expert
- DVD author
- Graphic designer

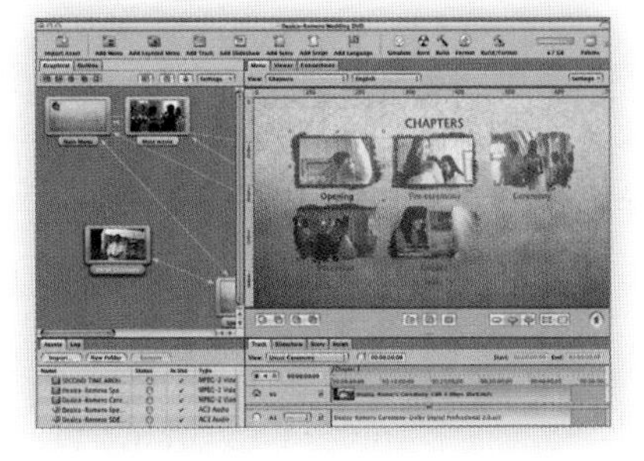

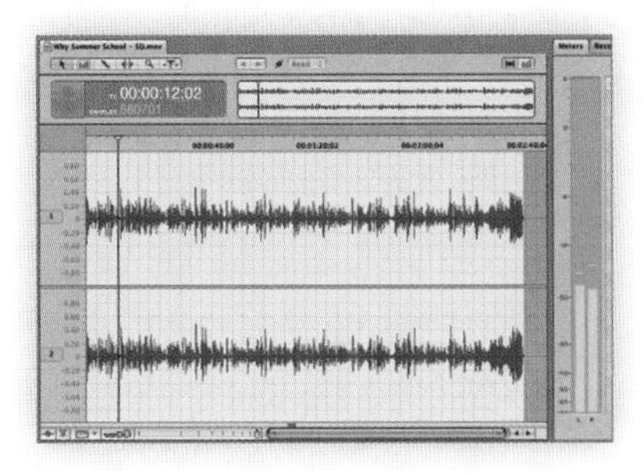

FIGURE 9.1 Event video producers need a varied skills set, from shooting and editing to sound mixing, DVD authoring, and graphic design.

Now ask yourself this: How much do you think a studio pays to have one of its DVD covers designed by a company that specializes in this service? $100? $200? Not even close. Yet, many of you are creating custom DVD cases and disc faces for your clients at rates equivalent to those above.

Likewise, how much do you think a studio pays a professional colorist to provide color correction on a feature film? Many of you spend hours adding filters and color correcting 90-minute event videos and charge less for the full video than you could probably be making if you just became a full-time colorist.

We hope you see where we're going with this. At the same time, we're not naïve. We understand that you're not producing a video that is going to generate millions of dollars in sales. We know that your clients aren't major global corporations (well, actually, for some of you, they probably are). That doesn't mean the work you do is any less difficult or time consuming. It still requires the same level of skill and time.

Once you embrace the real value of the skills you bring to the table, you're ready to start charging fees commensurate with those skills.

PICKING THE RIGHT PRICE

The next step in getting paid what your services are worth is determining a rate that adequately reflects the value you're providing and the work involved. For every service you offer (whether it's a wedding-day package or a day rate for corporate work) you need to have a clear understanding of everything that is included. In addition, you need to know what share of your company's general expenses each service will cover.

Here's a list of common expenses for which you should account:

Overhead. Rent, utilities, phone, Internet, employee wages, your salary, and so on. These are fixed expenses you'll need to cover whether or not you sell any videos. To adequately price your work, you'll need to have a good estimate of how many gigs you will do in a year so that you can distribute your overhead among your jobs.

COGS. Costs of Goods Sold (COGS) encompasses all the expenses directly related to each job. This includes tape stock, DVD media, packaging, rental fees, and any subcontractors you hire for a particular job.

Sales and Marketing. This includes advertising (online or print), e-mail marketing services such as Constant Contact or Vertical Response, blog services fees, Web site hosting fees, business cards and other collateral, demo DVDs, tradeshow (bridal fair) expenses, purchased e-mail lists, and thank-you cards and gifts (**FIGURES 9.2** and **9.3**). Don't forget to include the costs of any freebies or incentives you provide (for example, a free iPod to clients who book your top package).

One of the marketing tactics we've used successfully is producing promo videos for high-profile vendors and professionals. When we do that, any hard costs we incur from producing those videos is categorized as sales and marketing, even if they may normally be a different expense (travel costs, DVDs, subcontractors for those particular jobs). We know one photographer who purchased a $2,000 Harley-Davidson motorcycle as part of a promotional campaign. When his accountant confirmed that as long as he could prove that it was used as part of an ad campaign, he could write it off, the photographer's response was, "How about pictures? Is that proof enough?"

FIGURE 9.2 We created custom gift baskets for wedding coordinators in our area.

FIGURE 9.3 The baskets contained our uniquely packaged demos along with a variety of gifts to delight the senses.

Equipment. This includes cameras, audio gear, lights, computers, tripods, stabilizers, hard drives, monitors, decks, vehicles, and the list goes on and on. It's a traditionally accepted accounting practice to amortize or depreciate purchased equipment over its useful life. In such a case, you use the periodic depreciation or amortization when allocating expenses. However, we should point out that in certain circumstances, you may actually be allowed to write off the entire purchase price of the equipment, no matter how expensive. It's a little-known section of the tax code known as Section 137. Consult your tax accountant for details.

Software. As you already know, the software applications required to operate a production company can get pricey. These include nonlinear editing programs, effects plug-ins, graphic programs, DVD authoring programs, productivity software (such as Microsoft Office), and the like.

A NOTE ABOUT LABOR

A crucial aspect of calculating your COGS for a job is the actual amount of labor in billable hours. If you're not already doing this, you should be keeping track of how long it takes you to edit your jobs. We use a FileMaker Pro database to track hours attributed to a project. Many other tools are available as well.

Additionally, be sure the total billable hours of shooting time is the total number of hours worked on a job by each person assigned. Lastly, we suggest that you also determine how many hours you spend with typical clients. Calculate the total by including your time spent with them from start to finish, from the time you start courting them, to the time they hire you, to the time you spend corresponding via phone and e-mail, to the time you spend completing, packaging, and shipping their order. It may seem like a lot, but unless you get a good understanding of everything that goes into producing a job, you won't be able to obtain an adequate price for your services.

Let's use an average wedding videographer as an example. It's safe to say that you may invest as much as seven hours in a client on sales and customer maintenance. (This might include phone conversations before they hire you, in-person consultations and sales presentations, pre-wedding day calls to go over details of the day, e-mails back and forth over the course of the relationship, and so forth.)

If you have two shooters assigned to each production, each working eight hours, that's 16 billable hours. Then, add 40 hours of editing, another six hours completing the DVD (authoring, testing, designing the custom case), and one hour for packaging and shipping the final DVDs. All told, that adds up to 70 hours of labor.

If you're charging the national average for a wedding video, $2,000, you're receiving less than $29 per hour. That per-hour price has to cover all of the other expenses we mentioned. Considering that an independent contactor can easily make two to three times that amount, in this scenario it would make more sense to just hire yourself out as a freelancer than to run a full-blown production company.

This was a relatively simple exercise, but you'd be surprised at the number of small business owners in this industry who don't do this evaluation—they'll just pick a price out of thin air, something they think feels right. Or, worse yet, they'll see what a competitor is charging, then try to charge a little bit less. Which leads us to our next issue.

THE PITFALLS OF COMPETING ON PRICE

Many small video production companies make the mistake of picking a price for their services that undercuts the other guy. They compete on price, using discount incentives, lower rates, and rebates as a primary differentiator to their competition. In doing that, you eliminate your ability to stand out and be unique. You've reduced your business to a number: the price. All a prospect has to do is compare that price to another business to see which one to choose.

You've taken something that isn't a commodity—the unique experience and artistry your company brings to the table—and commoditized it. (A commodity is a product or service that is exactly like that offered by multiple other providers—for example, a bag of flour, a car, school supplies, or an oil change.) A surefire way *not* to be paid what you're worth is to compete on price and get paid less than what the other guy's getting paid. And let's be honest, chances are they aren't getting paid what they're worth either.

We should make it clear at this point that we're not saying a business has to be a higher-priced vendor in order to survive. In fact, if you've created a volume business in which you truly have turned the videos you produce into commodities, then competing on price may not be a bad strategy. If you aren't running a volume business and don't have the economies of scale and systems in place to run such a business, it's imperative that you don't make low prices a key selling point for your services.

Here are four key reasons why it's not a good idea to compete on price:

You undermine the branding experience. As we mentioned in Chapter 6, part of what sets you apart is the experience you provide. When price is your key differentiator, you weaken that individuality.

You set a pricing precedent for referrals. If you take Susie's wedding for a low rate just to get the job, all of Susie's friends will want the same, or similar, price if she refers them.

More difficult clients. Our experience has shown that clients who nickel and dime you, or who are chiefly concerned with how much you cost, will be the most difficult to manage. They'll often demand and expect more from you without expecting to pay for it, and they'll be the most picky when it comes to any review changes. Chances are they'll have a lack of respect for you and your work that may result in frustrating interactions.

Low-balling could backfire. In many circumstances, you could actually lose a gig if your price is too low. Remember the story we told in Chapter 4 about the corporate gig we bid on? Had we bid too low, we surely would not have been awarded the job.

It does make sense to use price as a competitive strategy in the following circumstances:

- You are selling a commodity
- You have a volume business
- You have economies of scale

REACHING THE RIGHT PRICE

Right about now you're probably thinking, OK, great. Now we know how to value our work and come up with a price, but how do we get people to pay it?" We're glad you asked. Let's cover some specific things you should be doing to charge and receive a fair rate for your services.

FISH IN THE RIGHT POND

The No. 1 mistake any small company makes with respect to charging what they're worth is selling to the wrong prospects. Here's a simple example to illustrate our point.

When we lived in Cupertino, California, every Sunday there was a flea market at the community college down the street. It's a fun place to find $1 DVDs, gently used toys and books, and fresh fruits and veggies at a fraction of their cost at the local market. Hundreds of people visit from near and far.

Imagine being at one of these outdoor markets, strolling along enjoying the beautiful weather and loving the deals, and finding a booth by Tiffany & Co. (We never did, but just imagine.) If they have the glass display cases, picture the impeccably dressed salesperson, and even a huge bodyguard named Bruno standing by. How many $10,000 earrings or $30,000 engagement rings do you think they'd sell that day? What are the chances their target client would really be strolling through, looking for a $30,000 ring?

We know this is an extreme example, but many of you are doing the equivalent. You're trying to sell a diamond ring at a flea market (FIGURE 9.4). Based on where you're advertising and how you're marketing your services, you aren't reaching the people who are willing to pay you what you're worth.

FIGURE 9.4 The jewelry stand at the local flea market will not be selling high-end jewelry.

So how do you reach those people you ask? Here are some ways:

Produce promo videos for professionals who are reaching your target market. Connecting with another company or individual who has already been successful selling to the clients you want to reach is a great source for referrals. It could be an event coordinator or photographer, a PR or ad agency, or magazines and other ad venues reaching your target demographic.

As we mentioned, one way we've been successful in reaching our target markets in wedding and corporate work is by creating promotional video work for vendors and companies who might refer us business. Then, when it is complete, as part of the deal, you get to include your credit and contact information in the video. Every time it's played on their Web site, or on a DVD they distribute to their prospects, you're getting advertising. What's nice about this tactic is that if the experience of making the video is a positive one, they may start referring your business even before the video is complete.

Join networking organizations. In both the event and corporate video worlds, there are organizations you can join that will expose you to individuals who can refer the right prospects to you. If you're a wedding videographer, find a local chapter for the National Association of Catering Executives (NACE) and the International Special Events Society (ISES). Getting involved with your local Chamber of Commerce can also be a great source of corporate referrals.

in many cases you may find that they're so busy planning their event that they haven't had a chance to respond. Build a follow-up routine into your sales process.

In some cases, the prospect may give you a specific time in which they plan to get back to you. If so, mark your calendar, then contact the prospect again the day after the deadline. If no specific deadline is given, call or e-mail back after an appropriate length of time. The amount of time varies depending on the service.

For a wedding or personal event, when you follow up will depend on how far out the event is. If a client is contacting you a year ahead of time, give him or her a couple of weeks to do more homework. Better yet, ask the prospect, after your initial contact, when would be a good

QUESTIONS TO ENGAGE YOUR PROSPECT

Following is a list of questions you can ask to get prospects talking about their events, while at the same time providing you with valuable information. Much of this information will give you clues about what the prospect can afford. This list of questions is geared towards event video producers.

When and where is your event? Get the name of the venue. Don't ask this question if they've already given it to you in a previous e-mail or contact form.

How many members are in your bridal party?

Who is your photographer?

If you have an event coordinator, who is it?

Which of the samples on our site or demo did you like the most, and why? It's important to confirm that they've seen your work. You don't want to engage with a prospect if he or she hasn't taken the time to view your work. If that's the case, you'll have nothing to talk about but rates. Make it a point not to divulge rate information until the prospect has seen your work. If a prospect asks about rates without seeing your work, say, "We'd love to give you an idea of how much you can expect to invest, but it's very important you view our work first so that we can give you an adequate estimate of our services." If the person continues to insist, it's a safe bet the prospect is not a good fit for you anyway. Give the potential client a high average rate then follow up from there.

With wedding prospects, ask, "What's the most important thing to you about your wedding? Not your wedding video, but your wedding itself?" The answer to this question will give you incredible insight. A common answer to this question is, "That everyone has a great time at the wedding." That opens the door for you to offer add-ons that can help the prospect achieve that goal. For instance, you could reply, "You know, our concept spoof videos have always been the talk of the wedding. Guests get a kick out of seeing you and your spouse in the video. They are often considered the most fun event at the weddings where we show them."

time to follow up. If the prospect doesn't know, ask if it's OK if you follow up in a couple weeks. If the event is less than three months away, reduce the follow-up period to a week or less.

The bottom line is that you must follow up. Don't assume that a prospect is not interested just because he or she hasn't called you back. One of the biggest wedding gigs we booked a few years ago came after seven months of back-and-forth e-mails, often with weeks of no communication in between. We were politely consistent and kept the "conversation" alive.

One thing you don't want to do is pull a *Swingers*. We're referencing the hilarious scene in the movie in which the main character, Mike (played by Jon Favreau) meets a woman at a bar and then calls her more than a dozen times, rambling into her answering machine, only a few hours after meeting her. You don't want to come off as desperate and pathetic.

THE SALES CONSULTATION

Let's cover some things to keep in mind during a sales meeting.

Pre-qualify your prospects. It's very important that you do not set up meetings with prospective clients without first making sure they have some idea of the minimum amount of money they can expect to invest for the services they need. This is a lesson we learned early in our business after spending up to two hours with a prospect, only to have them not hire us solely because we were too expensive.

You should also prequalify your prospects to ensure the kind of work you do is what they're looking for, especially if you have a distinctive style. Enough people have high-speed Internet access that there's no reason you shouldn't have samples of your work online. Don't spend an hour or more of your limited time getting to know a prospect, only to lose the gig because your style is MTV while they want A&E.

Hit the senses. Remember the Starbucks example we talked about in Chapter 6, "Building a Brand"? The minute you walk into a Starbucks, your senses of sight, smell, and sound are tantalized. Then, once you get your drink, your sense of taste is engaged. Whether you work from home or have a commercial space, you should be hitting your prospects' senses—all five of them. Make sure the meeting area is impeccable. Get a room freshener to create an inviting aroma. Have snacks available; chocolate is always a safe bet. Make sure the seats or sofas are extremely comfortable. Make sure the image of your meeting space lives up to the rates you're charging. If you meet your clients in the field, pick a location that is conducive to showing video clips. We've had success meeting at coffeehouses, but they tend to be a little loud.

Listen. It's been said that the person who does the most listening does the most selling. As much as possible, get your prospects to talk about their project. They want to talk about it. Chances are they *like* to talk about it. So let them. You can still drive and control the conversation by asking questions and follow-up questions. It is a good idea to have a list of your standard questions with you. Ask the prospect ahead of time if it's OK to take notes while they talk.

Be confident. Being confident in your work and your company when you tell clients how much they can expect to invest is key. Communicating without pausing, without stuttering, and with direct eye contact will speak volumes to your prospect and play a huge role in whether or not you get the job. If you're bidding on a five-figure corporate promotional video with a huge scope and it's obvious to the company that you're nervous or unsure of yourself, you can rest assured they won't trust their project with you. It's no different for personal milestone moments.

Show them what they want to see (and don't show them what they *don't* want to see). If possible, show the prospects samples similar to what they want for their project. If it's a corporate prospect, show samples similar to the kind of project or scope the company is looking to produce. If it's a personal event, show samples from the venue (if you have it) and show more samples of the kind of work from your site they said they liked. More importantly, don't show them something they've told you they don't like. I (Ron) once made the mistake of showing a 14-minute love story to a couple who told me up front they didn't like or want a love story. I was sure that once they saw *my* love story, they'd change their minds. Wrong! I could tell from the bored look on their faces that they were not buying it. And ultimately they did not hire me. Lesson learned.

Ask for the sale. The dreaded "close." Every salesperson worth his or her weight in gold will tell you that it's all about the close. You *have* to ask for the sale. Of course, asking for the sale isn't always about saying, "So, are you ready to hire us?" Early in our study of successful event vendors, we examined one successful photographer who had many great ways of subtly asking for the sale. Upon first meeting the prospect in the waiting room, he'd jokingly say something to this effect: "So, are we going to shoot a great portrait session for you or what?" He'd say it in a way that was obvious he was having fun with them. There are only two responses a prospect would have at that moment: "Well, we'll have to see" (or something to that effect); or, they might actually say, "Yeah. We loved what you did for Susie and want you to do the same for us." If they answer the former, he's in no worse position than when he first started. But, in the occasional instance when they said yes, he knew he could do a lot less work during the sales meeting, and even keep it shorter.

Ask for the sale. No, this isn't a typo or déjà vu. It's just our way of saying that you should ask for the sale multiple times during the presentation. You can do a "soft" ask at the first meeting as in the previous example. Then, after showing your samples, you can ask for the sale, especially if you're a wedding videographer and you see that they're emotionally moved by your work. Then, after you discuss the details of how you work and what the prospect can expect, ask one last time at the end. (See the "Asking for the Sale" sidebar for additional ways you can ask for the sale.)

ASKING FOR THE SALE

There are a number of ways you can ask for the sale that are not overt. Remember to ask the question and then be quiet. Wait for them to respond. Don't jump in with more questions, explanations, or excuses. Just wait.

1. "Hi, thanks for coming by. So, are we going to [insert service here] for you today?" Where applicable, say this in a fun way to keep the prospect at ease.
2. "So, now that you've seen samples of our work, do you think we're a fit for what you're looking for?"
3. "Now that you've seen samples of our work and our rates, shall we go ahead and book your date with a retainer so we can hold it for you?"
4. "Which package would work best for you?"
5. "Are you ready to make a decision today? We'd be honored to serve you."
6. "Now that you've reviewed our formal proposal, is your company ready to formalize a contract? We want to make sure we can get you on the calendar in order to meet your required turnaround time."

PRICING PRESENTATION

How you present your rates is almost as important as what they are.

To Web or not to Web. An age-old debate in this industry is whether or not to list rates on your Web site. As is the case with just about every aspect of marketing, there is no right or wrong answer. It depends.

There are a few schools of thought on this. Some say you should post rates on your Web site so that you weed out the clients who can't afford you. No use wasting your time. Some say you shouldn't because you could scare off a client that might potentially hire you once they see your work and get to know you. Some say you compromise yourself by posting a starting rate.

Our feeling is this: Unless you are so busy with the work you have coming in from other sources that you can afford to miss out on the potential business you might get from prospects that get to know you and your work, don't scare anyone off too soon. We distinctly remember one year, during the heyday of our wedding years, when we booked four jobs (representing almost 20 percent of our wedding revenue that year) from clients who admitted that their original budget for wedding videography was either zero or less than half what they ended up investing. After seeing our work and getting to know us, they opted to increase their budget. We're positive they would have never contacted us if they saw our rates online first (**FIGURE 9.5**).

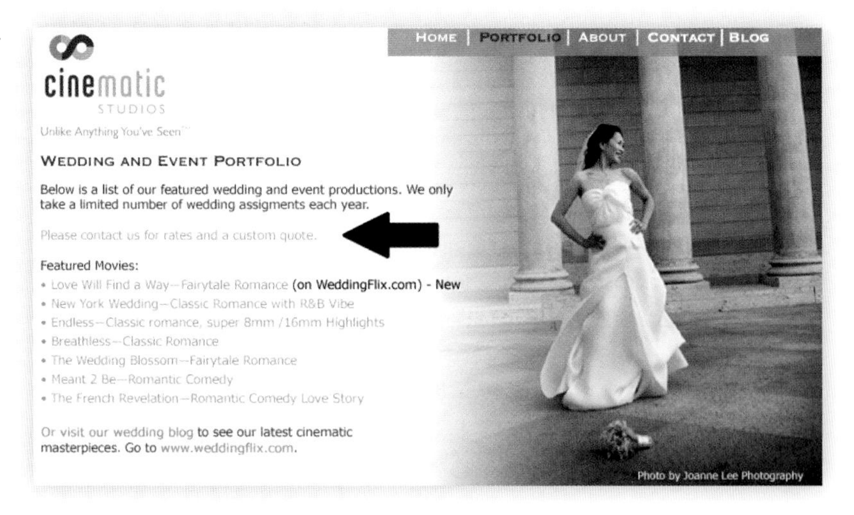

FIGURE 9.5 Our wedding Web site directs prospects to contact us for information about pricing.

Yes, you may have to weed through a lot of "looky-loos" before getting the jobs, but if you follow the steps we described, you can limit the amount of time spent. And as you'll learn in Chapter 12, "Customer Service and Support," there are systems you can put in place to manage these prospects.

Packages versus à la carte. The other big pricing debate is whether it's best to have package pricing or an "à la carte" (feature-by-feature) system. As you might have guessed by now, our answer is going to be...it depends.

First and foremost, whatever system you use, make sure you've created a pricing structure that accounts for all of the expenses and profits you need to cover (as discussed earlier in this chapter). Second, the concept of "packages" is better suited to wedding and event video producers. Corporate jobs are best bid on with custom estimates taking into account everything that will go into the job (in essence, an à la carte system).

With respect to event video pricing, we've tried it all, and our experience has shown that simplicity rules. The more convoluted and complicated your pricing, the more time and energy you'll have to spend explaining your rates to clients. This, in turn, costs you more in labor and also detracts from the client experience.

The system we've had the most success with is a straight hourly rate that takes into account both editing and shooting. Since we know on average how long it takes us to edit an event video based on the number of hours of coverage, and since we also know on average how many hours of raw footage we'd have based on the number of hours of coverage, we were able to come up with an hourly rate that covered everything. In our 2008 season, that amount was $900 per hour of coverage for two shooters with a five-hour minimum. That rate included an artfully crafted video of approximately four to five minutes for every hour of coverage (thus five hours of coverage would yield a 20- to 25-minute video); where applicable, the full ceremony uncut; and any toasts not included in the artistic edit. This system was easy to administer and explain. And it was all-inclusive.

The only additional investments would be for add-ons (love story, same-day edit, what have you). Again, the most important thing to keep in mind is to create a system that accounts for all of your costs. If you create packages, then calculate all the costs and profits associated and make the package rate the cumulative sum.

The order of your packages. If you use a package system, wherever you display those rates, list them from highest to lowest. Always. Why? Psychologically, it's easier for a prospect to go from high to low than the other way around. Furthermore, make your first package a package so high that you would never expect anyone to invest in it. Often referred to as the "whopper," the main purpose of it is to make the rates of the packages you really want to sell seem less severe. If you want to sell a middle package for $4,000, make your top package $10,000. We'll take it one step further.

If you're in a sales consultation presenting these rates, present them one page at a time so that all your packages do not appear simultaneously. Again, it's psychology. When you're on the "whopper," as you spend time talking about its benefits, one of two things will happen: Either the prospect will get used to the rate and start trying to think of ways in which they *might* afford it, or, they will be writhing internally with discomfort at the high rate. In either case, you win out. When you get to the next package, which is significantly lower, what's happened? They breathe a sigh of relief. Even though your middle package may still be significantly higher than your competition, if the prospects like you and your work, you'll have them seriously considering you and actually being excited that they can get you for only $4,000 (when they were worried whether they could afford $10,000). We know this may sound too good to be true, but it's a proven sales technique that has worked for us and for other vendors we've researched.

Keep your rates in-house. Do not give out a price list or menu of items for prospects to take with them. This reduces your services to just another vendor the prospect is going to shop around. You don't want prospects sitting in their living rooms with stacks of price lists from all of the other competitors, comparing packages on a pricing basis. If prospects insists on taking something with them, have them take notes on what the investment requires for their respective job.

FIGURE 9.6 Our pricing book started with our top package, The Criterion Collection.

Present your rates in a way that makes it obvious that they will not be able to take copies with them. You could provide this information in a PowerPoint or Keynote presentation, for example. Before we switched to the hourly rate system, we used to create a handcrafted scrapbook of video stills along with prices (**FIGURE 9.6**). We'd then hold the pricing book or place it on the table between the prospect and us. Remember, you don't want their focus to stay on your rates. So don't give them anything to take home that will keep their focus on rates.

NEVER F.E.A.R.

It goes without saying that the No. 1 obstacle that prevents most production companies from charging what they're worth—from you charging what you're worth—is fear.

Fear of rejection. Fear of not getting the job. Fear of losing business. Fear of not making ends meet. This fear is something that keeps so many from achieving the level of success they deserve.

FIGURE 9.7 Don't let fear prevent you from realizing your business dreams.

One of my (Ron's) favorite movies is Baz Luhrmann's *Strictly Ballroom* (FIGURE 9.7). In it, the main character, Scott Hastings, is one of the most promising dancers in Australia's ballroom dance subculture. His two "has-been" parents run a moderately successful dance studio. His dad is frequently shuffling on the sidelines somewhere, practicing some dance moves he hasn't done in years. His mom is a rather pathetic woman who is mean to his dad, bossy, and constantly pushing Scott to be the next Pan Pacific Amateur Grand Champion. She is vicariously living through Scott, trying to achieve something she never did.

There's one problem, though. Scott refuses to dance "strictly ballroom." His determination to infuse the dance with his own flashy footwork and showmanship is leading him down the road to losing the coveted Pan Pacific championships.

Along the way, Scott meets Fran—a rather plain girl who has been dancing in the beginner's class of the dance studio for two years. In a moment of bravery, Fran approaches Scott to be his dance partner (since his longtime partner dumped him due to Scott's rebellious ways). As they dance together and romance blossoms, Fran shares with Scott an old Spanish proverb taught to her by her grandmother: "Vivir con miedo es como vivir a medias." Loosely translated: *A life lived in fear is a life half lived.*

As we reach the end of the story, Scott has dumped Fran at the behest of his mother, and he reluctantly agrees to enter the championship with his ex-partner, having promised to dance the proper steps. He does this after being lied to by the ballroom dance chairperson about the reason his parents fell from grace.

At a climactic point in the film, seconds before Scott is to leap onto the dance floor and "sell out" his passion, his dad finally tells him something he'd been trying to tell him throughout the movie. Scott had been told that his parents were washed up because they danced their "non-ballroom" steps during the competition back when they were young. That resulted in them being dishonorably disqualified and forever shamed. Scott's dad reveals that what really happened was that they never danced their steps. In truth, Scott's mom danced with somebody else and lost anyway. They didn't stick together to follow their dream. And just before his mom pushes Scott onto the dance floor, his dad yells with a strength and conviction not shown in the entire movie, "WE LIVED OUR LIVES IN FEAR!" Scott stops in his tracks, the words echoing in his ears and throughout the dance hall. It is at that moment he realizes the truth of the Spanish proverb shared by Fran. He abandons his partner, finds Fran, dances an incredible Paso doble with her, which brings the crowd to their feet, and he lives (presumably) happily ever after.

To this day, that scene gives me goosebumps. We see throughout the entire movie the pathetic lives lived by Scott's parents. And at the end, we learn it was because of fear.

Throughout the movie, Scott is pushed by friends, judges, and his mom to stick to the steps—to dance "strictly ballroom," to do what everyone else is doing and toe the party line. It was that movie that helped me to realize an aspect of fear that affects us all. It's an aspect of fear that keeps you from taking chances in your business that could mean incredible success—a factor that, probably more than anything, is what's keeping you from charging what you're worth. It's an acronym I've coined to make it easy to remember:

Following

Everyone's

Accepted

Routine

Think about it. Many of you aren't charging what you're worth because people say you can't. You can't charge $5,000 for a wedding video, work for only five hours on the wedding day, and deliver a 20-minute video. No one would buy it. You can't double your prices overnight and expect to stay in business. You can't do [insert unpopular, aggressive marketing move that goes against the grain] and expect to survive.

F.E.A.R.—Following Everyone's Accepted Routine—will limit your success.

Don't live in F.E.A.R. Listen to your heart. Dance your flashy steps. Bring the crowd to their feet. Not only will you survive, but you may just live happily ever after.

IN FOCUS:
JOHN GOOLSBY

John Goolsby (www.weddingvideo.com) is a seasoned event and corporate video producer whose company, Cannon Video Productions in Riverside, California, has shot thousands of videos over a 25-year period (**FIGURE 9.8**).

FIGURE 9.8 John's business and systems are so efficient that he has time for afternoon catnaps in his editing suite.

John speaks at all the major event video conventions and is a business coach as well. He frequently teaches on effective pricing. I (Ron) wrote about this topic on my blog, and the following excerpt is a comment John left regarding the issue of "doubling your prices overnight":

> I've presented over 200 seminars over the last 20 years on the business of wedding and event videography, and I've told many audiences that if I could give you only one piece of advice that would have a positive influence on your business, it would be to double your prices.
>
> I did it 21 years ago and booked my new top package within two weeks. It revolutionized the way I looked at business and helped me understand how people relate quality to price.
>
> In 20 years of giving this advice I've had scores of videographers thank me and tell me what a positive impact doubling their prices overnight had on their business.

FIGURE 9.9 Taking risks and thinking big opens doors to possibilities you might never have imagined. John Goolsby and team in front of their business (Inland) "Empire."

This issue of doubling your prices overnight is a controversial one. It seems like such a radical move to make. Yet, as John can attest, it works (**FIGURE 9.9**).

Although we never doubled our prices overnight as John suggests, we were still aggressive in raising them. What worked for us in our early years of business was a 10 percent increase twice a season, once in fall and then again mid-spring.

But if you're feeling bold and F.E.A.R.-less, we encourage you to double your rates right now. Worse-case scenario is that you'd have to reduce them again.

III

SYSTEMATIZE YOUR BUSINESS

MANAGING YOUR TIME

THIS CHAPTER IS FOR YOU if you've ever made any of the following excuses for your business's shortcomings:

"I don't have enough time."

"I get too much e-mail. My inbox is overflowing."

"I can't find good help."

"We don't have the right resources, or enough money."

"My editing backlog is too big."

We all have the same amount of hours in every day. The only difference is how we choose to use them.

You've heard that before, right? You know it's true. But does it impact the way you operate your business? Does it alter your focus and change the way you prioritize your work and commit your time? If not, then knowing that it's true really does you no good.

The power of change is in the action.

That's what this chapter is all about. The principles and strategies for managing your time and taking back your life are not revolutionary, or even new, except for how you implement them in your life today. They won't make the slightest difference in the way you run your business if you just read through them, decide that they sound great, and then go back to your same habits of operation.

It bears repeating: The power of change is in the action—*your* action. It's up to you to change your behavior and habits. That is how you will transform your business and your life. That is what is possible if you make this *the* book that spurred you to implement what you know to be true.

Now is the time to make it happen.

BACK TO BASICS

Do you want to stand out in the crowd?

Are you ready to win awards for your groundbreaking productions?

Are you prepared to pass the million or multimillion-dollar mark in revenue?

I'm sure you answered a resounding "Yes" to all three questions. But are you really ready? Are you willing to focus on the small changes that are required for taking your business back to basics and covering the ground you may have skipped along the way? If not, then go ahead and skip this chapter.

If you're not willing to take a hard look at reality and what is working and not working, then this chapter won't help you. Don't waste your time reading something else about managing your time if you're not going to do something about it when you finish reading. We know you're smarter than that because you've already read this far in the book. So take the next step and decide what you will commit to for the next 30 days.

We'll give you some ideas. You'll come up with some on your own. Just choose one goal. Once you've accomplished that, come back and choose another. There is real power in focusing on one thing at a time. As you'll see in the following pages, multitasking is dead. But first, let's see where you currently stand.

Answer the following questions (or keep a running log for a day to get real data). Even if it's just a 10-second glance at something, count it. Only count the interruptions during the first eight hours of your workday.

- How many e-mails do you get per day?_____
- How many e-mails do you send per day?_____
- How many times do you check e-mail each day?_____
- How many times do you check Facebook each day?_____
- How many times do you check Twitter each day?_____
- How many phone calls do you receive and make each day?_____
- How many meetings do you have each day?_____
- How many IMs, text messages, or chats do you send or receive?_____
- How many Twitter notifications do you see each day?_____
- How many times a day are you interrupted by someone while working on something else?_____

Add up your results and divide by eight for an average eight-hour day in order to determine the average number of interruptions per hour. We know most video producers and small business owners work much more than a typical eight-hour day, but wouldn't you like to get it down to that? Keep this data in mind as we explore multitasking.

MULTITASKING IS DEAD

Do you ever have difficulty focusing on the task at hand? Or do you find your mind wandering to your endless to-do list while listening to someone talk? If so, you're a victim of multitasking.

Dave Crenshaw, author of *The Myth of Multi-Tasking: How "Doing it All" Gets Nothing Done*, asserts a basic rule about multitasking: "The more responsibility you have, the more hats you wear, the more likely you are to become inefficient."

That description sounds like nearly every video producer we have ever met.

Crenshaw goes on to explain how the purported benefits of multitasking are a lie. Multitasking robs us of time, energy, and joy. It damages rather than enhances productivity. And it destroys relationships.

You may be wondering if it's really that serious. Let's do a simple exercise adapted from Crenshaw's book to find out.

1. Get a timer and a pen.
2. Time yourself while writing the sentence *Multitasking wastes time and costs money.* on line 1. After each letter that you write, write the corresponding number.
3. For example, after you write *M* on line 1, go to line 2 and write *1*; then write *u* on line 1 then go to line 2 to write *2*; go to line 1 and write *l*, then go to line 2 and write *3*; etc. Make sure you write a number for every letter. You do not need to add a number for punctuation.
4. Record the time it took you to write the sentence and numbers.
5. In the second round, you will time yourself as well. First, write the complete sentence on line 3, then move to line 4 and write the numbers *1* to *35*.
6. Time yourself completing both lines and write the number in the box to the right (**FIGURE 10.1**).

FIGURE 10.1 Create a table like the one shown here.

	Multi-tasking wastes time and costs money.	Time
1		
2		
3		
4		

Do not skip the activity. It is enlightening. If you haven't done it, go back and try it. It will take less than five minutes.

When I (Tasra) had Ron do this activity when we were sitting in the Starbucks café at Barnes & Noble, he was shocked. It took him more than twice as long to do the multitasking on the first effort. It's likely you had similar results.

If one small activity like this takes more than twice as long when multitasking, imagine how much time is lost over the course of a day, a week, or a year. The amount of wasted hours is astonishing.

People are proud of their multitasking prowess, like they're proud of their perfectionism. However, it's not the answer and it won't bring you what you really desire—more time, which equals more life. When you boil it down, all we really have is time, and we're throwing it away.

Even if you consider yourself an expert at multitasking, which I did, you can't argue with the facts. Research from Vanderbilt University offers neurological evidence that the brain cannot effectively do two things at once (René Marois, Ph.D., Department of Psychology, Vanderbilt Register).

The act of switching back and forth between different tasks will always result in a loss of productivity and time.

THE MANY FACES OF MULTITASKING

There are two types of multitasking: outside interruptions and self-imposed distractions. Let's tackle outside interruptions first.

Whether working at home, in a small business, or at an office, it's easy to get interrupted. Studies have shown that the average worker is interrupted 32 times a day. That adds up to 126 minutes of lost productivity each and every day, according to Jonathan Spira of Basex Research. More than two hours per day? Wouldn't you rather do something else during those two hours?

After reading about Spira's results and research, we immediately implemented a no-interruption zone. That's a block of time that will be interruption-free—no phone, e-mail, Facebook, Twitter, chat, or knocks on the door. We've got a three-hour block in the morning and a four-hour block in the afternoon. In between we have regular "open" and "closed" hours (**FIGURE 10.2**).

FIGURE 10.2 Set specific open and closed hours to minimize interruptions and increase focused work time.

In order to enforce no interruptions, we instituted "open" hours. Open hours are consistently scheduled times each day when we are available for ordinary interruptions, meetings, questions, inquiries, and so forth. People need to be trained to respect your time. That starts with training yourself to respect your time as well, which leads us to self-imposed distractions.

So let's talk about *self-imposed* distractions. When I (Tasra) worked at Apple, it was not uncommon to hear jokes about the entire workforce having ADHD (Attention Deficit Hyperactive Disorder). Although we don't mean to downplay the challenges faced by those who genuinely suffer from this disorder, we'd argue that many video producers deal with attention-deficit issues from time to time, but not so much as a chemical or biological condition than as a natural response to a technology-dense, information-saturated world. What's a distractible, highly creative individual to do?

Get real about what distracts you and set limits for yourself. If it's an open tab for Twitter, Facebook, and e-mail, set a strict boundary on when you'll get online, and then stick to it. If boredom strikes while working, focus on what you can do after hours with the extra time if you stay focused now. Not sure what to work on next? Set one day a week where you plan your entire weekly calendar. Then stick to it! Afraid you'll miss something in social media? You won't. It will be right where you left off the last time you checked. You've got the idea. Now use some of your creative genius to find solutions to remaining on task throughout your workday.

Go to the next level by finding an accountability partner. Start a thread on your favorite online forum and give regular updates on progress. But post your results only once a day. You don't want productivity-tracking to become another distraction that steals your time.

THE POWER OF SINGLE FOCUS

If multitasking is dead and we're wasting our lives on unnecessary interruptions, the solution is nurturing single focus. Single focus can be described in numerous ways: working in flow, finding the zone, finishing what you started. They all represent a state of being where things are moving and progressing. That's where you want to spend most of your days.

Single focus will prevent job burnout. Working long hours and dedicating your life to a company or industry can last only so long. When the dust clears, you need something more to show for your time than a few awards and some paid bills.

NOTE

Let's be real. Eliminating multitasking, ending interruptions, training ourselves and others to respect our time—it's all going to take some serious, focused effort. While we know the power of focus and the reality of wasted time due to interruptions, we still fall prey to the "I just need one minute" thinking. In truth, while I (Tasra) was writing this chapter, Ron stopped by my office three times for a quick question, I checked e-mail three times, and visited Facebook twice and Twitter once. Learning to focus and use time more efficiently is a process, so be patient with yourself as you break bad habits and implement new ones. But don't give up. Just keep that goal of recapturing more than two hours.

Single focus will prevent stress and accompanying illnesses. Popping pills for headaches, getting stronger prescriptions for glasses, gaining weight from lack of exercise—do any of these sound familiar? It's the price paid by overworked individuals, and it won't change until you make the time to relax, unwind, and let work go. You don't have to let go forever, just for a time. Single focus will help you do that.

Single focus will enhance your vision, creativity, and clarity. Every video producer who wants to transform his or her business will find these three qualities invaluable. Without them, feelings of being overwhelmed, overworked, and underpaid will rapidly rob you of job satisfaction.

What is single focus? It's simple: Focus on the task at hand. Finish that task. Move on to the next.

Remember to break your projects into bite-sized tasks, so they can be completed in a reasonable amount of time. Getting out from under your backlog is daunting, but finishing one section of a current production is doable. Build on the small things and you'll end each day with a sense of accomplishment instead of feeling utterly exhausted, unable to even remember what you did.

If this one strategy reclaimed even one hour of time each day for you, at five hours per week times 50 weeks a year, that's 250 hours. If you use a fair market rate of $75 per hour for the roles we mentioned in Chapter 9, "Getting Paid What You're Worth," this one new habit will save you $18,750 over the course of the year. If you reclaim 2.1 hours per day as suggested by Basex Research, we're talking about 525 hours and nearly $40,000!

Isn't that worth the effort to change your ways? We won't even get into the numbers if you have more than one person working in your company, and you *all* pursue the single-focus approach. The results are staggering.

Just think of what you could do with that extra time and money:

- Build your brand
- Stay connected to your current customers
- Market to the right clientele
- Start a podcast
- Begin a personal project you've been putting off
- Get in shape
- Take a vacation
- Buy another copy of this book for someone who needs it!

GETTING THINGS DONE

We're not talking about the national bestseller *Getting Things Done* by David Allen, although it is a fantastic book on productivity. What we're talking about are the nitty-gritty details of getting things checked off your to-do list.

We've found two techniques that work well in keeping us on track of our ever-expanding project list. The techniques are *block scheduling* and *time tracking*.

BLOCK SCHEDULING

For our schedules, we each use Google Calendar. This allows us to keep everything online and share our calendars seamlessly. It also allows for easy editing and flexibility.

Because one of my (Tasra's) strengths is organization and project management, I manage all calendars and projects for Dare Dreamer Media. At least once a week, if not more frequently, I rearrange when tasks and projects are worked on. From there, all of our calendars are connected via RSS in ShootQ (**FIGURE 10.3**).

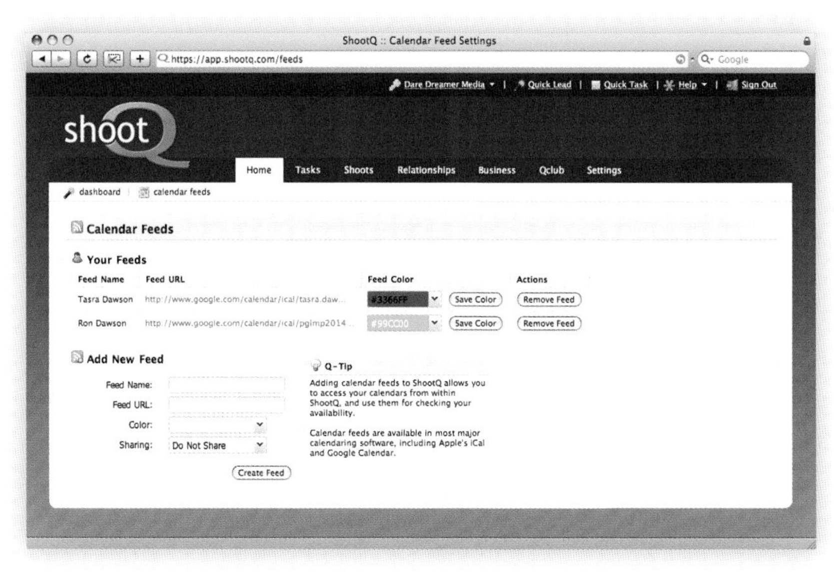

FIGURE 10.3 You can add multiple RSS calendar feeds directly into your ShootQ database.

In scheduling tasks and projects, we chunk them into blocks of time. Blocks of time are rarely less than an hour. Common blocks we use every week include the following:

- Processing e-mail (one hour each day with the goal of getting the inbox down to zero. For tips on reducing your inbox, do a Google search on "inbox zero.")
- Administration tasks
- Recurring meetings (we have a weekly Monday morning meeting at our local coffee shop)
- F-Stop Beyond interviews (weekly photo industry podcast)
- Editing (we'll insert the name of the project in each editing block)
- Blogging (two to three blog posts per week, written at one time)
- Podcast editing

As new projects and tasks are added to our workload, we create new blocks to account for the addition (**FIGURE 10.4**). For example, when writing this book, we added a block for writing and another block for editing.

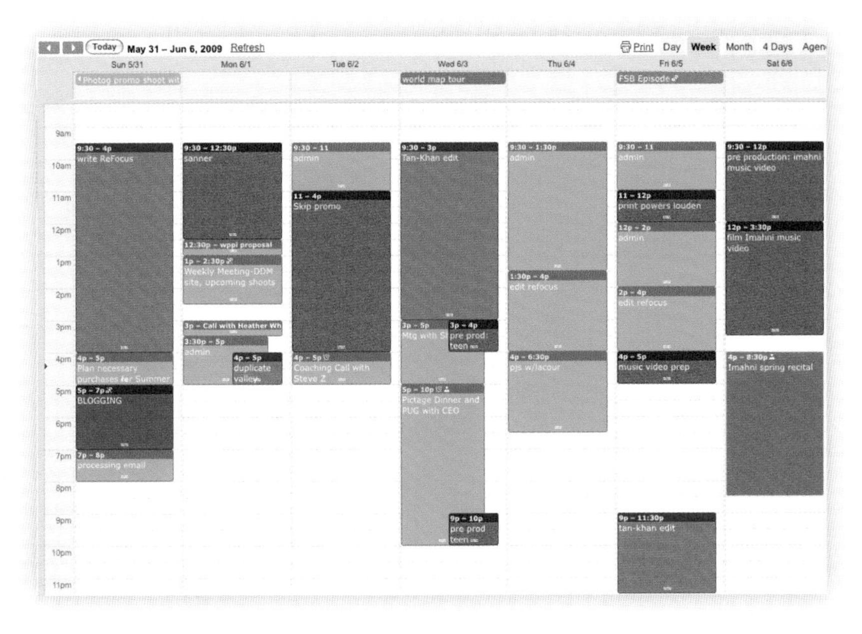

FIGURE 10.4 A page from our Google calendar.

Create a weekly or monthly block schedule with all recurring projects and tasks. The more consistent the times are for performing certain tasks, the better chance you'll have of creating a habit and training your mind to be prepared for the task at hand. Ron's *F-Stop Beyond* interviews are almost always scheduled for Tuesday afternoons. That way, every Tuesday Ron knows he's got an interview. The predictability allows for one less thing for you to remember and for more focus on the important aspects of running your business.

TIME TRACKING

One of the many side effects of multitasking is distorting your ability to accurately measure time. If you're always doing five things at one time, you really have no idea how long each individual task takes.

Now that you have (we hope) committed to single-tasking, it's time to get back on track with time. One of the ways to stop underestimating time is to keep track of it. This serves four main purposes:

1. Time tracking allows you to provide clear estimates to clients.
2. Time tracking allows you to charge what you're worth. If you know your time is worth a certain dollar amount, and you know how much time a given task takes because you're performing it exclusively, it's easy to figure out the cost of any project or job.
3. Time tracking provides you with a picture of where your time is going. On days you feel like nothing was accomplished, you can review your time tracker to see what happened.
4. Time tracking provides a sense of urgency in completing tasks. When you know you will give an account of how you spent your time, it helps you keep moving forward when you might otherwise become distracted.

We use a simple system. We have a FileMaker Pro database in which each day is one record (**FIGURE 10.5**). There is a running column in which we enter start and stop times for each activity; we round to the nearest five minutes. The database then does the calculation to add up the number of hours per day and per activity.

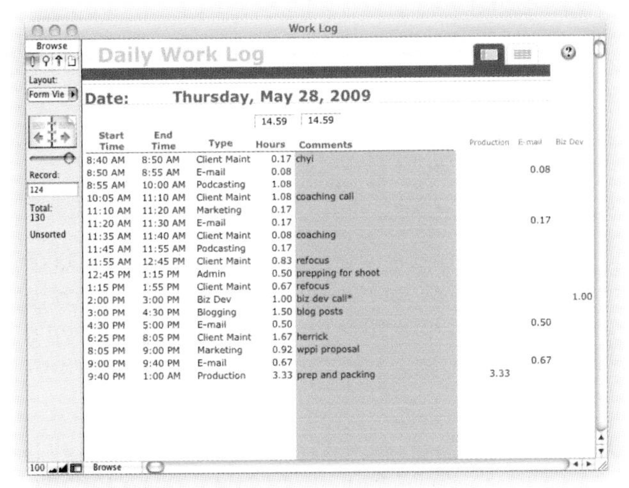

FIGURE 10.5 Tracking your day with a simple database allows you to increase efficiency and eliminate time-wasters.

From there, we can run reports on how many hours are worked in a given week, on a given activity or task. We have a similar database to track time spent on post-production for any projects, where each record is a project, and the activities tracked are categories such as logging tapes, editing highlights, and DVD design. (If you'd like a free blank copy of these databases, visit http://bladeronner.com and click the REFOCUS link.)

STOP BREAKING THE LAW

You probably didn't even know you've been violating basic laws and principles of business and time management. Chances are if you're like most small business owners, you have been, and it's affecting your business and bottom line.

The two laws we're talking about are *Parkinson's Law* and *Pareto's Principle* (also known as the 80/20 Rule).

PARKINSON'S LAW

"Work expands so as to fill the time available for its completion."

Cyril Northcote Parkinson, a famous British historian and author, discovered this law in 1955. It was first published in *The Economist* and later became the title and subject of Parkinson's book.

The essence of this statement is that any given task or project will take whatever amount of time you allow for it. Give yourself a week to complete your latest video project and it will take a week. Allow yourself a month and that same project will rapidly expand into a month's worth of work, worry, and stress.

This is exactly why time tracking can save you countless hours and help you avoid significant stress. By knowing how much time a specific task should take and assigning that time in a block schedule, you prevent the unnecessary expansion of work.

It's tempting to give yourself a buffer when estimating the time it takes to complete a certain task. When providing estimates or bids for clients, it's actually a wise thing to do to prevent underselling yourself. However, in setting your own schedule, don't add in that extra time. Set a reasonable time based on what you've assessed from your time tracker and force yourself to work quickly and effectively to complete the task in the given time.

One advantage of not working in a corporate environment is the relief from having to appear busy at all times of the day. When you're working for yourself, you have the advantage of working hard when you're working and not pretending to work when you're really taking a break.

Consider using a timer to spur you on and provoke your competitive nature. Give yourself less time than you think you need in order to complete a specific number of tasks. If you beat your estimated time, reward yourself.

Much of what we do is really not exciting or particularly transformative for our businesses. If you have mundane tasks that you need to get done, power through them quickly and move on to something more meaningful.

PARETO'S PRINCIPLE

Tim Ferris, author of the *4-Hour Workweek*, credits economist Vilfredo Pareto with changing his life forever. After reading about Pareto's Principle, commonly referred to as the 80/20 Rule, Tim Ferris stopped everything and spent an entire day answering two questions:

1. "Which 20 percent of sources are causing 80 percent of my problems and unhappiness?"
2. "Which 20 percent of sources are resulting in 80 percent of my desired outcomes and happiness?"

Asking and answering those two questions could transform your business and provide you with answers you've been seeking for years.

You can apply the 80/20 Rule to nearly everything, from your personal life to your video production company.

- 80 percent of customer complaints are caused by 20 percent of your products or services.
- 20 percent of your marketing efforts generate 80 percent of your marketing results.
- 20 percent of your projects or customers will generate 80 percent of your profitability.

Pareto's Principle should serve as encouragement about the enormous room for increased productivity and profit. It is a constant reminder to focus 80 percent of your effort on the 20 percent of your tasks that matter the most. Identifying and focusing on these vital few tasks allows you to maximize your return on investment. Reallocating resources from unproductive sources to productive uses can be liberating.

Give it a try. What do you have to lose—except for 80 percent inefficiency and lack of productivity?

IN FOCUS:
CHRIS P. JONES

Early in 2006, Chris P. Jones (www.masonjarfilms.com) had a backlog of 18 edits with more to come in the following months. As a team of one, he did not have the requisite time to perform all functions of the business while keeping his delivery time under one year. While contracted to finish in a year, he began to discover that while clients were contractually OK with delivery in that time span, they were not emotionally OK with the wait once it became their reality. Client satisfaction was not what it should be.

After 10 months, when one client decided she had waited long enough and did not to allow Mason Jar Films to complete the edit, Jones decided to make changes to reduce the likelihood of this occurring again.

First, Jones sharpened his workflow so that the moment he ingested footage to the moment he burned DVDs was as systematized and efficient as possible. By importing entire tapes, placing all footage chronologically on one timeline, combing through the footage while selecting the final shots, and copying the best shots to another timeline, he found that he saved plenty of time by not needing to constantly revisit footage in the bins. Logging and capturing into a hyper-organized set of folders was the enemy to getting things done. Once he had a teachable plan, he trained two part-time editors to share his editing responsibilities, allowing Jones to sharpen other aspects of the business (**FIGURE 10.6**).

FIGURE 10.6
Chris P. Jones trains one of his editors to follow his system.

Despite having an A–Z plan for editing his product, the key component to speeding up the editing process was eliminating distractions that keep him and his editors from getting intense in the edit. He disconnects from the Internet and does not answer the phone while editing, keeping himself from being tempted to allow the urgency of others to dictate his schedule. E-mail, Facebook, and Twitter are all off-limits for the editor, period.

While editing, Jones sets a timer for one hour and then rushes to accomplish as much as possible in that hour. After every hour of editing, he allows himself a timed five-minute break to stretch, eat, and record what he accomplished in the last hour. Setting a goal for the next hour, he dives back into the edit with focused intensity. After four hours of editing, Jones allows himself time to go online or tackle some other important business matter.

With two part-time editors sharing his approach to editing, Jones began to reduce his promised delivery time, putting it in writing to clients to keep everyone on track:

- For contracts signed in 2007, Mason Jar Films guaranteed delivery in eight months.
- For contracts signed in 2008, Mason Jar Films guaranteed delivery in four months.
- For contracts signed in 2009, Mason Jar Films guaranteed delivery in two months.

Now that he is delivering before his contracted deadline, Jones spends his time thinking forward about the business rather than looking back at what should've been done yesterday.

If you'd like to learn more about his success, Jones is sharing this information at local PVAs and at upcoming In[Focus] video events (www.infocusvideoevent.com).

ADMINISTRATION AND STAFFING

THE BANE OF EXISTENCE FOR every artist/businessperson is administration and staffing work. We dare to say that of all the hats the small business video producer wears, this one will be the most frustrating, the least enjoyable, and the most spirit-draining. However, it's a necessary evil for running any business.

In this chapter, we endeavor to give you ideas and insights that will help you evolve your business, and perhaps even bring back a joy you may have lost.

A TEAM EFFORT

No matter what size business you run, there is one unchanging truth about running a video production studio: It is a collaborative process. Very rarely (if ever) will you find a one-man (or one-woman) show where the sole proprietor does absolutely everything: shooting, editing, accounting, marketing, and so on. Even if you are a sole proprietor, chances are at some point you'll hire a second shooter for a gig, or get your spouse involved in some way. And if you haven't done that, you need to.

IF YOU WANT SOMETHING DONE RIGHT...

You know how this saying ends, right? "If you want something done right, you have to do it yourself." This is a common mantra among entrepreneurs, especially ones in the creative field. Because it's your vision, your company, your baby, you feel that *you* are the one who needs to do everything (or most things) to make sure nothing bad happens or goes wrong. We're here to inform you that if you keep that attitude, you will never evolve your business to its full potential (**FIGURE 11.1**).

You must adopt a level of trust that will allow others to help you in areas in which you may not be as capable or inspired. There are areas in your business where your talents and skill sets are best suited. Maybe it's the creative direction of the videos you produce. Maybe it's the sales and marketing. Whatever it is, if you try to do it all, the area where you are the strongest will actually be weakened. Or rather, it will have a less powerful effect on your company.

FIGURE 11.1
Don't let yourself get to the point that you dread going to work each day.

BUILDING YOUR TEAM

In reality, your "team" goes beyond the people you directly hire or contract to help you specifically with the business. You should also think of your team as those vendors and suppliers with whom you consistently work. They too can be a valuable source of assistance with your business, whether it's referring you clients, helping you manage costs, or working with you to service your clients. However, for the purposes of this chapter, we're going to focus on building the team you specifically hire.

CONTRACTORS VS. EMPLOYEES

How do you engage your shooters, editors, and administrative staff? There are two ways to do it—as contractors or employees—and if you choose wrong, or handle either in the wrong way, you could find yourself in trouble with the government. Local, state, and federal laws are very particular about how you handle the treatment of those you hire (**FIGURE 11.2**). Issues such as how much work you give them, where they work, how many resources you supply, and how much freedom you give them, all affect whether someone you hire is a contractor or an employee.

FIGURE 11.2 Hiring contractors and employees can free you to work "on" your business, rather than "in" your business.

The reason the classification matters is because there can be a significant financial impact on your business if you have employees versus contractors. The primary additional expense of employees is the Social Security tax you must pay in addition to salary and wages. Many states also require an employer to provide workers compensation insurance. Then there are additional administrative costs such as payroll service fees, additional tax and accounting paperwork, and the like.

For all these reasons, most small companies prefer to classify hired help as contractors whenever possible. However, just because they say they're an independent contractor and you sign a contract to that effect, doesn't necessarily mean the government will see it that way.

According to the Internal Revenue Service (IRS), three things affect whether a hired individual should be treated as an employee instead of as a contractor. (If you answer "yes" to any of these three, the IRS could re-classify a contractor as an employee.)

1. **Behavioral:** Does the company control or have the right to control what the worker does and how they do it?
2. **Financial:** Are the business aspects of the worker's job controlled by the payer? (These include things such as how the worker is paid, whether expenses are reimbursed, and which party provides the tools or supplies.)
3. **Relational:** Are there written contracts or employee-type benefits (such as pension plans, insurance, or vacation pay)? Will the relationship continue, and is the work performed a key aspect of the business?

Following is a list of parameters that must be met for hirees to be classified as contractors:

- They provide their own equipment.
- They have the freedom to make decisions on how a particular job is done. (This doesn't mean you can't provide some instruction, but keep in mind that the stricter your control over how they do their work, the closer to the "employee edge" they will be.)
- They have a viable business that serves other clients besides you. This establishes that they are in the business of providing that service, as opposed to serving just you.

- They work at their own place of business (home, studio, or office).
- There is a quantifiable precedent in the industry that defines the company/contractor relationship.
- There is a contract in place that describes the work as "work for hire" and establishes the points made previously.

For the most part, given the nature of the industry, most of the shooters you hire will easily fall into the contractor category. There's definitely a precedent set for freelance shooters, and most will have their own equipment. But hiring freelance editors is a different story. There is less of a precedent here, and therefore more of a potential for studios to get into trouble.

If you hire editors as contractors, but they come to your home or studio to work, they edit on your equipment, and you give them extensive instruction on how to edit your projects, you run the risk of having them re-classified as employees. The result can be that you end up paying back taxes, penalties, and interest. A worst-case scenario would be your contractor (who's deemed to really be an employee) gets hurt at your place of business, and you don't have the required workers compensation insurance. Or an ex-contractor gets upset with you, then sues you for overtime or for benefits that you gave actual employees who did the same level and amount of work.

The moral of this story is clear: Be sure that anyone you classify as a contractor truly meets all the parameters the law requires to be classified as such. It's not worth the pain or financial penalties down the road if you do inaccurately classify someone.

WHY YOU MIGHT WANT EMPLOYEES

Even if you can classify someone as a contractor, it may still be a good idea to hire them as an employee. Why? Loyalty and competitive advantage.

As we discussed in Chapter 6, "Building a Brand," a key way to create a distinctive brand is to produce exceptional work. If you come across a shooter or editor who is keenly talented, it might behoove you to offer that person stable employment in exchange for his or her loyalty to your studio. The added cost of having the person as an employee may be worth it if he or she can elevate your work to a level that sets you apart.

Create an employment contract that stipulates what the employee can and cannot do with respect to the work he or she produced for you. However obvious it might seem that the copyrights of anything employees or contractors shoot for you belong to your studio, protect yourself by making it explicitly clear in a contract. Beyond that, you will want to ensure that the employee's strongest areas are reserved for your studio only.

CONTRACTS

Make sure you put a contract in place for anyone who works for you, even employees (**FIGURE 11.3**). Lack of communication and unmet expectations are perhaps the two most common causes for disputes between employers and employees. We create a yearly agreement with contractors we frequently hire. It is specific with respect to the relationship, legal rights, handling of taxes, copyrights, and such, but has broad strokes with respect to payments. For payments, we state a general range in the contract and stipulate that specific payment for a job will be made on a case-by-case basis and mutually approved.

Following are some key elements you want to make sure are addressed in your contracts:

Resources. Stipulate whether the contractor/employee provides his or her own equipment, supplies, and the like.

FIGURE 11.3 A signed contract from every employee and contractor is essential.

Work-for-hire and copyrights. Make it clear that each job is a "work for hire." This is key because according to federal copyright law, unless stipulated otherwise in a contract, whoever creates an image owns that image. Don't get caught in a situation in which you hire someone to shoot a gig for you, and there's nothing in writing stipulating that your studio hired the individual as a "work for hire" and that you retain the copyrights.

Dress code. Make sure the contract stipulates that the contractor/employee will dress appropriately for the project assigned. Just don't get too specific in saying *what* they must wear.

Taxes. Make it clear in subcontractor agreements that the contractor is responsible for his or her own taxes.

Usage rights. If someone works as a freelance shooter or editor, their ability to get additional work relies on being able to show prospective clients what they've done. This can be a sticky area for obvious reasons. It's quite possible that, at times, you and a contractor will vie for the same business.

On one hand, you want to have some control over what a contractor can show. On the other hand, you should be the kind of studio that cares for its people (whether or not they are employees). Think of the Golden Rule. How would you like to be treated? If at all possible, incorporate some way in which a contractor can show some work they've done for you, without necessarily jeopardizing your own business.

We know it's likely that some studio owners completely disagree with this line of reasoning, but our feeling is that if you treat your freelancers and employees well, they'll generally be loyal and work hard for you. (Granted, that's not always the case, as even we've discovered. But we do believe that disloyalty is the exception, not the rule.)

Confidentiality. State somewhere in the contract that any information the contractor comes across while working on your job, unless it becomes public knowledge in some other way, will be held confidential. This clause will most likely be more important for corporate work.

Self-promotion. Stipulate that contractors working on a job for you are not to do any self-promotion of their own business. Any business inquiries on a job should be directed towards the owner or other studio representative. If you send a contractor out on a job alone, make sure he or she has generic copies of your business card to hand out to anyone on site who asks. If you can't give them business cards to hand out, at least ensure they know to give out *your* contact information.

Ownership of files. Your contract should stipulate that any project files (and any other deliverables) created by or given to contractors with respect to a project remain in your ownership, and that any copies remaining on their computer systems should be destroyed upon your request.

Federal ID number. Have your contractors include their Federal ID number under their signature on a contract. For most contractors, this is most likely their Social Security Number. As of the writing of this book, any payments in excess of $600 in a year must be reported on your taxes via form 1099 (thus the term "1099 Contractor"). Since you'll need their Federal ID when filing 1099s, it's best to get it up front rather than scrambling to find it at tax time.

OUTSOURCED LABOR

Most of the contractors you hire will be for production-related purposes. Yet, there are necessary duties in your business that have nothing to do with shooting or editing. These include everything from running errands to bookkeeping to answering e-mail and phones. This is the area in which you'll quickly find your soul drained from work you may find anathema to your creative sensibilities. Tracking income and expenses, filling out government paperwork, paying quarterly taxes—these and many more duties are ones that you can hand over to someone else. In fact, you probably should hand over these duties. As the visionary and owner of the company, your time is better spent drumming up more business and doing the creative work.

So, how should you handle all these administrative jobs that inhibit you from growing your business? Outsource them.

Outsourcing is the act of hiring companies or individuals outside your business to handle work that would normally be done inside. Hiring a subcontracted editor is a form of outsourcing. But with respect to administrative work, there are two other forms of outsourcing you may find helpful.

FIGURE 11.4 Virtual assistants can relieve many of your repetitive administrative duties.

VIRTUAL ASSISTANTS

As the name suggests, Virtual Assistants (VAs) are administrative assistants who work virtually. That is, they do work for you from their home or office via the phone or computer. Anything that can be done via a phone or computer can be passed on to a VA.

These include the following:

- Replying to e-mail or phone inquiries (**FIGURE 11.4**)
- Doing online research
- Managing voicemail messages
- Writing and sending letters
- Answering the phone
- Handling travel arrangements
- Managing your calendar
- Checking and managing your e-mail box

That last duty may be one of the hardest to share due to privacy issues. Naturally, before handing over the user name and password to your e-mail account, you'll want to make sure you can completely trust the VA. But once you get to that point, you'd be surprised at how much freedom and efficiency it can give you. The way we look at it is this: regardless of the size of your company, you are its CEO; and if the CEO of a Fortune 500 company feels comfortable letting his or her administrative assistant manage e-mail (which CEOs do), then so can we.

FIGURE 11.5 Consider letting a VA deal with general e-mail inquiries and responses.

About 18 months into our relationship with our VA, we felt comfortable enough to give her access to our e-mail. If we had the chance to do it over, we wouldn't have waited that long. We're not big fans of e-mail auto-responders, so if we're away on a trip without frequent access to e-mail, we instruct the VA to check our e-mail twice a day, and reply to any time-sensitive e-mails. We use Gmail, so we're able to have multiple accounts. One of them is "Donna on Behalf of Ron Dawson." So, it's Ron's actual e-mail address, but the name lets the recipient know it's not Ron personally writing.

If you just can't get past the idea of handing over the "keys" of your e-mail to a VA, at least create an e-mail address for him or her with your company's URL (**FIGURE 11.5**). Then, have certain types of e-mail forwarded to your VA. We have all of our service inquiries go directly to our VA. She will then either answer the e-mail herself if the inquiry is simple and she has the knowledge to answer it, or she will forward it to one of us as necessary.

The cost of a VA can range from $10 per hour to two to three times that for more-seasoned VAs who are given more complex tasks. However, you must weigh the opportunity costs of not having a VA versus having one (see the "Power of Outsourcing" section later in this chapter). Due to the popularity of Timothy Ferriss's *4-Hour Workweek*, in which he writes extensively about VAs, they have become more popular and it's relatively easy to find one. Ideally, if you can get a referral, do so. If not, you can do a Google search and find exhaustive resources. Or, start with the International Virtual Assistants Association (www.ivaa.org).

FIGURE 11.6 If your inbox is overflowing, it may be time to hire some help.

ACCOUNTING AND BOOKKEEPING

This is easily the most dreaded aspect of our business. Despite the fact that Ron has a degree in finance from the University of California at Berkeley's Haas School of Business, taking care of the books and doing the accounting is absolutely loathsome. The time and energy involved combined with the monotony make this task at times unbearable (**FIGURE 11.6**). Whenever feasible, we hire a bookkeeper to come in and take care of bank reconciliations as well as enter invoices and expenses.

This is another area in which some level of trust is required on your part to allow an outsider to look at your books and handle bank statements. If you can afford a full- or part-time bookkeeper, it is very much worth it. If you can't, consider engaging a company such as Accountemps (www.accountemps.com) that specializes in placing temporary bookkeepers with businesses of all sizes.

THE POWER OF OUTSOURCING

Whether you're outsourcing administrative work or even creative jobs such as editing, outsourcing is a powerful way to evolve your business. It allows you to refocus your time and energy on areas that are required to keep the business running—and running efficiently.

Let's look at a simple example of how the costs associated with outsourcing can be justified.

Let's say that you spend eight hours a week (just over 90 minutes per weekday) handling random online tasks that you could hand over to a VA. These are tasks that are not directly related to generating business or finishing up a client's project. You decide to hire a VA for five hours per week (just one hour per weekday) to help with these administrative duties. Conservatively, let's say you pay this person $20 per hour. For $400 per month, you regain 10–12 percent of your time—time you can put towards marketing your business. How many more prospects could you connect with if given an extra hour per day? If that extra 20 hours per month helps you land even one additional job, you may have paid for multiple months of a VA's time.

Another way to look at it is how much your time is worth. Conservatively, your time is worth at least $75 per hour. If that's the case, then it makes no sense for you to spend multiple hours doing work that could be done at the $10–$20 per hour rate. When you do gain extra hours back, make sure you are using them for the most impactful aspects of your job, marketing and client relationships.

HIRING AND TRAINING

The last point we want to address is the importance of creating systems to identify, hire, and train the contractors and employees who will help you grow your business.

HR ISN'T JUST FOR BIG COMPANIES

Many of you may have experience in a corporate environment where there was a human resources division of the company. HR personnel were there to help orient you to the company culture, answer questions about company benefits, ensure the company was in compliance with any employment laws, and provide training for new recruits.

All of these duties are necessary for your company as well. Even if most of the people who work for you are independent contractors, you need to have strong HR policies in place to help maintain efficiency, quality standards, and compliance with the law.

HIRING

No decision you make in your business will have as profound an effect on your company's success, and your state of being, as who you hire to work for you. In many cases, these individuals will represent the face of your company.

Whether it's an administrative assistant answering the phone or replying to e-mail, or a shooter in the field interacting with clients, you need to make sure you have strong systems in place to attract and acquire talent that will appropriately represent your brand and the experience you want to give your clients.

Here are some things you should be doing:

Job descriptions. Have a detailed job description for all the major roles available in your company—from gopher to senior editor to marketing manager/VP. Even if you perform most of these duties for now, you should have their descriptions written down somewhere. That way, when you're ready to hire someone to take over a particular duty, you will already have the information to provide to the applicant. Your description should also include required and desired qualifications and approximate pay.

Job applications. Even if you plan to hire contractors, it's a good idea to have some sort of application system. We use an online form where prospective employees or contractors can give us basic contact information, work history, links to demo reels, and even upload a resume (FIGURE 11.7). We also have them answer a few essay questions to gauge their level of commitment and sincerity.

Interviews. If you're hiring anyone who will have access to your work, your clients, or your finances, you should conduct a rigorous interview process before hiring. Whenever we've hired key personnel or contractors too quickly, we've been burned. Either their work ethic turned out to be less than we required, or we didn't get a clear picture of their expectations and as a result their job dissatisfaction caused conflict. Take the time to get to know the people you plan to entrust with your branding experience.

DARE DREAMER media
Formerly Cinematic Studios

Back home

JOIN OUR TEAM!

Dare Dream Media (formerly Cinematic Studios Inc). is an award-winning new media marketing agency specializing in providing creative productions for its clients using narrative filmmaking techniques and sociall media marketing consultation. Our cinematic approach to digital video production, combined with top notch customer service, has contributed to the meteoric growth and success of our company. We are growing so fast we need your help.

We are looking for creative and energetic filmmakers and artists interested in helping us change the face of video production. Contractor and part time positions are available in the following areas, with opportunities for growth to full time employment and profit sharing. Payment is on a job-by-job basis.

- **Producer/Director/Editor**: this position needs an entrepreneurial individual with a creative eye, experience in wedding and/or live video production, strong organizational and producing skills, and strong interpersonal skills. He/she will lead a small team consisting of an assistant camera, production assistant, and editors to conceive, shoot, and bring to completion one of our cinematic style wedding or event digital films. Must be an experienced and creative editor (preferably Final Cut Pro) and experienced camera operator/cinematographer. Must have a friendly disposition and strong interpersonal skills as there will be significant client interaction.
- **Editor**: we are in need of highly creative and experienced Final Cut Pro editors who have a strong command of traditional narrative filmmaking editing, but are capable to push the creative envelope. Experience in After Effects or Motion is not necessary but a huge plus.
- **HD and 8 mm/16 mm Shooters**: we're in the process of establishing a specialized division that will focus solely on HD and film productions. We need individuals with their own equipment and experience. Must have an artistic eye, be RELIABLE, and have strong interpersonal skills.
- **Camera Operator and Assistant Camera**: we're in need of professional camera operators with experience shooting live events and documentaries. Must have a friendly disposition and strong interpersonal skills as there will be significant client interaction.
- **Apprenticeship Program**: we are starting an educational apprenticeship program for those of you aspiring filmmakers and digital video producers who want real world experience. This 6 to 12-month non-paid position will give you hands-on experience in the fields of cinematography, production, and editing. The only qualifications necessary is a passion for filmmaking and a hunger to learn.

FIGURE 11.7 Our online job application form. This part of the form is followed by a questionnaire.

Trial periods. You might want to consider assigning trial periods to key roles. If you hire a new editor, before putting her in charge of that $20,000 corporate project, give her a period of time to prove her abilities, loyalty, and work ethic. This is another area in which we've had to learn the hard way. Some of our biggest disappointments have come from seasoned Hollywood professionals that we didn't put through a standard trial period before assigning high-level work. The results ranged from substandard quality to major deadlines being missed. If you know you're going into a season when you'll have a backlog, start looking to hire help well before you get into a position where you have to bypass a trial period.

TRAINING

In a creative business such as video production, you'll come across a wide range of candidates with varying skill sets and aesthetic tastes. Remember, it's your company and your branding experience. Therefore, it's up to you to make sure that the people you hire are equipped and ready to produce work that lives up to the standards you've set. Here are some ideas:

Training DVDs. Maintain a library of training DVDs that you can use for new hires. These could be DVDs you create yourself or DVDs from other professionals (see the "Training Resources" sidebar).

Samples of your work. Provide new hires (whether employees or contractors) with DVD samples of your work. Give them a wide diversity of work you've produced, and point out any specific videos you want them to emulate.

Shooting/editing guidelines. One of the best time investments we ever made was to create eight pages of guidelines on editing wedding movies to send to new editors. It gives a brief history of our company and the industry. Many of the editors we attract do not have specific experience editing wedding movies. So they may have some of the same prejudices and stereotypes of wedding videography that the average layperson does.

Our guidelines set the record straight, and give detailed information on everything from our style to how we want our files named and our Final Cut Pro projects organized. It's all about creating systems. When you get a project back from an editor, anyone else who works for you should be able to open that project and be able to navigate the media and sequences without getting lost or confused. That can only happen if you create a standard way for organizing your projects.

On-the-job training. Consider an apprenticeship or internship program for hires that are not only new to your company, but new to the industry as well. Provide an opportunity for these people to help out as a production assistant (PA) on a job. Give them safe and basic tasks, while at the same time allowing them to observe you (or a senior person on your crew) in action.

Reviews and post-mortems. Once someone has completed a job for you, if you plan to use that person again, it's a good idea to review the work and your experience working with that person. Often referred to as post-mortems, these reviews help you consistently improve your company's output. You're also providing opportunities for your hires to grow, as well as an opportunity for them to provide feedback to you so that you can grow as a manager.

TRAINING RESOURCES

Following are some solid training resources worth adding to your educational library.

Digital Juice (www.digitaljuice.com): This company is one of the most prolific producers of multimedia products such as digital backgrounds, motion graphics, layered still-image graphics, and various audio and music collections. They also have a terrific educational video series called DJTV that covers every major category of video production.

Ripple Training (www.rippletraining.com): This site is an invaluable source of education on Mac production software. The pieces are available as both digital downloads and DVD.

CreativeCOW (www.creativecow.net): This is perhaps the most comprehensive collection of knowledge on the Internet with respect to all forms of media production. They have everything you need in online and offline education: forums, podcasts, blogs, articles, DVDs, online video tutorials, and more. And they cover all major (and minor) creative production systems for all major computer operating systems. Spend a few hours on CreativeCow.net and your head will surely spin.

Safari Books Online (www.safaribooks.com): Safari Books Online is an on-demand digital library that provides access to thousands of technology, creative, and business books; training videos; and expert reference and learning materials from leading publishers such as Addison-Wesley, Peachpit Press (Apple Pro Training and Adobe Press), O'Reilly Media, lynda.com, and many more.

Mark and Trisha Von Lanken (www.vontraining.com): Award-winning videographers, and four-time EventDV 25 honorees, Mark and Trisha Von Lanken are powerhouses in the world of wedding and event video training. They have an excellent array of training DVDs in shooting and editing techniques, including samples of their award-winning work (**FIGURE 11.8**).

PixelPops (www.pixelpops-shop.com): In addition to providing the company's own assortment of Photoshop training DVDs, the team at PixelPops also sells popular titles from just about every major event video producer with a training product to sell.

FIGURE 11.8
Complete training series from Mark and Trisha Von Lanken.

IN FOCUS:
BRETT CULP

Brett Culp, based in Tampa, Florida, is one of the most celebrated and award-winning event video producers in the industry. He's an author, speaker, educator, and extremely creative individual. The predecessor to his current company, Brett Culp Films, was Creative Video Productions (www.cvpexperience.com). His company remains one of the top five all-time winners of the coveted WEVA Creative Excellence Awards. The team's cutting-edge style, creative use of music and motion, and out-of-the-box approach to shooting and editing help raised the bar in the industry and quickly elevated Brett and his staff to national success (**FIGURE 11.9**).

What makes their success all the more interesting is that when Culp hired the two key employees who helped grow the business and win all those awards, he selected people with absolutely no video experience. That's right. Nada. Zilch. Zero.

As Culp tells it when he speaks to standing-room-only crowds, he made it a point to hire individuals who had creativity, but in other fields. He had a particular style he knew he wanted to instill in his studio's work, and as far as he was concerned, the best way to ensure that was to work with a clean slate.

FIGURE 11.9 From left to right: Emily Whittlesey, Brett Culp, JT Fannin, and Monica Crafts.

In tennis, coaches prefer it when they get new trainees who have not been taught how to grip a racket incorrectly. It can be a very frustrating to get students to unlearn what they've learned. Likewise, Culp didn't want his recruits to be already set in their ways of shooting and editing. The results and the "method to his madness" speak for themselves.

Naturally, not everyone can go out and hire complete novices and train them from scratch to become top-notch video producers. If you have an established studio with a full slate of important gigs to film, you may have no time to train new recruits to the level Culp did. However, if there is any way you can work with absolute video novices in your training regimen, you not only have better control over the quality of your finished product, but you may also have a higher retention and loyalty rate.

CUSTOMER SERVICE AND SUPPORT

NOT TOO LONG AGO—in fact, during the writing of this book—I (Ron) was on an extended business trip to shoot a gig in Santa Cruz, California, then a second gig a few days laters in Ohio. While in Silicon Valley, I stopped by the popular camera store Keeble & Shuchat to buy a couple of 16 GB compact flash cards. I was purchasing one card for each shoot.

A few days after the purchase, I was prepping for the second shoot and noticed that the second CF card was only an 8 GB card. There apparently was an 8 GB package behind the 16 GB one when the sales associate grabbed them off the shelf. (Note to self: Always double-check your purchase at a camera store before walking out.) I was irked with myself for not checking the order and was certain they'd give me a hard time trying to exchange it. I was already 2,000 miles from the store and my next stop was back home in the Atlanta area.

I called Keeble & Shuchat to explain the situation and was prepared to hear the person on the other end say, "Sorry, I can't help you, all sales are final." Or, "Sorry, unless you come in person, there's nothing I can do." Instead the associate said, "No problem, just return the 8 GB card with a copy of your receipt and we'll send you out another."

Due to a packed production schedule, it was two weeks before I got around to sending back the card. I called them again to confirm it was still OK. The original gentleman I spoke with was on vacation, so a new guy (this time, the associate who actually sold me the card) was on the phone. I explained the situation again, this time more certain than ever he'd say no because it was now two weeks since I made the original purchase. Again, he said, "No problem," and told me to ship back the card. When I did so, he even made a point to call me when he received it and shipped out the replacement.

I can't tell you how many times I've been in similar situations in which it was darn near impossible to get either a refund or exchange. In today's competitive business environment, I'm still baffled at companies that will make you jump through hoops to resolve a problem, especially when the product's price seems negligible. Keeble & Shuchat got it right.

IT'S NOT ABOUT THE WIDGETS

One thing we've learned over the years as we've read books about great customer service, and studied companies that offer it, is that the businesses that get it right all understand one thing: You're not selling widgets. That is, you're not selling whatever it is you're selling. What you're really selling is customer service. You're selling an experience (there's that word again). The companies that get it right focus on making the customer service experience the best it can be.

We recently read an *Inc.* magazine cover story about Tony Hsieh, CEO of online shoe retailer Zappos. In less than ten years, he grew Zappos to $1 billion in sales and profitability, and he created a corporate culture that is the envy of Wall Street. Everything about the company is centered around creating an amazing customer service experience, from free overnight shipping and returns to call center reps empowered to perform services such as sending a vase of flowers to a customer who was returning boots she got for her husband who was recently killed in a car crash. We would say that Zappos isn't selling shoes, they're selling customer service.

In the same issue was an article about Circuit City's demise. The CEO of the struggling electronics retailer blamed the terrible economy for the company's liquidation. However, as the article's author pointed out, other electronics retailers (such as the Apple Store and Best Buy) are flourishing. The bulk of the article was actually about a company you probably have come into contact with repeatedly: B&H Photo and Video (**FIGURE 12.1**). This popular resource for both professionals and consumers provides amazing customer service at terrific prices. And get this: Because the owners are Orthodox Jews, both the store *and* the Web site are closed every week during the Jewish Sabbath and also each year during Jewish holidays. How can an electronics store afford to close both their store *and* Web site during a 24-hour period each week during these tough economic times? Because their service has helped build a loyal customer base that gives them more than enough business the rest of the week.

If you think you're in the business of selling event or corporate video production, we encourage you to rethink that approach. As far-fetched as it might seem, what you're really selling is customer service.

FIGURE 12.1
B&H's service and competitive pricing has made it a globally recognized leader in the worlds of both professional photography and video production.

MANAGE YOUR RELATIONSHIPS

Vital resources for any business looking to deliver amazing customer service are *customer relationship management* (or CRM) solutions and project management solutions. These are database-driven software programs that allow your company to track clients and prospects. Here's an example of a common CRM workflow:

A prospect fills out a form on your Web site (**FIGURE 12.2**) with all the information about the project. That information gets e-mailed to you and stored in your CRM program. Your sales rep (or whoever handles client inquiries) can log in to the CRM, go to the record for the prospect, then call him or her back to discuss the project. While on the phone with the prospect, the sales rep can take notes about the project and enter them into the prospect's record.

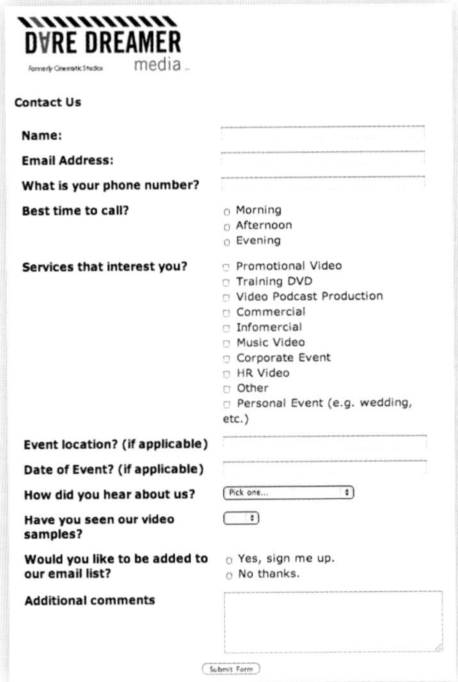

DARE DREAMER
media

Contact Us

Name:

Email Address:

What is your phone number?

Best time to call?
- Morning
- Afternoon
- Evening

Services that interest you?
- Promotional Video
- Training DVD
- Video Podcast Production
- Commercial
- Infomercial
- Music Video
- Corporate Event
- HR Video
- Other
- Personal Event (e.g. wedding, etc.)

Event location? (if applicable)

Date of Event? (if applicable)

How did you hear about us? Pick one...

Have you seen our video samples?

Would you like to be added to our email list?
- Yes, sign me up.
- No thanks.

Additional comments

Submit Form

FIGURE 12.2 A quick contact form on our main Web site. Information is submitted directly into our CRM program.

When the prospect decides to book our services, a contract is created within the CRM (based on the parameters set earlier) and e-mailed to the client. The client can sign the contract electronically. During the relationship, any e-mails sent to and from the client are added to the CRM database, thus maintaining a record of all the important correspondence.

A CRM solution such as ShootQ also provides an online project calendar where the client can log in and check on the status of the project, see which milestones are pending, and so forth. People on your team can log into the system and see the calendar as well as get e-mails when certain project due dates are pending.

Files are uploaded to a central location. These include photos, graphics, audio files, documents, and the like.

When it's time to send the client an invoice, it's generated in the CRM. An e-mail is then sent to the client, giving him or her the option to pay online or send in a check. Once payment is received, the information can be exported to your accounting program (e.g., QuickBooks).

Clients can also use the system to update their contact information.

Once you have all this information aggregated in one spot, you are much better equipped to deliver amazing customer service by doing the following:

- Keeping up to speed on a project
- Following up with phone calls or e-mails
- Sending holiday, birthday, and anniversary cards
- Providing surprises in your product delivery based on the preferences of your clients (for example, you know your client loves macadamia nut cookies, so you put a box in with her DVDs)

Client communication is an important part of customer service and support, and a CRM solution makes that communication very easy and efficient.

CRM AND PROJECT MANAGEMENT SOLUTIONS

CRM solutions are so important that Fortune 500 companies spend millions of dollars each year on systems such as Oracle or Salesforce.com. Fortunately, you don't have to spend that kind of money to get powerful solutions. Here are just a few suggestions:

ONLINE SOLUTIONS:

Basecamp (www.basecamphq.com): This online project management solution by 37signals Inc. is a leader among small businesses. It's completely Web-based, simple to use, and affordable.

Highrise (www.highrisehq.com): From the creators of Basecamp, Highrise is specifically for tracking clients and prospects.

ShootQ (www.shootq.com): This is the solution we use. In the past, we used both Basecamp and Highrise, but ShootQ is designed specifically with photography and videography studios in mind and offers all the features we need in one system. We also like the fact that, like Basecamp and Highrise, it's accessible online. It handles everything from online booking, customer e-mail newsletters, custom package creation, the ability to track the profitability of packages, online contracts, download information into QuickBooks, sync with your iPhone, and much more.

OFFLINE SOLUTIONS:

Successware (www.successware.net): This is a studio management software solution designed specifically for professional photography studios, but with features that are transferable to video businesses.

FileMaker Pro (www.filemaker.com): If the monthly subscription costs of the aforementioned services don't fit your budget, FileMaker Pro is a great alternative. This is a very popular, flexible, and affordable application that gives you the ability to track just about anything. The downside is you'll need to invest the time to design a database that fits your needs. Or, perform a Google search online to find pre-made databases that need just a little tweaking.

QuickBooks Customer Manager (http://quickbooks.intuit.com/product/add-ons/cmdesktop.jsp): Intuit provides a desktop CRM solution that naturally integrates well with their popular accounting program. As of this writing, it is only available on Windows®. A beta version of an online solution is also available.

ACT (www.act.com): Last but certainly not least is ACT, one of the original CRM software solutions that made such features accessible to the small business owner. As of this writing, it is only available for Windows® systems.

MAKING UP FOR MISTAKES

If you've been in business long enough, there will come a time when your studio will drop the proverbial ball. You'll make one of those mistakes, or be subject to one of those mishaps, that you dread. But some of the greatest customer service stories come out of misfortune and mistakes. It's not so much trying to implement a system in which nothing bad can happen—despite all your best efforts, bad things *will* happen. But it's how you react when they do that counts the most.

THE BUCK STOPS WITH YOU

In January 2005, a few years after we started our business, we were booked for a wedding in Lake Tahoe, Nevada. The groom's family was a loyal client for whom we'd already produced a couple of wedding videos. We had one of our trusted contractors shooting the gig along with his partner (our son Joshua was due soon, so we didn't do any traveling that month). For more than a year-and-a-half, we had been using contractors to shoot jobs for us when we couldn't be there. So there was no fear or trepidation about sending out a team without us.

A few days after the wedding, I got a call from our contractor regarding the shoot. Everything went really well except for one mishap: Just as the bride was coming down the aisle, his camera stopped recording, and his was the camera angled on the bride. Perhaps the most important shot of any wedding video (second to maybe the kiss) is that shot of the bride coming down the aisle. We didn't have it—or the rest of the ceremony—from that camera.

Perhaps it was the cold weather. Perhaps he accidentally double-clutched (hit the Record/Pause button twice). Perhaps it was just a fluke of nature. Whatever the reason, it didn't matter. The footage wasn't there.

For a while I was in denial. I'd watch the tape over and over again, hoping the footage would magically appear—maybe God would come down and save me by creating a miracle. But there was no miracle, no magic.

I then had the very unpleasant task of calling the bride to inform her of the mishap. Naturally, she was very disappointed, but took the news relatively well. I apologized and assured her that the footage from the other camera was intact and that we could still make a beautiful ceremony video from that. I told her we'd work with the photographer to get photos of her coming down the aisle that we could incorporate into the video.

What I *didn't* do was blame my shooter. It didn't matter if what happened was his fault, an equipment failure, or an act of God that no one could've prevented. It was *our* company and we needed to bear the full brunt of any consequences.

In the long run, the client absolutely loved what we produced for her (**FIGURE 12.3**). In fact, she wrote us a long and thoughtful e-mail about how amazing her video was and all that we had done for her:

> I LOVE IT!!!!!!!!!!! I have watched the video 3 times in a row and I can't stop crying with joy! The video is fabulous and I can't thank you enough for all the time and effort you have put into making our wedding memories everything that I hoped for and more. I am looking forward to sharing the video with all of our family & friends!

FIGURE 12.3
The bride was a scrapbooking enthusiast, so we took that into consideration and created a handmade custom-designed DVD case.

STEPS TO MANAGING MISHAPS

When you're faced with the unfortunate task of telling a client something's gone wrong, here are some actions we suggest you take:

Take full responsibility. The client hired *your* studio to do the job. If something goes wrong on that job, it doesn't matter to them who may or may not have been specifically responsible. It's *your* company they paid.

For example, once we ordered Super 8 film stock from a respected company. The sales rep sent the shipment two-day instead of overnight. To make matters worse, the shipping company they used didn't make deliveries to our address on Saturdays (which would have been day two). As a result, we weren't able to use the film on our scheduled shoot. When we called to express dissatisfaction and ask for a refund of the shipping costs, the only thing this film supplier would say was that it was the shipping company's fault and that we should deal with them. When we explained that we didn't pay or choose the shipping company, the owner said we still had to call the shipping company. When we did call the shipping company, can you guess what they said? Because we paid the supplier, we'd have to deal with them for a refund.

Needless to say, we never did business with that film stock company again. There's nothing worse than when a company refuses to accept responsibility, but instead wants to pass the buck to someone else. (It should be noted that we're deliberately not mentioning the name of this company. However, if they had treated the situation differently, and had made the mishap into an amazing experience, we *would* be praising their name and mentioning it here.) The moral: You never know what terrific benefits you'll miss out on if you deliver terrible service.

No excuses. As much as you may want to offer an excuse for what happened, don't. It's human nature to want to defend yourself, especially if something happens that's not personally your fault. But this can only aggravate the situation, and communicates to clients that you don't care as much about their feelings. (This is a valuable lesson we learned in our marriage that just happens to be terrifically applicable to business.) Feel free to explain what may have caused the mishap, but not in such a way that you're trying to absolve yourself of fault. And definitely don't dwell on it.

Go above and beyond. It goes without saying that if your company screws up, you need to make amends. Depending on the severity of the situation, there are a number of things you could do to make up for it. In some cases, a partial (or even full) refund may be warranted. But that doesn't need to be your first (or even last) option. You could offer extra DVDs of the final project, if applicable. Upgrade their service. Provide a credit for future services. For the aforementioned Lake Tahoe bride, we offered credit toward another video (either a baby video or an extended edit of their wedding movie), unlimited changes (as opposed to our traditional hour of complimentary editing changes), and unlimited DVDs. Ultimately we gave them about ten DVDs and spent about three hours re-editing an opening sequence.

Be wise. Depending on the situation, you need to be wise about when you deliver information. You never want to knowingly conceal important information from a client, but timing is everything. It would not be a good idea to tell a bride on her wedding day that you screwed up a significant part of the video. If something like that happens the day of and you find out, don't ruin the most important day of her life by telling her you missed a key shot. There's nothing that can be done that day anyway. News like that may be better communicated after the honeymoon. However, on a corporate shoot, it may be totally different. If your camera malfunctions while filming an interview with the CEO—a CEO who's leaving on a plane back to the main office that night—as hard as it may be, you may *have* to tell the client what happened so you can redo the shot. Whenever and however you decide to inform a client of bad news, use wisdom and discretion.

Be sensitive. Lastly, show that you care. In the long run, people just want to be treated fairly, and to know that you care. That alone will sometimes be all the customer service you need.

IN FOCUS: RITZ-CARLTON

The first time I (Ron) ever had a gig at a Ritz-Carlton (FIGURE 12.4), within minutes of driving up I knew why they are the world-renowned customer service leaders they are. When I drove my car up to the front, someone rushed over to open the door and greeted me by name. I had never been there before and as far as I knew, I had never met the guy. Then it occurred to me. At the entry gate to the property, the guard asked for my name. At the time, I thought it was to check it against a list of vendors for the event. (Maybe he had done that too.) But it was now apparent that he had also "phoned in" my name to the bellhops at the front door. All I could think of at the time was, "Wow! That's cool."

I'm sure a number of you reading this have worked a gig or two at a place like the Ritz-Carlton and probably have your own stories to tell. Do a Google search on "ritz-carlton + customer service" and you'll find no shortage of amazing stories. The company has legendary customer service because it trains and educates its employees to deliver it. It's paramount to the business and the company's foundation. Here are the 12 Service Values listed from the Ritz-Carlton site as part of its "Gold Standards":

FIGURE 12.4 Shot of the Ritz Carlton Half Moon Bay, about an hour south of San Francisco.

1. I build strong relationships and create Ritz-Carlton guests for life.
2. I am always responsive to the expressed and unexpressed wishes and needs of our guests.
3. I am empowered to create unique, memorable and personal experiences for our guests.
4. I understand my role in achieving the Key Success Factors, embracing Community Footprints and creating The Ritz-Carlton Mystique.
5. I continuously seek opportunities to innovate and improve The Ritz-Carlton experience.
6. I own and immediately resolve guest problems.
7. I create a work environment of teamwork and lateral service so that the needs of our guests and each other are met.
8. I have the opportunity to continuously learn and grow.
9. I am involved in the planning of the work that affects me.
10. I am proud of my professional appearance, language and behavior.
11. I protect the privacy and security of our guests, my fellow employees and the company's confidential information and assets.

    I am responsible for uncompromising levels of cleanliness and creating a safe and accident-free environment.

That is quite an impressive list. And you may say to yourself, "Sure they can do all of that. Guests pay for it." True, but you don't have to charge Ritz-Carlton prices to offer a Ritz-Carlton experience.

Recently, our family stopped by a local pizza restaurant after doing some shopping. CiCi's Pizza was offering a $3.99 "recession special," an all-you-can-eat buffet. The food was just okay, but the service was great. The person behind the counter was friendly and said if there was pizza we wanted that wasn't at the buffet, let her know and she'd have it made. Lucky for them, I'm easy. I came up a few minutes later and requested a Hawaiian. She told me to grab a red cone and she'd have someone bring it out to me.

I must tell you, I was quite surprised. At a fast food-service price, I received 5-star restaurant service. It just proved the point that great customer service can come from any business, at any price. If CiCi's Pizza can do it for a $3.99 all-you-can-eat buffet, you can do it too.

PRODUCTION AND DELIVERY

WE COULDN'T WRITE AN ENTIRE BOOK about the video business without including at least one chapter on production.

It's no coincidence that this chapter is near the end of the book. As much as we appreciate art and passion, when it comes to building a business, all the things we've talked about to this point will have a greater impact on your success than the actual productions.

We know this makes a lot of you uncomfortable. Maybe it even ticks you off. However it makes you feel, the truth is, a decent video producer who is excellent at business and marketing will be exponentially more successful than the consummate artiste who's terrible at business. (They don't call them "starving artists" for nothing.)

With that said, some aspects of the production process can actually aid your business's evolution.

PRE-PRODUCTION

Any successful filmmaker or video producer will tell you that pre-production is one of the most important elements of any shoot. The planning and preparation that go into a video production will obviously have a significant impact on the shoot itself. What happens in pre-production will continue to impact the project all the way through post-production as well.

If you've been in business for a while, it's easy to get stuck on automatic. Dane Sanders, author of *Fast Track Photographer*, is an accomplished speaker and business coach who often talks about "getting off automatic." That is, stop, look, and listen to the world around you, at the people you're serving, at the internal workings of your business. Putting time into pre-production requires switching gears and getting off automatic.

I (Ron) must admit that when we focused on wedding and event work, I was frequently caught on automatic. I didn't have the same issue with corporate work, since every project is so different. But when it came to wedding work, I got to a point where I'd show up ready to shoot and realize I hadn't even read the wedding coordinator's schedule. This is not something I'm proud of.

When I first started, I spent considerable time prepping for each shoot. I'd go to the rehearsal, prep my lists of shots, and call the photographer, the DJ, the venue manager, and any other vendor I would need to significantly interact with.

Then, a few years into it, I stopped attending the rehearsal because I realized 99 percent of them were the same: the rehearsal started 30 minutes to an hour late, the actual walkthrough took about 20 minutes, I'd put my cameras in the same location, and so forth. So I did what most event video producers do and stopped attending rehearsals. I made up for it, or so I thought, on the day of the event by showing up a bit early. But when I stopped going to rehearsals, I also stopped performing some other important pre-production tasks. In retrospect, I shouldn't have stopped calling the vendors ahead of time to introduce myself. When I was focused on weddings, I shouldn't have stopped doing a lot of things that were part of my routine as a new business owner.

Following is a list of pre-production tasks every video producer should consider working (or as in my case, reworking) into their production.

Create shot lists. It's not necessary to have a detailed list of every specific shot you plan to shoot, but it's important to have a general list of key shots. For corporate jobs, this list may be more detailed, especially if you're working from a script. But even for event work, there may be some establishing shots or b-roll you know you'll want to use in the storytelling process.

Get connected. Meet with, in person or over the phone, all key personnel and vendors related to the project. For event work, this includes the photographer, DJ, coordinator, and venue manager. For a commercial job, as we suggested earlier, it's best to have one point of contact—but the people you want to ensure are aware of you varies: product managers, brand managers, creative directors, PR managers, marketing managers, clients of the company who may be involved (for testimonials), and the like. We use FreeConference.com to schedule conference calls. It's easy to use and you can set it up so that everyone calls a toll-free number (which, as of this writing, costs $0.10 per minute per caller); or you can set up a regular number (depending on the location of the callers, it may be a long-distance call).

Give instruction. If you have anyone else besides yourself shooting or working on set, make sure everyone has specific written instructions. Hopefully you've taken our advice from Chapter 11, "Administration and Staffing," and you have a contract in place that spells out certain expected behavior. In addition to that, you should have specific instructions for the job at hand. Are there any particular shots you want them to get? If you're shooting a wedding or event, what time are they supposed to arrive, and where? Where do you want them during the ceremony? Do you want them to set their cameras to certain setting to get a particular look or style? It's a great idea to not only send your shooters written instructions, but to have a conference call with them as well.

Plan for travel and weather. I can't tell you how many times we've left for a job, but given ourselves just enough time to get there based on Google or Yahoo Maps—only to realize that those maps didn't take parking into consideration. Have you ever shown up at a job and discovered that it took longer to find parking than to get to the location? Plan ahead for issues such as traffic, parking, weather, baggage check-in, and the like (FIGURE 13.1). When flying with equipment, plan on being delayed longer at security. Some video equipment, when disassembled, looks awfully suspicious on X-ray machines.

When traveling overseas, you also have to deal with passports, IDs, and foreign laws. You may even have to plan for different ways to power (or recharge) your equipment. Many countries outside the United States use a different electrical current system, so the traditional electric plug and ground you're accustomed to using may not work abroad. You don't want to show up for that luxury Italian wedding only to find that you can't recharge your camera batteries. Bottom line: Whether your job is 30 minutes away, or around the world, plan for everything and anything related to getting there on time and being ready to work.

FIGURE 13.1 Whenever traveling, we use video gear and bags that are compact enough to take on the plane with us.

Equipment needs. Plan in advance for any additional equipment needs. You don't want to find out the day before a big corporate shoot that the jib or dolly you planned to rent was just checked out. Whether it's additional equipment you need to rent, purchase, or borrow, make arrangements with the rental facility to have the equipment you need reserved and ready to go when you need it.

Plan B. Every good producer has a backup plan in case something goes wrong. If you're shooting a once-in-a-lifetime event, definitely make sure you have alternate shooters in place in case the main shooters cannot attend. This is another reason that it's a good idea to get involved with a local videographers association—so there's a pool of talent you can tap in emergencies. It's also smart to have backup equipment with you on a shoot (such as an additional camera, replacement bulbs for lights, additional batteries and chargers, as well as an array of audio equipment and accessories). While you're making Plan B, we suggest you go ahead and make Plan C, too.

PRODUCTION

On the day(s) of your shoot, keep in mind that the impression you make on site is a key part of the "branding experience" we talked about in Chapter 6. The way you and your crew interact with the client will have a profound impact on the brand you create for your business. You need to be deliberate about all aspects of the shoot.

Attire. Crew members don't need to wear uniforms, but there should be a dress standard that supports your brand. For our wedding shoots, we require shooters to wear all black with a buttoned-down shirt (FIGURE 13.2). Tie is optional, but the outfit must look contemporary and stylish. Our corporate shoots are a little different. For a large crew, we allow casual dress, but no ripped jeans or unprofessional T-shirts. We require the "director" on the set to be more formal. (Of course, depending on your company's branding, ripped jeans and a "rocker" T-shirt may be required attire.) The point is to make sure that people who represent your company wear clothing that is an accurate reflection of your brand. Make sure you're clear with them in advance about what's appropriate and what isn't.

FIGURE 13.2 Ron filming a high-end wedding at The Ritz-Carlton, Half Moon Bay in the early years of our company.

Attitude. Every person working on your set (whether it's a personal event or a corporate shoot) is an extension of your studio. Even if everyone is a contractor, in the eyes of your client, they are your employees. Make sure your shooters and crewmembers have good people skills, friendly dispositions, and a customer-centric mentality. The last thing you want is a shooter representing your company who balks at the idea of doing anything that isn't specifically in their job description. Even if you have to pay extra for a contractor you know will have that level of professionalism, it's worth it. We once had a wedding shoot in Mexico for which Ron was already booked for another gig and unable to be the main shooter. We paid extra money for a nationally acclaimed shooter to be the lead—someone we trusted and knew had the experience to represent our company well. When his camera failed to operate the morning of the wedding, he took the initiative to drive two to three hours out of his way to the nearest Sam's Club to purchase an HD camera as a replacement.

Attention to detail. In business and in life, it's often the little things that make all the difference. In fact, Seth Godin wrote about it in his book *Small is the New Big*. Leo Babauta frequently mentions the idea on his blog, Zen Habits (http://zenhabits.net/), and in his book *The Power of Less*.

Paying attention to details on a shoot can make the difference between a good production and a great production. I (Ron) will never forget a wedding shoot we had during our first year in business. Tasra was shooting with me at the time, and the father of the bride had just given an eloquent toast in honor of his daughter. After the applause died down, I turned off my camera. Tasra, being in tune with the vibe of the room and paying attention to the details, kept her camera rolling. She stayed focused on the father and captured him seated in his chair, hands folded in a prayer-like position, just as he started to break down at the thought of losing his "little" girl. His wife put a reassuring hand on his shoulder.

No one else in the room (including me) saw this. But we captured it on tape, and to this day it's by far one of the most emotionally powerful clips I've seen. Pay attention to the people, places, and things around you. You never know what might happen.

POST-PRODUCTION

Many would argue that most of the "magic" that happens in a video production happens in post. Give the same footage to ten different editors and you'll get ten vastly different final products. So how you handle post-production is of utmost importance. We want to give you some idea of the logistical process that you may find helpful in evolving your business.

Assembly-line editing. One approach to editing we've seen used quite effectively is a sort of editing assembly line (and by this we don't mean the "automatic" approach we discussed earlier). Have an assistant editor take care of any editing tasks that require less skill and complexity. This includes capturing and logging tapes, color correction, editing out extraneous raw footage, and piecing together a simple cut matched to a soundtrack.

Have a more senior editor take over and do the more creative work. In many small production companies, the owner is also the main editor, the marketer, and the bookkeeper. If that's you, it may be more cost-effective to have an assistant do the simple production work, freeing you up to work on more important tasks.

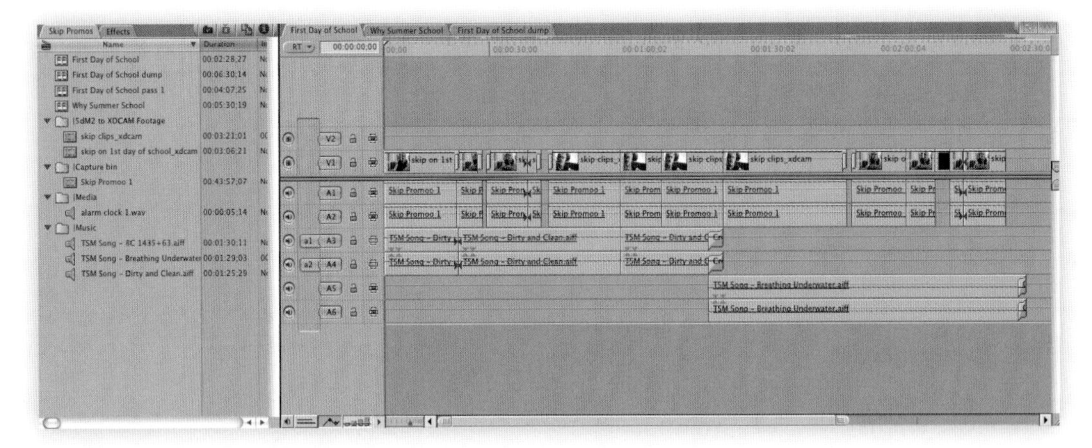

FIGURE 13.3 Our naming conventions make it easy for the editor to navigate files and folder in our nonlinear editing system.

File organization. Create an editing process that makes it easy for any person who is looking at a project to navigate his or her way through it. This includes having systematic naming conventions for files and assets (**FIGURE 13.3**). It also includes organizing files and assets in your project in a consistent and organized manner (**FIGURE 13.4**).

Server systems. If you have a large editing team and work on projects that may involve multiple post-production personnel (such as colorists, motion graphic designers, audio experts, narrative editors, and the like), you may want to look into a file-server version of your editing software. When using multilicensed versions of NLEs software, all the assets are stored on a single computer that all the "satellite" computers can access via a centralized server.

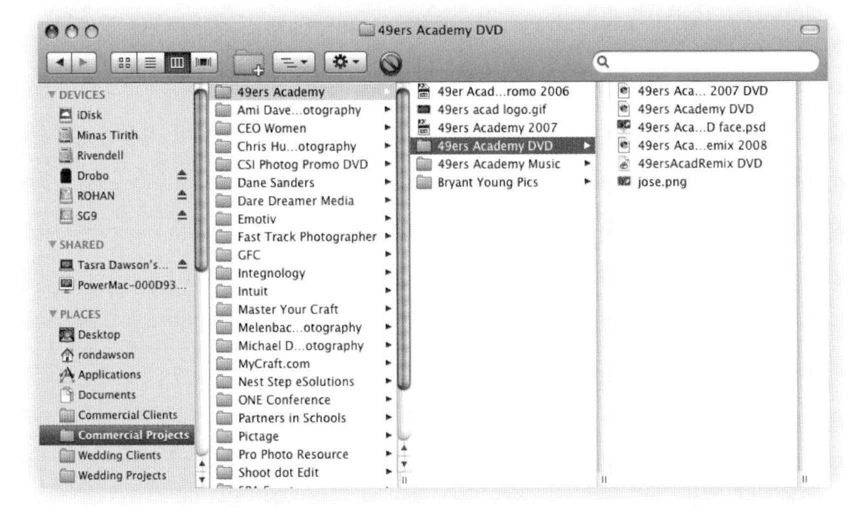

FIGURE 13.4 Media and assets organized in our standard file tree for the 49ers Academy project.

Disparate house drives. An alternative to having a physical studio where all your editors work is to have contract editors who work in disparate locations. This can significantly cut your office overhead. This is the type of system we use. The cost of hard drives is so low that we can buy a new drive for every project. An additional $60–$80 expense on a $10,000–$20,000 job is insignificant. Even on a $5,000 wedding it's worth it.

We then capture all the tapes and media to the hard drive, pack it up, and FedEx it via two-day or three-day air. Our editors are instructed to make the hard drive the scratch disk for all additional media used as well as render files. That way, when the drive is returned, we have all the assets. We use a Google Docs spreadsheet as our online library for tracking all of our drives (**FIGURE 13.5**).

Review videos. Videographers often debate whether it's wise to give clients an opportunity to review their video before it's finalized. Some say that it opens you up to hours upon hours of extra work to deal with picky clients. Our philosophy is that clients are investing their money to get a video and it should be something they are absolutely thrilled to have. We therefore always have some sort of review video for them to watch (either a DVD or a clip posted online). We build into our contract a set amount of complimentary editing time for changes. Our contracts also state that any time after that will be billed at our standard hourly editing rate. We try to build a similar arrangement into our contractor agreements, so that if a contractor does the editing, we're covered. As long as you're charging a fair rate for your work, and communicating clearly up front to the client how the process will work, it's worth using this system. Remember, it's all part of that branding experience.

Hard Drive Library

File Edit View Format Insert Tools Form Help

	A	B	C	D	E	F	G	H
1	**Drive Name:**	**SG6**						
2	Make:	Seagate Free Agent Portable						
3	Connection Type:	USB 2.0						
4	Serial No.							
5	Capacity:	250 GB						
6								
7	**Editor**	**Project**	**Tapes**	**Date Out**	**Date In**	**Phone**	**Email**	**Address**
8	JD	FSBTV - Becker	A1-2, B1-2	11/1/2008		555-555-5555		
9		FSBTV - Colón	A1-4, B1-4	11/1/2008	12/15/2008			
10		Aranda Wedding		11/1/2008				
11		Valley-Williams Wedding						
12	Joe	The Longest Day Opening	C1, A2	12/5/2008	12/10/2008	555-555-5555		
13								

FIGURE 13.5 We have implemented a check-in and check-out system for our hard drive library.

DELIVERY

When all is said and done, how you deliver the final product will be almost as important as the product itself. In Chapter 6, "The Branding Experience," we discussed the importance of packaging in establishing your company's brand. Here are some ideas on how you can deliver your final product in a way that makes the client say, "Wow!"

Beyond the Amaray case. Consider presenting your client's final DVDs in a folio album or other high-quality case (**FIGURE 13.6**). Folio albums are often used by photographers to deliver slideshows, but they're great for personal event DVDs as well. Get a couple of high-resolution images from the photographer that you can use on the case and design the disc face. What's particularly nice about this idea is that the client will be more inclined to leave it out on a coffee table or living room shelf where more people will see it. If you use a conventional DVD case (like the kind you find in a video store), you run the risk of your hard work being lost among all the other DVDs in your client's library.

Popcorn and peanuts. Include conventional movie snacks such as popcorn, chocolate-covered raisins, or other similar treat. Or, if you've been keeping good notes about your clients in your CRM database, and you know they like macadamia nut cookies, for example, include a batch of those. That will really win you some points.

FIGURE 13.6 These black folio cases include space for two photos and come in a presentation box.

FIGURE 13.7
For one of our first wedding clients, we created custom cards with an image of their "getaway" car. Each card included a CD of their wedding to give to friends and family.

The personal touch. When applicable, include a handwritten note with the final discs (FIGURE 13.7). This personal touch shows your clients that they are more to you than just a number.

Customized Web site: The delivery of your final product isn't always physical. Consider creating a customized Web-viewing experience. We surprised one of our clients, for whom we produced a love story and a wedding-day trailer (also known as a "save the date" video), with a "movie trailer" Web site designed to look like the trailer Web pages on Apple's QuickTime site (FIGURE 13.8). The clients included a link to it from their personal wedding Web site.

The name of the game is to wow your clients—by taking the mundane and making it meaningful.

Visit wedding website

"Hot Dogs and Harmony"

The Love Story of Elaine and Riva

Copyright © 2006 Cinematic Studios, Inc.

Riva had no idea that there was so much time and energy that went into planning a wedding (what do you expect, he's a man!) With less than a year from the time they would hope to be husband and wife, nothing had been done yet, least of which the proposal. So, Elaine "gently" let Mr. Han know that if "certain things were to happen next year" (i.e. get married), well, he had better start planning. There was no time to wait for a proposal. Make sure you're there, Saturday, August 5, 2006, to find out the whole story.

At St. Francis Winery: August 5th, 2006	Videos
Romantic Comedy Not Rated Ron Dawson (dir.) Elaine Hsieh Riva Han Brad Schneider	Teaser Preview "Joking Around" Love Story (Flash) Same Day Edit (Flash)

FIGURE 13.8
The movie trailer-style Web site for our client's love story and save-the-date video.

SECRETS TO SUCCESS

OUR JOURNEY TOGETHER IS COMING to a close. But before we go, we want to leave you with something we hope will encourage you.

OUR TOP TEN SECRETS TO SUCCESS

This list is by no means an exhaustive list. And in truth, what you're about to read here aren't really "secrets." They're just very specific things we've done to help us achieve success in this business.

One thing to keep in mind is that by "success" we mean making a living at something we love to do, growing in the process, and being happy. If your only concept of "success" is financial, then you stand the chance of being really disappointed in life. Yes, financial freedom and not having to worry about the necessities of life can contribute to a lifestyle and bring you some level of happiness. But you've no doubt heard enough stories of wealthy individuals who take their own life to know that having all the money in the world means nothing if you're not happy.

So, if you've adjusted your perspective—and are ready to pursue the sort of success that goes beyond financial reward—as our four-year-old would say, "LET'S DO THIS THING."

1. FIND YOUR 'ONE'

First and foremost, find the one thing that you're absolutely passionate about. If you do that, no matter what it is, you'll find a way to make a living from it. This reminds us of a scene from the comedy film *City Slickers*, starring Jack Palance and Billy Crystal. Palance plays Curly, an age-worn, grumpy, and rather menacing old cowboy, leading Crystal (Mitch) and a rag-tag team of "city folk" on a cattle drive. During the film, Curly reveals to Mitch the secret of life: He holds up his index finger to make the number 1—the one thing that means more to him than anything else in the world. Find that one thing and you'll find the secret to life...and happiness.

FIGURE 14.1
Like an eagle that flies to a mountain-top or aims for the sun, your success will be only as big as your dreams.

2. SHOOT FOR THE STARS TO HIT THE MOON

In my (Ron's) college application essay, I told the story of two eagles, each looking to fly farther than any other eagle. One decides he's going to fly to the summit of the highest mountain. The other decides to fly to the sun (**FIGURE 14.1**). At the end of the story, they rendezvous back home and the first eagle brags about reaching the highest mountain and seeing the whole countryside. He then cynically asks the second eagle if he ever made it to the sun. The second eagle says, "No, I only made it as far as the moon. But I'm going to try again tomorrow." The moral of the story is clear. Aim higher and you'll go farther in life. Your success will be only as big as your dreams.

3. THINK OUTSIDE THE BOX

Yes, thinking outside the box is very cliché. But that doesn't make it any less true. We always strive to do things in a way that either bucks convention, or is just plain "out there." Whether it's shooting at a shutter speed of 1/30 (versus the traditional 1/60) for most of our weddings because we like the softer look, launching an audio podcast primarily about photographers (versus doing one about videographers), or using pop-culture movie references throughout a book about business, in everything we do we look for a way to do it differently.

4. SURROUND YOURSELF WITH WINNERS

We used to call this one "build a great team." But at its core, it's really about surrounding yourself with people who have a winning attitude. That includes employees, contractors, vendors, suppliers, and other colleagues with whom you can collaborate to achieve your goals. We've learned and gained so much from motivated, successful people in many walks of life that we would not be where we are today without that inspiration. And we've always tried to hire and work with individuals who have a similar mindset.

5. GIVE. GIVE. GIVE.

We used to call this one "Give 'em more than they expect." In other words, always give your clients more than they're expecting—give them positive surprises. But as our business has matured (and as we have matured), we've learned that it goes beyond just giving more to your clients. Give to everybody. Allow your *giving* to outweigh your *getting*, and you'll be surprised by how much more *getting* you'll actually experience. Whether it's helping others in your area with their business, sharing your knowledge and experience on a blog, or starting a podcast that makes no money but just helps and inspires, you'll see rewards down the line you never expected—not the least of which is the feeling you get by doing something positive in the world.

6. STAY IN SCHOOL AND STAY INSPIRED

You should always be learning. Hopefully, if you've gotten this far in our book, you've learned a lot. Continue to educate yourself on business and your craft. And look to industries outside of your own. Read magazines that span a wide range of topics. Look for inspiration not just in other people's work, but in their lives.

7. EMBRACE FAILURE, CELEBRATE SUCCESS

One of the most famous quotes on the topic of failure is by superstar basketball player Michael Jordan (**FIGURE 14.2**).

> *"I've missed more than 9,000 shots in my career. I've lost almost 300 games. Twenty-six times I've been trusted to take the game-winning shot and missed. I've FAILED OVER AND OVER AND OVER again in my life. And that is WHY I SUCCEED."*

FIGURE 14.2
We can't all be Michael Jordan, but we can all learn something from his idea that how we deal with failure is part of our success.

You will fail in life. It's a given. In fact, rejoice in your failures. That means you're one step closer to greater success. Don't be afraid or ashamed to fail. As we discussed in Chapter 9, F.E.A.R. will keep you from achieving as much as you can. So, don't let fear of failure stop you. Likewise, when you *do* succeed—land a big job, reach a certain revenue level, and the like—celebrate it. Early in our business, we'd take the whole family out to dinner every time we booked a new gig. It was a great opportunity to get the whole family excited about the business, and it was added inspiration to work hard and close those sales.

8. RE-EVALUATE. RE-ADJUST. RE-INVENT.

You should evaluate every aspect of your business to see what's working and what's not. Then make adjustments and tweaks where necessary. The "re-" prefix suggests that this is an iterative process. There will be times when you should completely re-invent yourself. When you look at music stars that have remained powerhouses for two decades or more (Madonna, U2, Sting, Prince), you see that they all constantly re-invent their look, their music, and sometimes even their bands. For us, it was switching our focus from weddings to commercial work. Then in early 2009, we changed our company from a *production* company to a new media marketing *agency*. As we've entered this new field, it's like starting from scratch. But re-invention keeps life exciting, keeps the business fresh, and keeps us on our toes.

9. ENVISION WHERE YOU WANT TO BE

Many texts from a variety of different belief systems, philosophies, and sciences have attested to the power of the mind in shaping your life. When you start envisioning your life and your business where you want them to be, your mind will actually start making you act and interact with people as if you were already there (**FIGURE 14.3**). Those actions will then manifest themselves in your life and business in ways you wouldn't expect.

FIGURE 14.3 If you can envision yourself where you want to be, you're much more likely to get there.

10. JUST DO IT

This is a philosophy we held long before Nike made it famous. After you've done the planning, completed your research, and received input from your colleagues and peers, there will come a time when you will just have to do it. It may require a leap of faith. It may require increasing your failure percentage. But, if you wait too long to do something, you stand the risk of someone else doing it first. So, what are you waiting for? Just do it already! Whatever "it" is.

THIS LIST GOES TO 11

In the spirit of No. 5 and giving positive surprises, we have an 11th "secret" of success. It may be the thing you'd least expect.

Prayer.

Why? Because it can't hurt.

FIGURE 14.4 Pray, relax, meditate—whatever it takes to keep things in perspective and make all your goals seem attainable.

Seriously, prayer has been a big part of our life and business. When you're faced with the stresses of running your own business, trying to stay ahead, and keeping up with all the strategies we've mentioned in this book, you'll find personal reflection and quiet time a welcome respite. For some of you, it may mean praying specifically as it relates to your personal faith. For others of you, it may mean taking time to stop, relax, and meditate (**FIGURE 14.4**). However you choose to do it, take that time. It's not only a great way to stay grounded and keep all things in perspective; it's a good way to recharge.

CUT. PRINT. THAT'S A WRAP.

When filmmakers finish capturing the last shot while making a movie, the director calls, "Cut. Print. That's a wrap." So it's time for us to do the same.

It's been an honor to share with you, but your journey is far from over. As with any movie just wrapped, it's now time to take this "raw footage" and go make something great.

Amaze your clients. Astound your colleagues. Surprise *yourself*. And, in keeping with our propensity for pop-culture references, dare we say, "May the force be with you."

INDEX

C

D

N

O

P

T

U

V

W

Y

Z

Special offer for *ReFocus* readers!

Refocus your business and keep it *in* focus throughout the year!

A subscription to *EventDV* provides you with the tools to make that happen. Each issue highlights the business and marketing strategies, shooting and editing techniques, gear, and emerging industry trends you need to master to make your business thrive, evolve, and grow.

EventDV features regular contributions from *ReFocus* authors Ron & Tasra Dawson and many of the video professionals profiled in this book!

Get your subscription today. *ReFocus* readers receive a 1-year subscription (10 issues!) for only $17.95 (basic rate $29.95).

Subscribe online at
www.EventDV.net/subscribe.
Please use priority code RFCS to receive your discount.

Offer valid for U.S. subscribers only.
Offer expires 4/30/2010.

Subscribe online today!
www.eventdv.net

Get free online access to this book for 45 days!

And get access to thousands more by signing up for a free trial to Safari Books Online!

With the purchase of this book you have instant online, searchable access to it for 45 days on Safari Books Online! And while you're there, be sure to check out Safari Books Online's on-demand digital library and their free trial offer (a separate sign-up process). Safari Books Online subscribers have access to thousands of technical, creative and business books, instructional videos, and articles from the world's leading publishers.

Simply visit www.peachpit.com/safarienabled and enter code ERQPFDB to try it today.